IMAGES
of America

WAKEFIELD AND BROOKFIELD

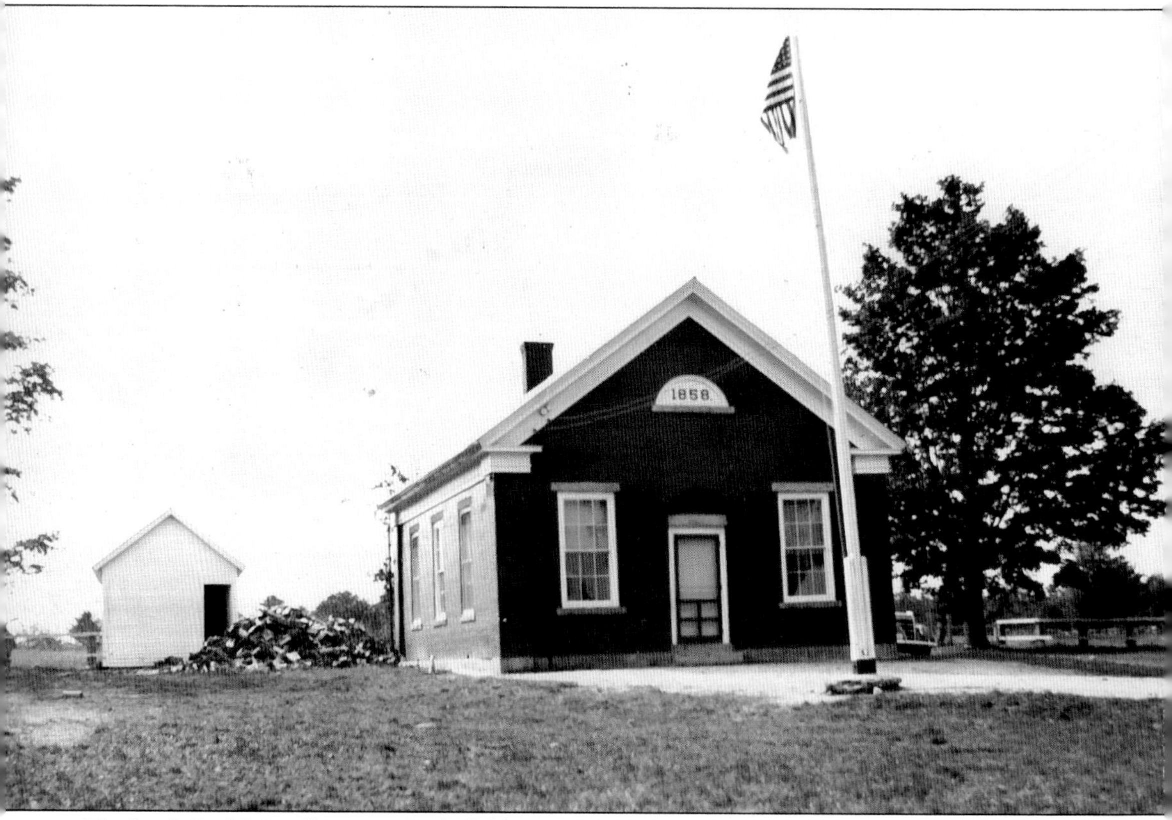

The Little Red Schoolhouse in Wakefield Corner has housed the Wakefield-Brookfield Historical Society since 1947. Built in 1858, the red brick schoolhouse had been attended by generations of neighborhood children before it closed in 1943.

On the cover: Staff members and patrons of the G. W. Armstrong Restaurant were photographed on the platform of the Sanbornville railroad station in 1900. Included here are Frank Graves, Ernest Williams, Annie Fellows, Edna Downs, Mary Ahearn, Nettie Fellows, Carrie Knight, Grace Lamontagne, Kate Foley, and Annie Hanson. (Wakefield-Brookfield Historical Society.)

IMAGES
of America

WAKEFIELD AND BROOKFIELD

Wakefield-Brookfield Historical Society

ARCADIA
PUBLISHING

Copyright © 2006 by Wakefield-Brookfield Historical Society
ISBN 978-0-7385-4479-3

Published by Arcadia Publishing
Charleston, South Carolina

Printed in the United States of America

Library of Congress Catalog Card Number: 2005937497

For all general information contact Arcadia Publishing at:
Telephone 843-853-2070
Fax 843-853-0044
E-mail sales@arcadiapublishing.com
For customer service and orders:
Toll-Free 1-888-313-2665

Visit us on the Internet at www.arcadiapublishing.com

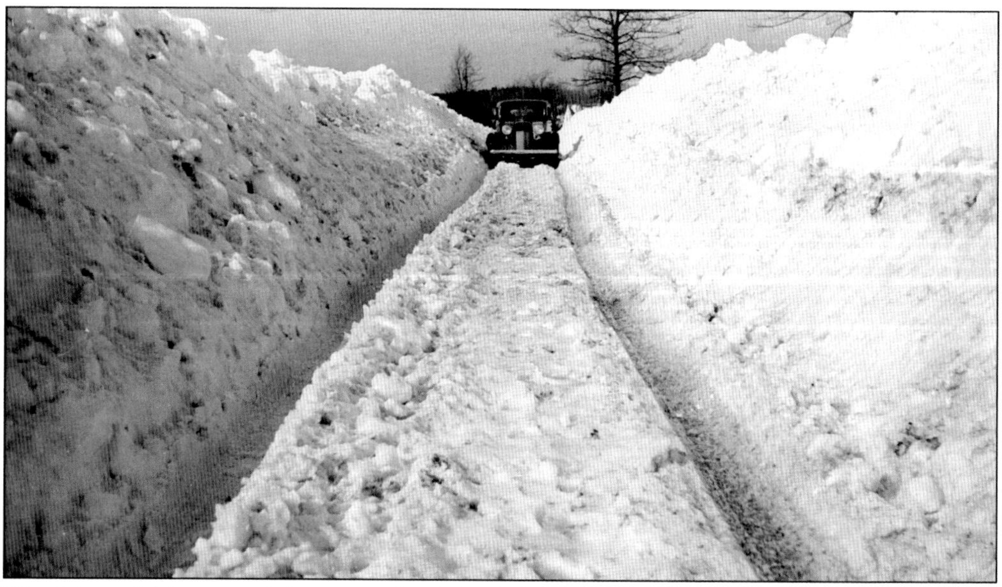

The driver of this automobile, pictured on March 1, 1936, certainly would have hoped not to see another car coming in the opposite direction.

Contents

ACKNOWLEDGMENTS

Members of the Wakefield-Brookfield Historical Society Book Committee were Carolyn Chase, Patricia Golden, Rev. George Harvey, Gerry Hastings, Ann Hatch, Ron Prior, Jessica Sobti, and Paul Winckler.

We wish to thank the many individuals and organizations whose assistance, generosity, and encouragement made the work possible, including all the members of the historical society since its founding in 1938.

We are very grateful to the following people, who provided photographs and/or information: Nancy and Chris Bancroft, Victor Becker, Marjorie and Warren Berg, John Bowker, Peter Brown, Vivian Chick, Craig Evans, William Gaver, Gary Hackett, Donald Hanson, Gerry Hastings, Ann Hatch, Paul Hatch, Sigi Hays, Thom Hindle, Pam Judge, Jim Keating, Cathy Kinville, Dorcas Knight, Ann Martin, Jim Miller, Mary Lou Monnat, Ronald Murray, Larry Nason, Chris Pinkham, Norman Royle, Adeline Russo, Arlene Tibbetts, Timothy Tibbetts, Janet and Paul Twombley, Monty Warman, and Virginia Wentworth.

The following organizations also provided assistance: the Wakefield Public Library, the Gafney Library, the Wakefield Heritage Commission, the town of Brookfield, the town of Wakefield, and the Walker Transportation Collection of the Beverly Historical Society and Museum in Beverly, Massachusetts.

We are grateful to Erin M. Stone, our helpful and very patient editor at Arcadia Publishing.

We also thank Elizabeth Banks MacRury for writing *Footsteps of Pride to the Past: Wakefield, New Hampshire*, a remarkable compendium of information about Wakefield's past. MacRury's hard work preserved much of the town's history for future generations.

Finally, we wish to thank all the people who have remembered, recorded, and shared stories and images over the years and continue to do so; without them, history would be nothing but a series of dates and names.

Introduction

Wakefield is a town of many villages, many lakes, and many changes. From a forested area delineated only on maps grew a collection of villages, shaped and changed by population shifts and the arrival of the railroad and related industries. In the early and mid-1900s, the railroad caused more changes with its departure. However, Wakefield remains a thriving community, home to both year-round and summer residents who appreciate the beauty of the land, the waterways, and the strong community spirit that unites the multiple villages into one town.

Earlier known as East Town, Ham Town, and Water Town, Wakefield was incorporated on August 30, 1774, a year before the Revolutionary War broke out. The origin of the name is unknown; some have guessed it was taken from the novel *The Vicar of Wakefield*, popular at the time. Although Native Americans and white explorers had visited the area, the first settlers arrived just a decade before the town's incorporation.

In the late 1700s, those who had invested in the purchase of vast tracts of land in interior New Hampshire were eager to profit from their investments. They promoted the sale and settlement of these densely forested holdings among young families in the province's coastal towns, where land was already becoming crowded and expensive. Wakefield provided plenty of lumber for building, spacious land for agriculture, and abundant water for the running of mills and other purposes.

The initial phase of the town's development involved clearing the forest to create fields for growing hay, corn, and other crops and to provide pasture for horses, cattle, and sheep. As fields were cleared, stone walls became abundant and the first modest houses were built. Almost immediately upon its establishment, the new town responded to demands for soldiers to fight in the War for Independence.

By the early 1800s, Wakefield Corner had become the most prominent village in town. Larger houses were erected by prospering farmers and business folk, inns were constructed to serve those traveling through by stagecoach, and the first town hall, academy, and fine village church were soon added.

A second stage of development in Wakefield began with the arrival of the railroad in the mid-1800s. Investors were eager to open the interior of the state to commerce, and Wakefield was a benefactor. The first appearance of the trains brought them, in 1854, as far as the village of Union at the southern tip of the town. As the slave issue embroiled the states to the south, the people of Union watched their village prosper, with new businesses that relied on waterpower to produce goods and the railroad to transport products to market. Excelsior mills, for example, used the abundance of wood to produce the packing material essential to commerce until the advent of plastic.

Although the town had provided its share of men to the Union army in the Civil War, development continued at home. The railroad continued its move northward, reaching Sanbornville in 1871. The new village was at the time called Wolfeboro Junction, as a branch line led to Wolfeboro while the main railroad line continued north. Previously, this area between South Wakefield and Wakefield Corner had been largely undeveloped, described in the *History of Carroll County* as "full of ravines and huge bowlders [*sic*], and covered with a dense forest."

John W. Sanborn is credited with bringing the railroad and related industries to Wolfeboro Junction. He oversaw the construction of a large station with a restaurant for the traveling public, freight services, and an extensive service and repair facility located on what is today called Turntable Park. The village developed rapidly, with factories, stores, churches, schools, and a new town hall, and became the town center. A short spur track to Lovell Lake, just south of the village, served the growing ice-harvesting industry and allowed tons of ice to be shipped to Boston for over a half century. In 1895, Wolfeboro Junction was renamed Sanbornville in honor of its benefactor and most prominent citizen.

The railroad wound its way northward by a curving route to avoid the large hills, and so opened East Wakefield to development. Lumber and produce from the area were shipped out by train, and inns were built to accommodate summer visitors. Before automobiles were prevalent, horse-drawn carriages met the trains at the station to transport passengers and their trunks to their chosen vacation destination.

The railroads survived two world wars and the Great Depression, but could not survive the next phase of development: construction of a massive highway system to serve a population that had fallen in love with the automobile. The relocation of Route 16 (the White Mountain Highway) was completed around 1960. By that time, all passenger service and virtually all freight service had disappeared—along with most of the stations that had served so well for so long. The town of Wakefield, however, survived, prospered, and doubled its population.

The neighboring town of Brookfield was originally known as Middle Towne. A portion of Governor's Road wound through the Second (or Northern) Division to Wentworth House in Wolfeboro. Governor Wentworth's wife, Lady Francis, was terrified by the journey to the estate, writing in 1770 to a friend in Portsmouth that her husband would "ride over the trees of Moose mountain, while poor I even tremble at passing through a road cut at the foot of it." The residents of the Second Division found it equally difficult to travel south to the First Division for worship and town meetings, and petitioned to be un-annexed from Middle Towne as early as 1785. In December 1794, the two divisions were separated, with the First Division remaining Middle Towne, or Middleton, and the Second Division incorporated as Brookfield.

Settlers were drawn to Brookfield's fertile soil, and farms spread across the landscape. Later, visitors came to enjoy the hills, fields, and ponds, and some built summer homes. Rural retreats such as Mountain Lake Camp brought wealthy "city folk" to town by train and later by automobile. While the town has added new homes and the occasional small business over the years, it has never lost its rural character and retains many small farms.

The Wakefield-Brookfield Historical Society, formed in 1938 and still active today, has selected these images from its archives and from the collections of many generous local residents. The society hopes the reader will find these glimpses into the towns' pasts both informative and entertaining.

One

Wakefield Corner

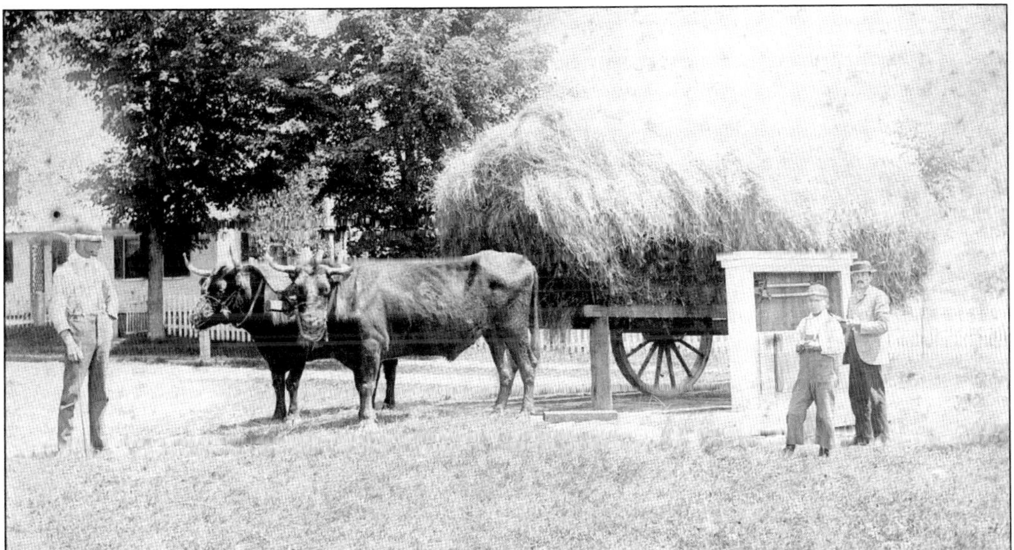

The hay scales are now Wakefield's logo and one of its most recognizable landmarks. Used to weigh loads of hay, they originally included a stone well and floor to hold the wagon, but these have been lost due to road widening. The scale mechanism is still operational, though the weights, once kept at the local store, have disappeared.

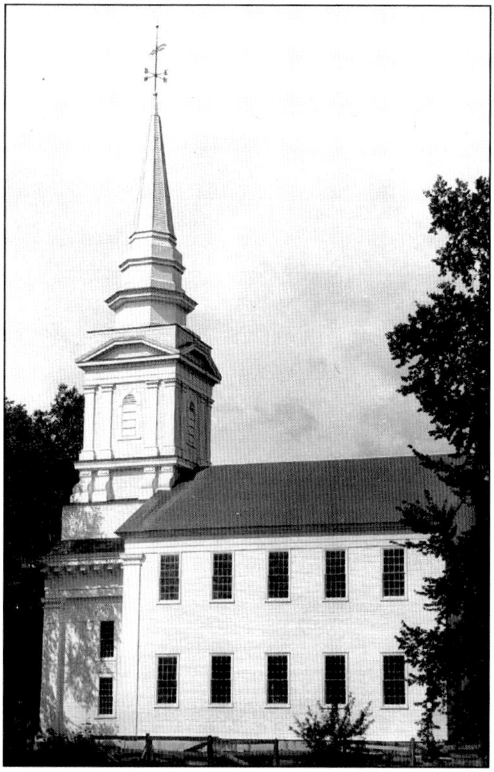

This beautiful old church graced the village of Wakefield Corner for 125 years before being struck by lightning and burning. The only record states that the church was raised on this site on July 22, 1816, and framed the next day. It was finally completed and dedicated in 1831. The steeple was raised in 1854.

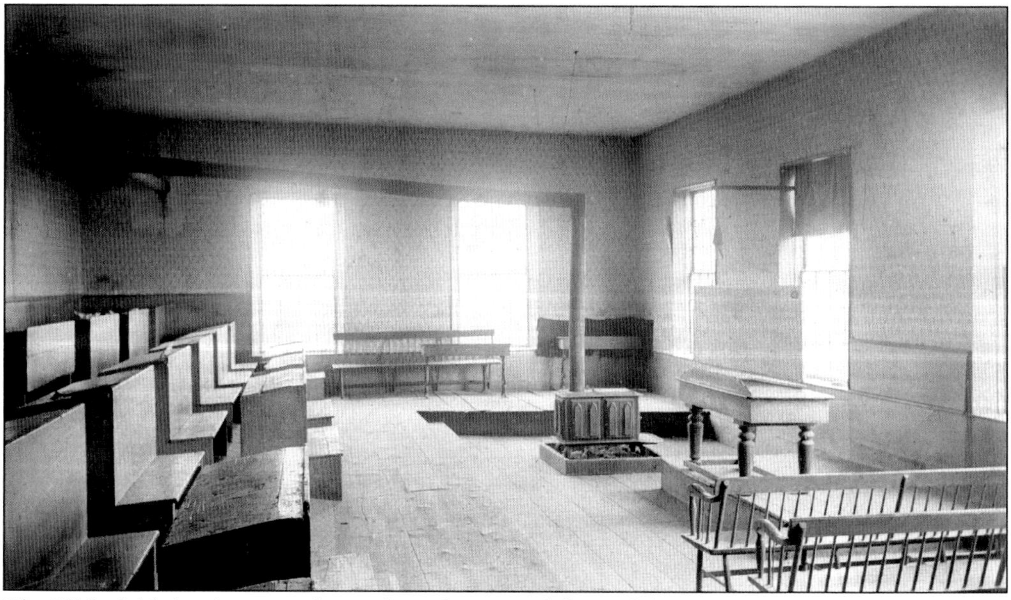

The Wakefield Academy was located on the second floor of the Congregational church, above the sanctuary. As the ceiling below was barrel-vaulted, the floor above sloped toward the fronts of the rooms. The academy was incorporated in 1827 and opened in 1832 with 32 male and 26 female students.

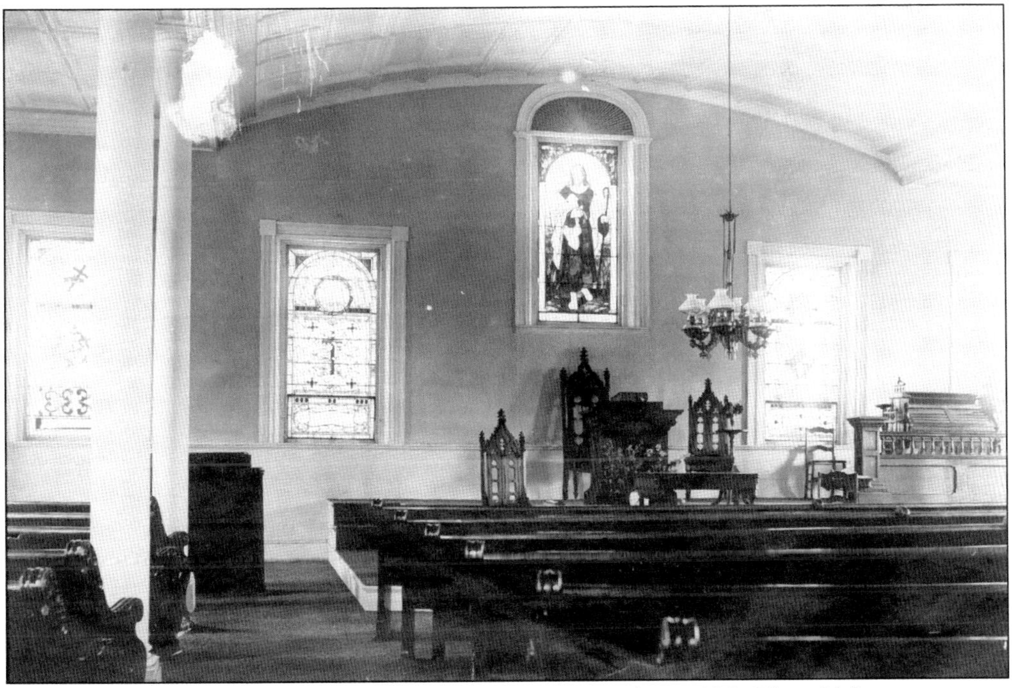

The interior of the Congregational church was renovated in 1900. The old box pews were removed, along with their doors, and the seating was reversed so that worshippers entered at the rear instead of the front. The chairs, pulpit, and communion table are still in use, and four of the original stained-glass windows remain.

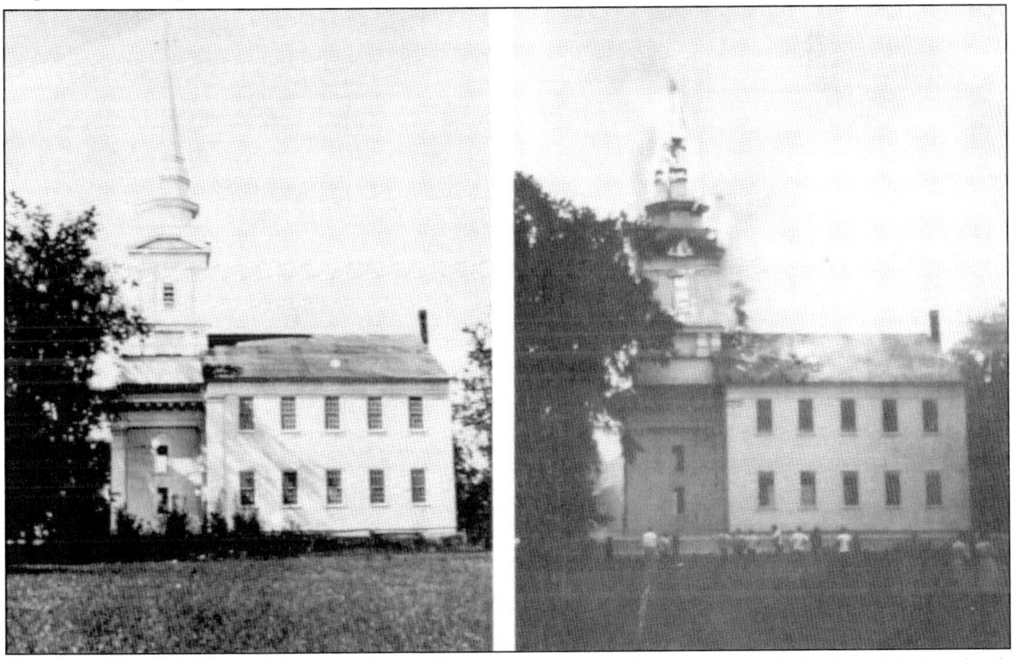

Fire claimed the beautifully constructed, historic church on September 2, 1956. The 119-foot-high spire attracted a lightning bolt that destroyed the heart and soul of the village. Within two years, though, a new edifice had risen in its place.

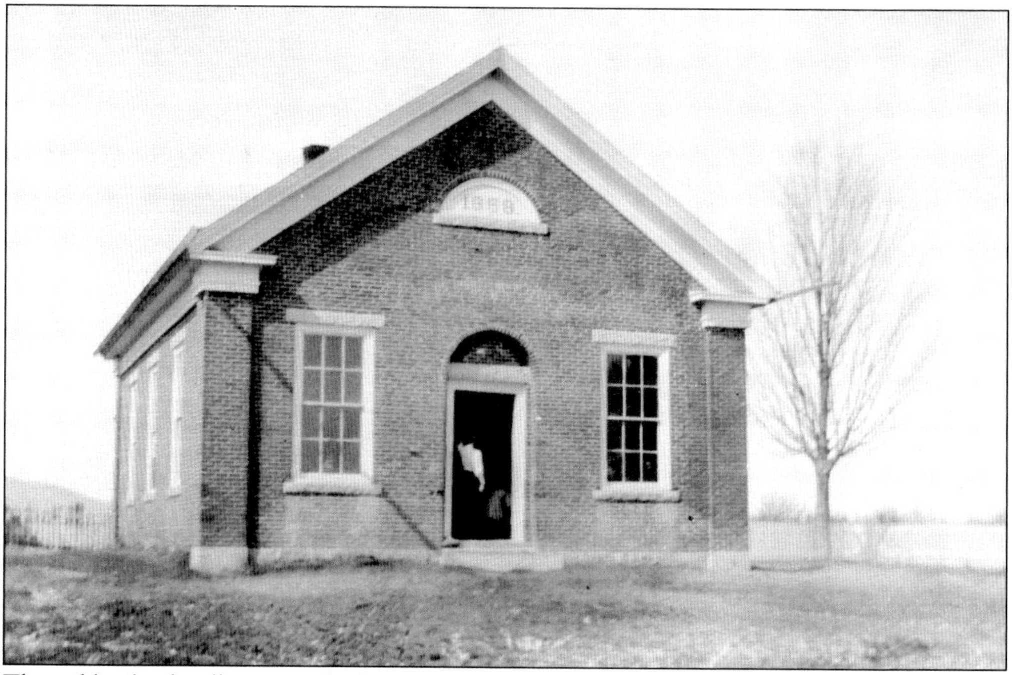

The red-brick schoolhouse was built in 1858 as a replacement for two previous structures that had burned. Attended by three generations of neighborhood children, it closed in 1943. Purchased from the town in 1956, it now houses the Wakefield-Brookfield Historical Society. The former woodshed to the rear contains an intact cobbler shop.

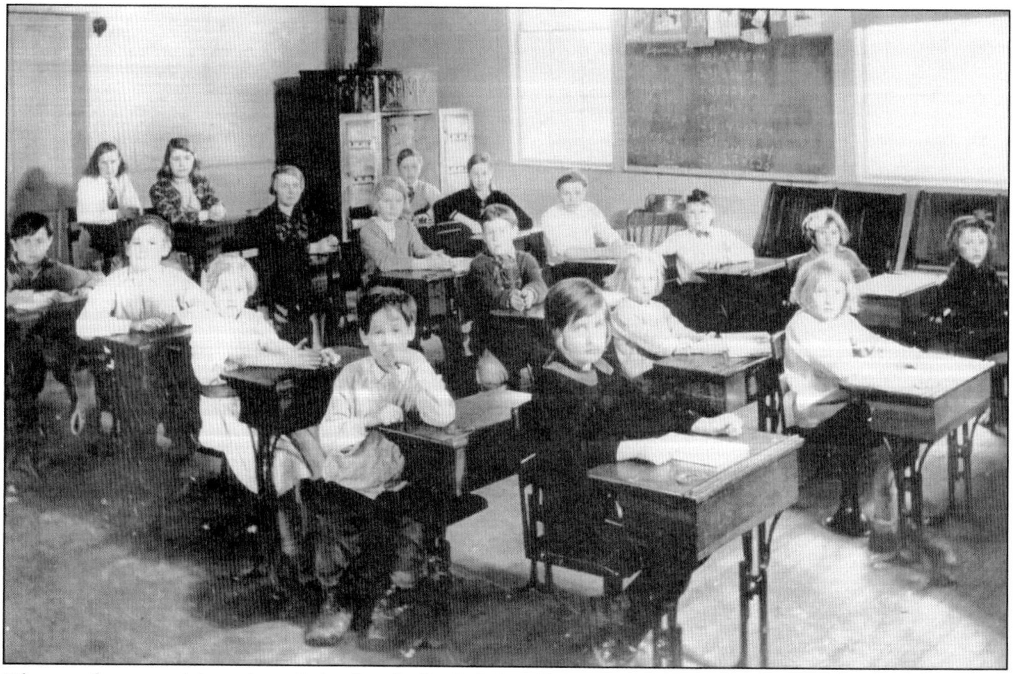

The students and interior of the Little Red Schoolhouse are pictured here in the early 1930s. Note the "number work" on the blackboard and the artwork above it. The large woodstove in the back corner really kept the room hot.

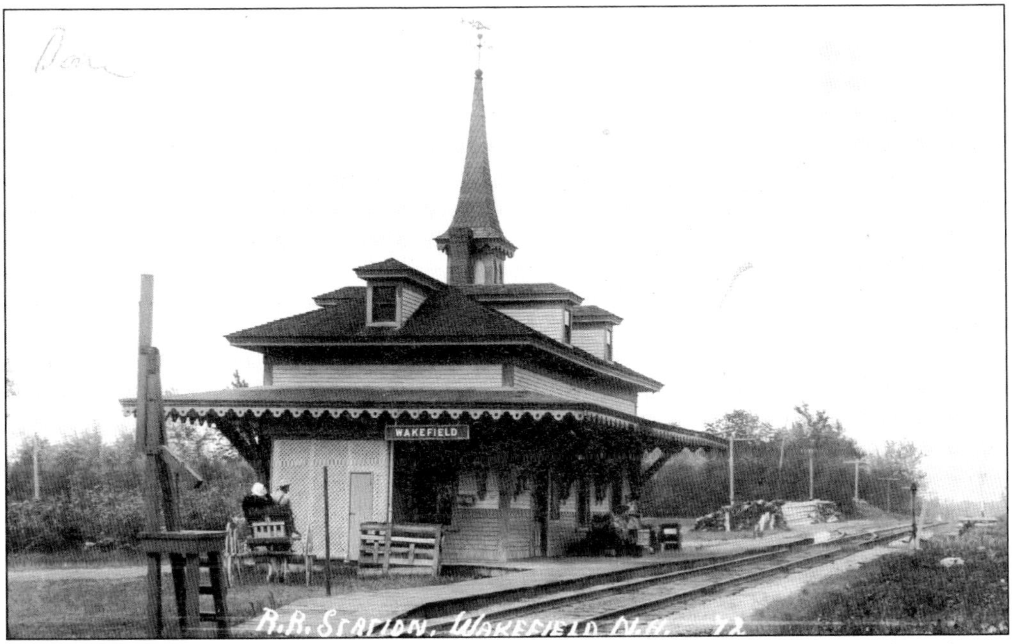

The Wakefield railroad station handled lumber, passengers, and mail. Note the mail catcher at the left of this image. If there were no passengers, the mailbag would be hung on the arm and "grabbed" by the train as it passed, making a stop unnecessary.

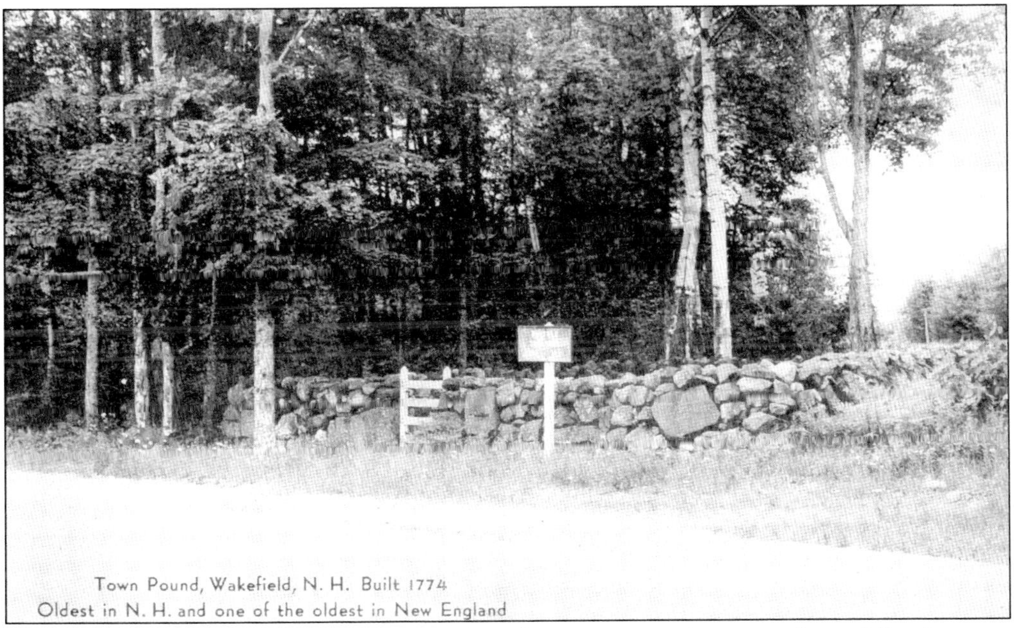
Town Pound, Wakefield, N. H. Built 1774
Oldest in N. H. and one of the oldest in New England

The original Town Pound, built in 1774, stood on the same site as this restored one. All early towns had common land set aside in perpetuity, and the inhabitants' animals were allowed to graze there. Should the animals wander and destroy property, they would be incarcerated by the pounder.

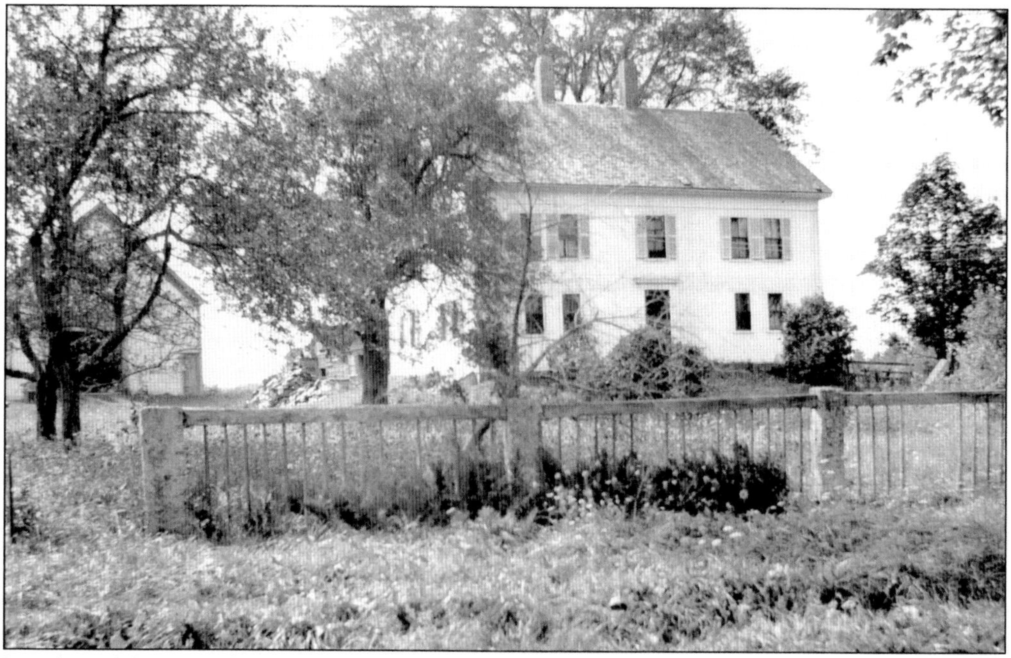

Joseph Maleham purchased this land in 1768. The house was originally a cape, but in 1888, the owners "riz" the roof, adding five bedrooms. The long, low ell behind the residence at one time housed Sarah Maleham's hat factory, where several women of the town were employed.

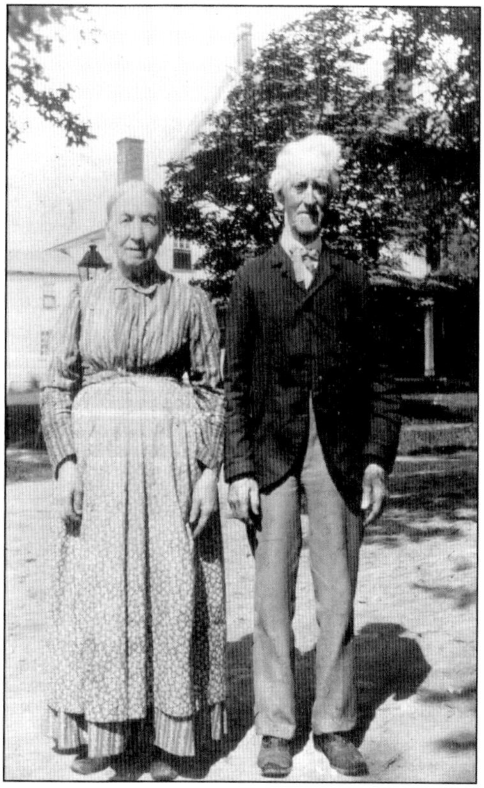

Olive Rollins Brown and her husband, Asa, lived in the house north of the church. Asa kept the post office and a small store in a separate building for a number of years before the building was moved.

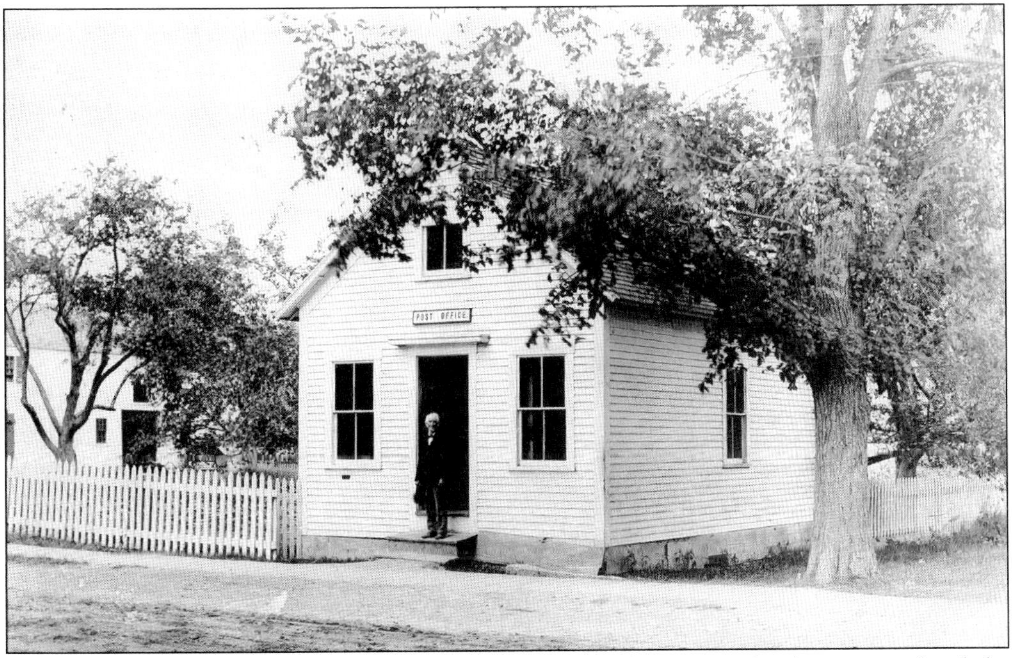

The old post office originally stood on the property of the Brown family, just north of the Congregational church. Asa Brown operated it, along with a small store, for many years. In 1915, the building was purchased by Fred Elliott and transferred up the street to its present location opposite the Little Red Schoolhouse.

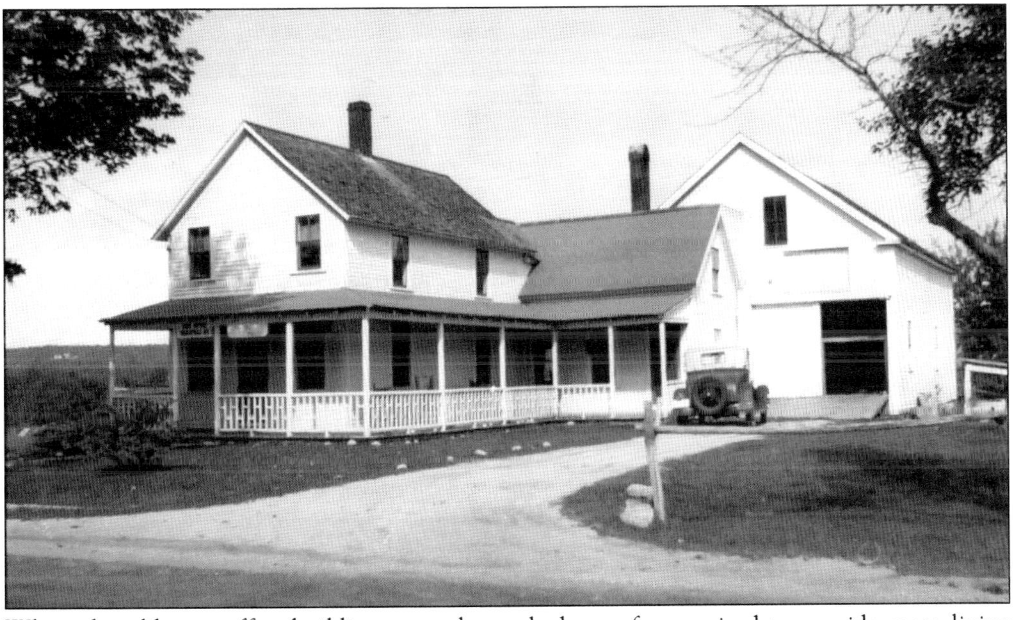

When the old post office building was relocated, the roof was raised to provide more living space. In 1938, after the death of Henry Tibbetts, Goldie Elliott became postmistress. The post office remained open until 1976, when Wakefield Corner lost it for good due to a change in the zip code.

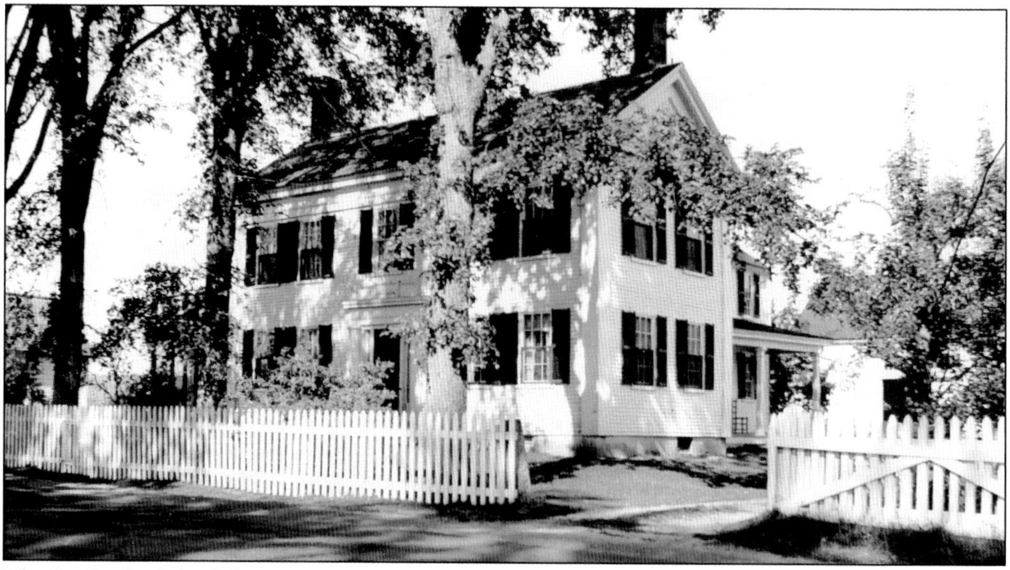

The back ell of the John Wingate House is the original dwelling, built around 1798. The main house, in front, was added in 1881 after the ell was moved to the rear. At one time, George Gage operated a pants factory in the barn. Near the side entrance, a "parson's cupboard" enabled the parson to obtain his dinner without disturbing the occupants of the house.

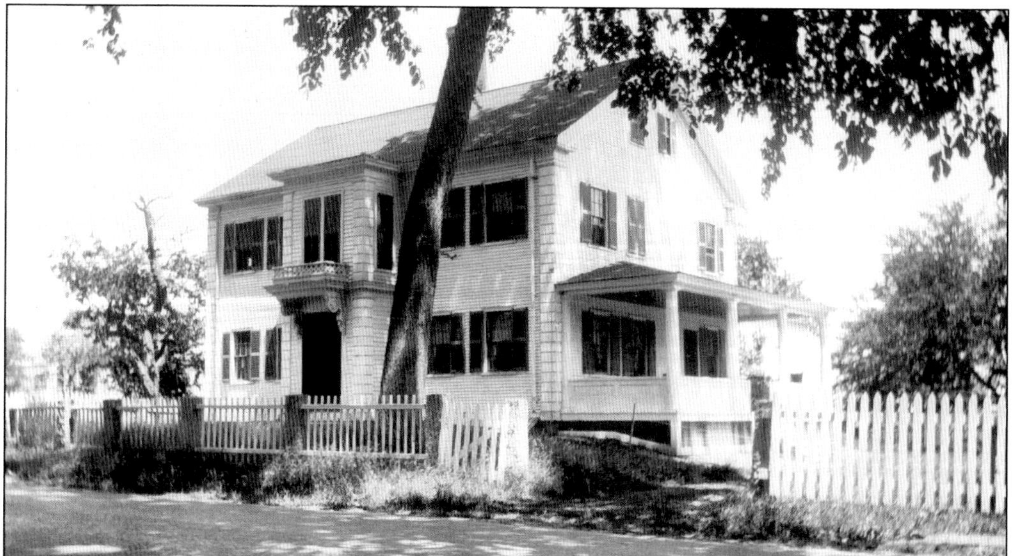

This house was originally built by John Wingate, who sold it to his son. He in turn sold it to the Sawyer family. In 1860, Elisha Rollins purchased the home for his daughter Olive and son-in-law Asa Brown. It remains in the Brown family.

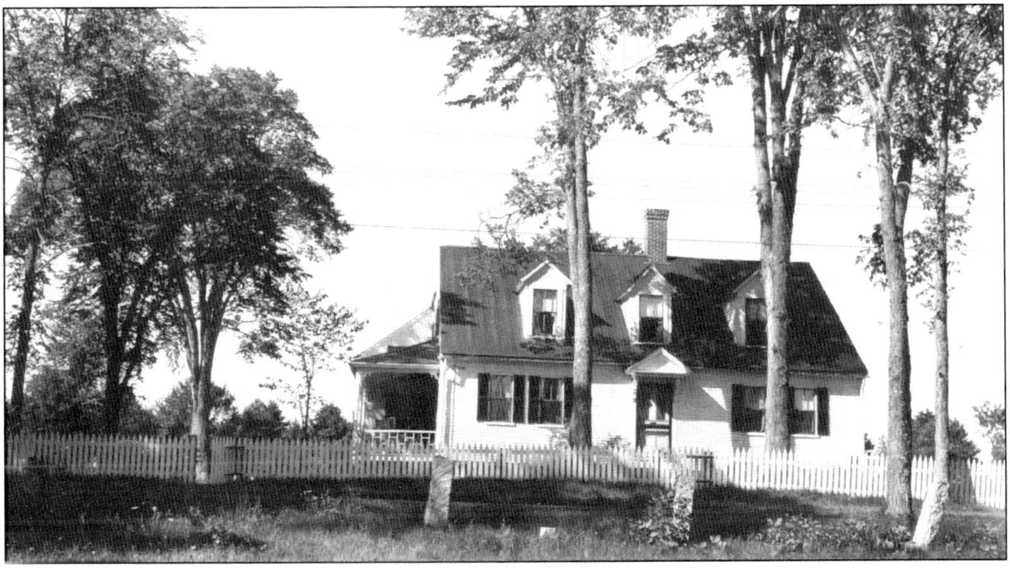

John Wingate also constructed the Thomas Mordough house, one of the earliest and best examples of cape architecture in the village. Owned at one time by Susan Pike Sawyer (Mrs. Charles Henry Sawyer), it was eventually sold to Maj. Samuel Smith and descended through three more generations of Smiths.

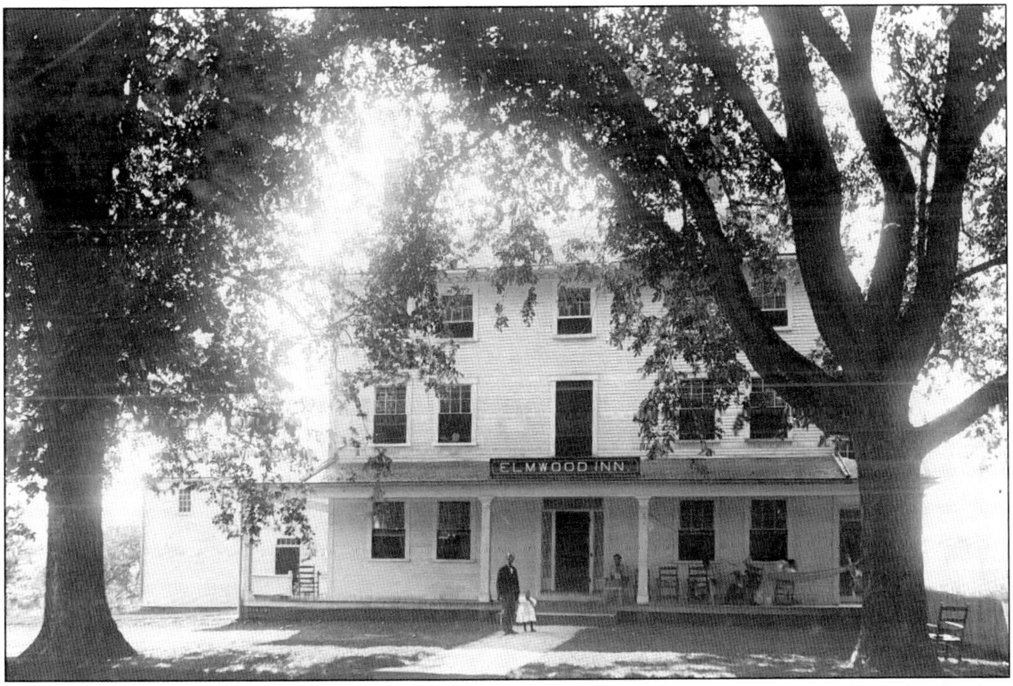

The Wakefield Inn was built for William Frost in 1816 by twin brothers Isaac and Jacob Chesley. When payments were not made, the Chesleys took the building back and lived there for many years. Eventually, it was sold to the Tibbetts family. Henry Tibbetts completely refurbished the structure, opening it to the public in 1890 as the Elmwood Inn. It has also been known as the Carriage Stop Inn and the Spiral Staircase, after the beautiful architectural feature that rises to the top floor.

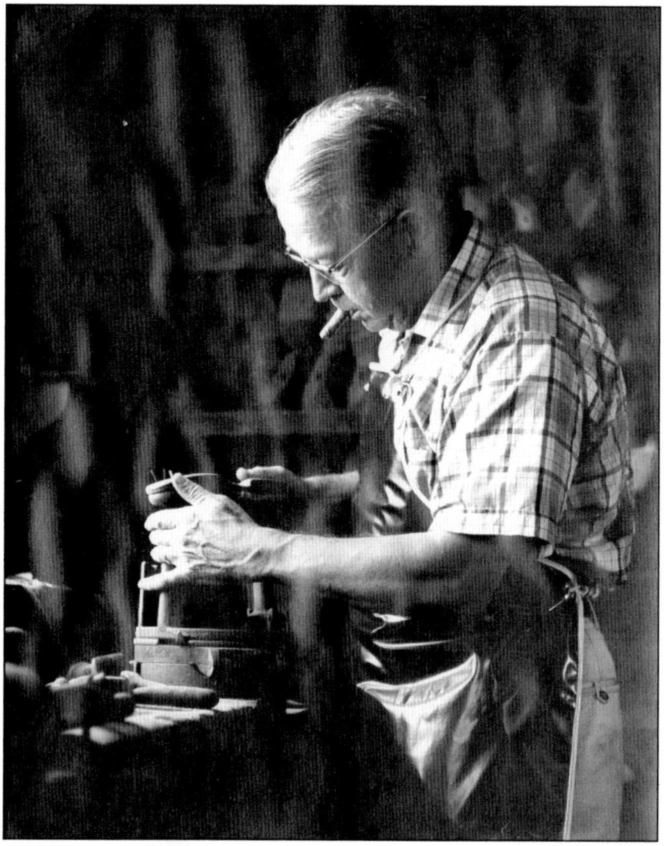

The cobbler shop stood on land owned by the Pike family of Brookfield. The cobbler, Freeman Pike, apparently closed the door one day and just walked away. Much later, the cobbler shop was purchased intact and donated to the Wakefield-Brookfield Historical Society. The shop was then moved to the former woodshed behind the society's Little Red Schoolhouse. Dr. Frank Heck learned what he could about cobbling so that he could give demonstrations.

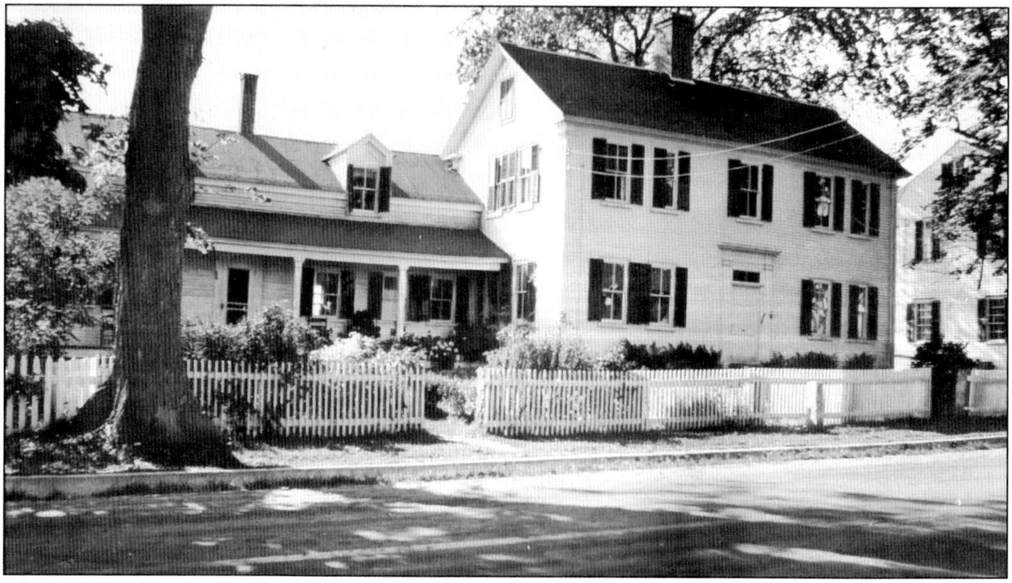

The Doctors' House is notable for having housed, at different times, three local doctors: Samuel Twitchell, Samuel Roberts, and Gijs Bozuwa. It is unknown by whom the house was built, but at one distant time a gentleman by the name of M. J. Smith operated a carriage shop here. Between the second and third doctors, it was a successful dairy farm for many years.

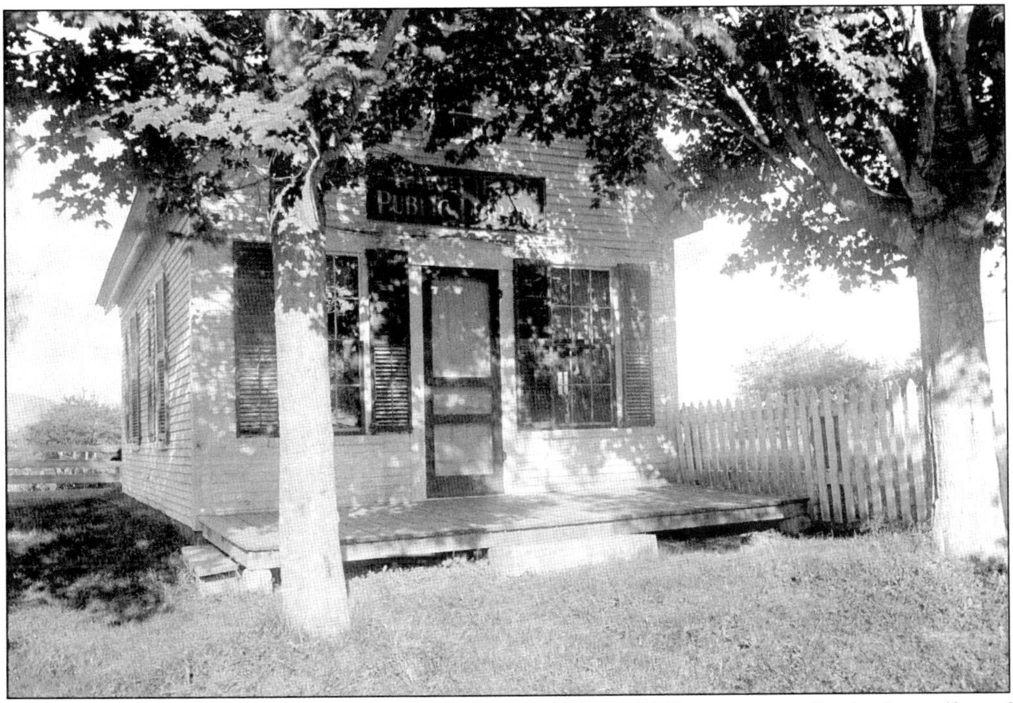

This back portion of the Wakefield Public Library, built in 1797, was originally the law office of Chesley, Carter, Hobbs, and Sawyer. In 1894, Seth Low, president of Columbia University and later mayor of New York City, purchased it to build a library in memory of his mother, Ellen Almira Dow Low, who was born in Wakefield.

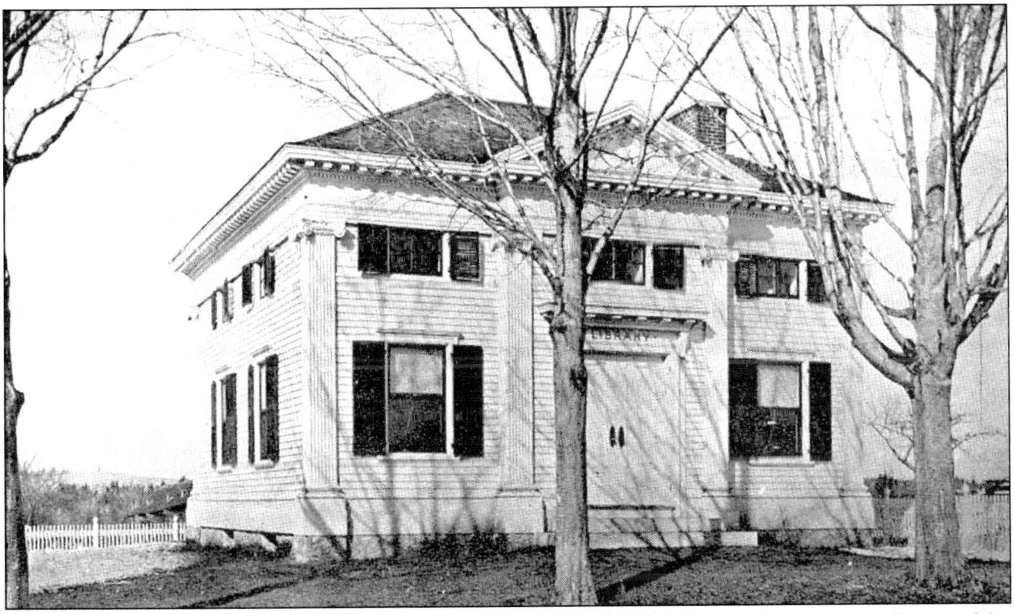

Funded by Seth Low and built in 1902, the present Wakefield Public Library was designed by architect Ernest Green of New York. Low also financed the construction of the Low Memorial Library at Columbia University, designed by McKim, Mead, and White. This beautiful little library resembles that great building.

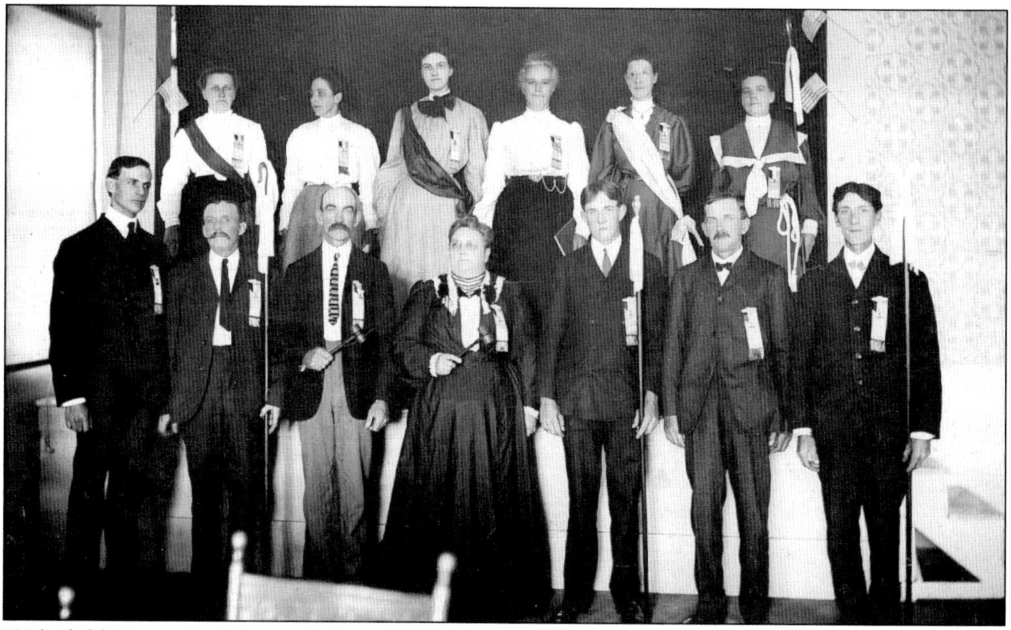

Wakefield Corner's old town hall was erected in 1837 for a sum of $525. It served the town until 1895, when the new hall was built in Sanbornville (then Wolfeboro Junction). Here, officers of the Lovell Union Grange No. 178 pose in 1905 at the old town hall, where they met until they built their own space in 1918.

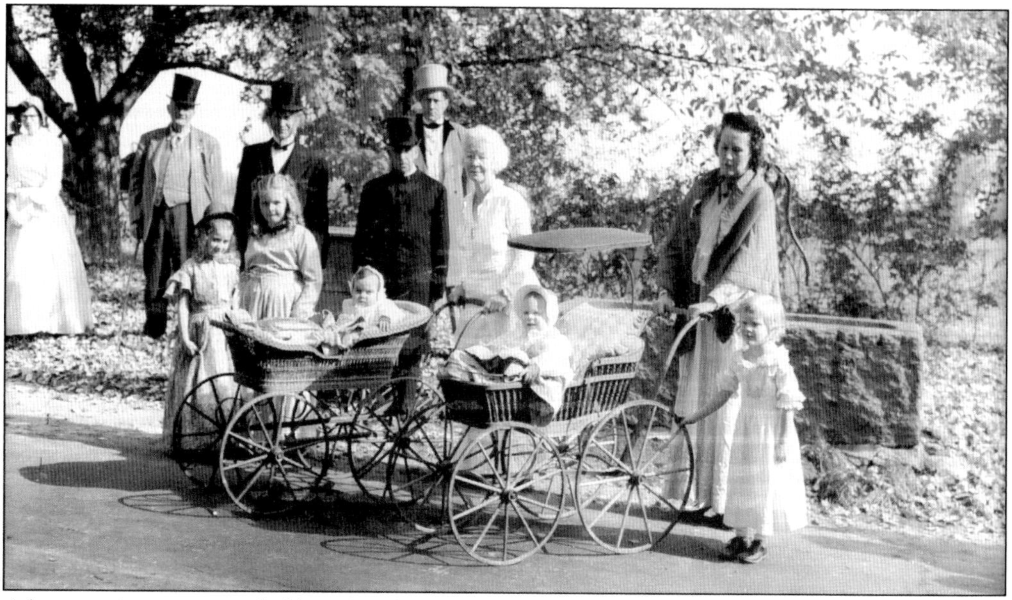

A historical pageant was held on October 13, 1956, to call attention to the ruined Congregational church. The performance attracted many participants of all faiths and several thousand spectators. Television stations filmed vignettes throughout the village. Pictured here, from left to right, are the following: (adults) Ida Maleham, Frank Garney, Samuel Paul, George Doe, Carlton Spencer, Dr. Louise Paul Heck, and Frances Belknap; (children) Darlene Maleham, Marion Elsie Maleham, Nora Kelley (first carriage), Debra Belknap (second carriage), and Marsha Belknap.

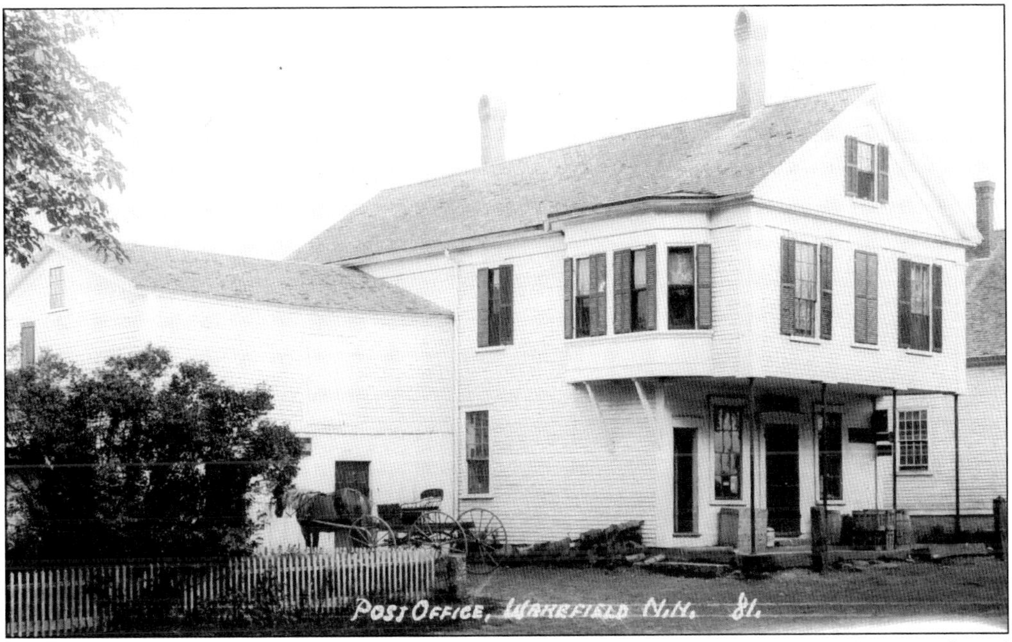

This building was originally constructed as a wheelwright's shop. Samuel Smith then purchased the structure, added a second story, and turned it into a store. Also kept over the years by George Gage, George Yeaton, Andrew Milliken, Henry Tibbets, and Robert Palmer, it additionally served as the village post office at different times.

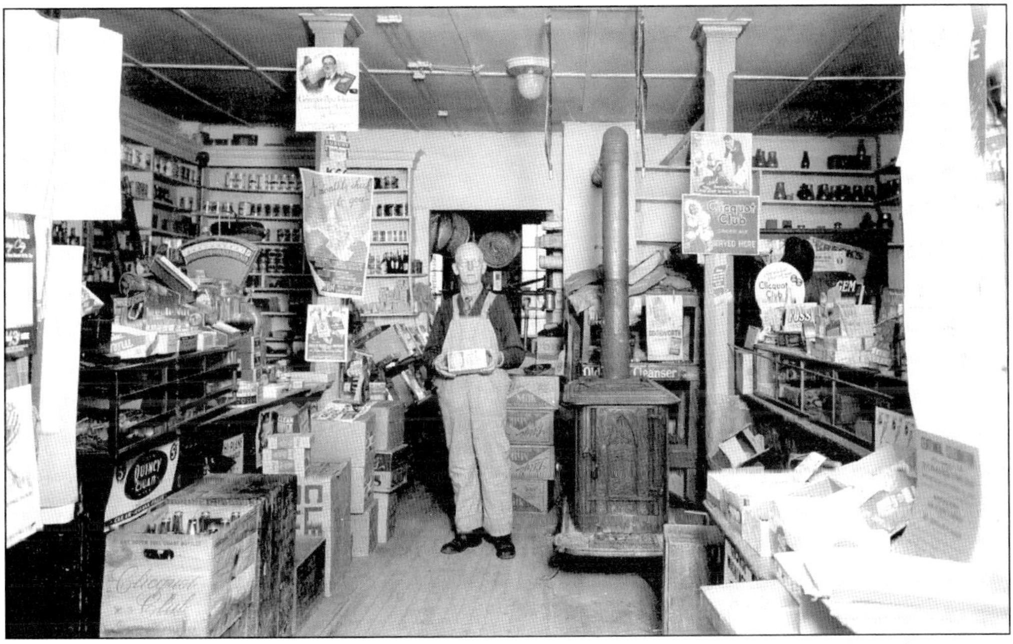

This early photograph shows a typical country store and post office from the early 20th century. Longtime proprietor Henry Tibbetts stands among his wares. An advertisement of the time promised "Groceries, Flour, Grain, Feed, Boots, Shoes, Rubbers, Dry Goods, and in fact everything usually found in a First-Class Country Store." Tibbetts was also keeper of the weights used at the hay scales across the road.

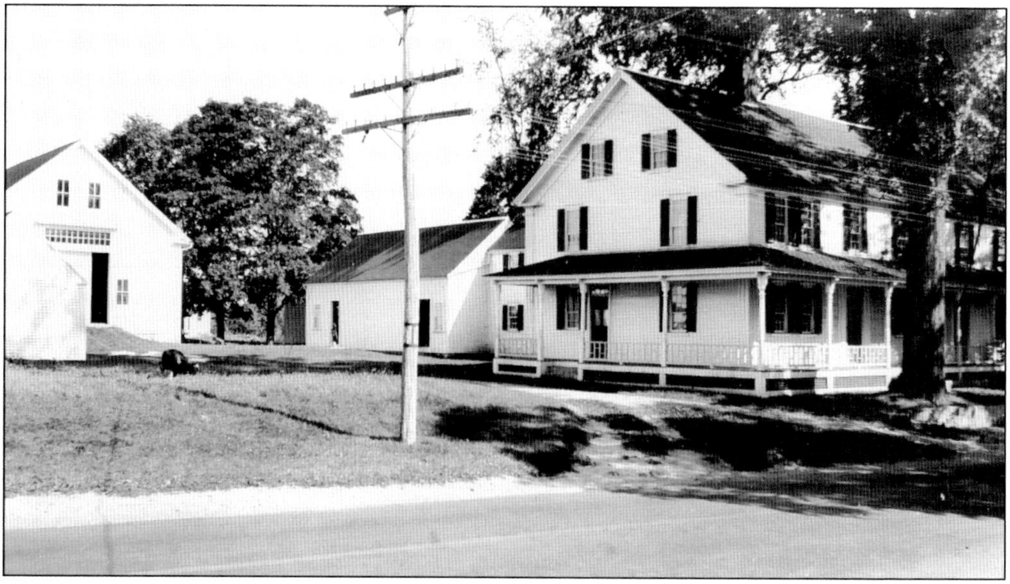

The former National House was an early stagecoach stop in Wakefield Corner. Here, six lines stopped regularly to discharge passengers, parcels, and letters. It then became a private home to the Wiggin family and is probably the only house in town to remain in the same family.

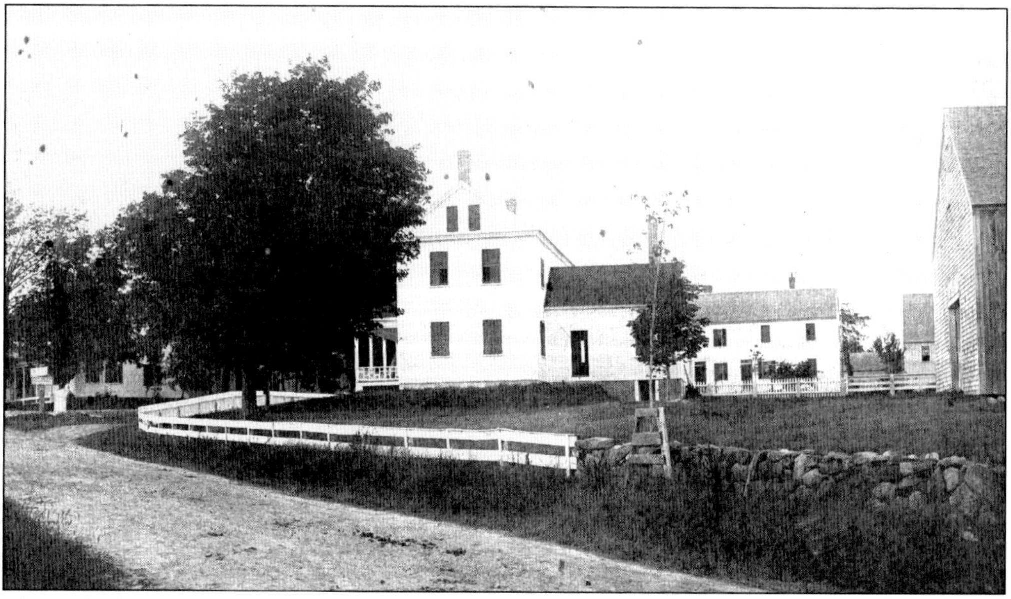

The Wakefield House was one of the stagecoach stops en route to the North Country. Originally much larger than it is today, the house once stood facing the Check Road, which stretched across woods and fields to Wakefield Corner. When that road closed, owner Hiram Paul had the structure turned 90 degrees to face as it does today.

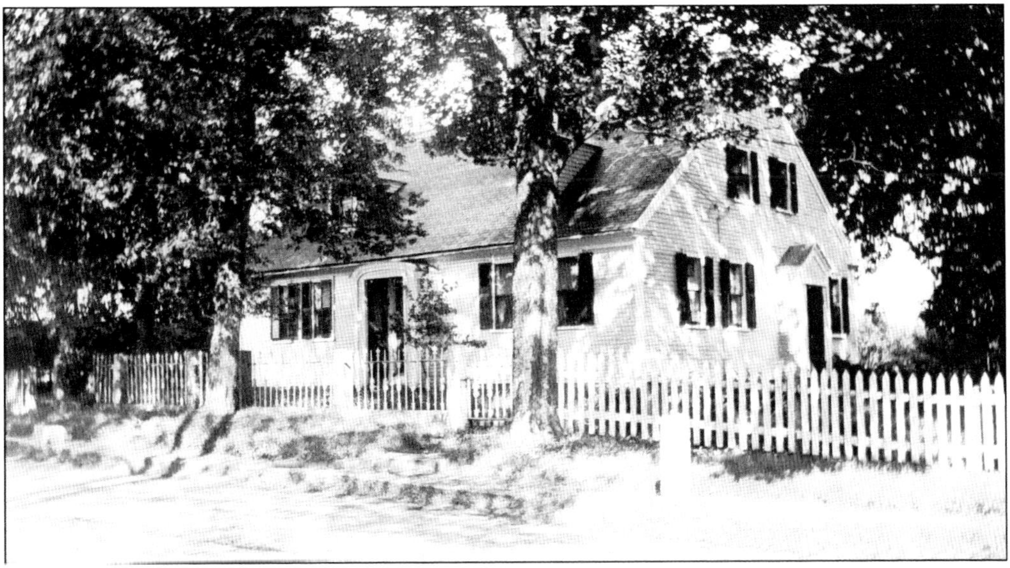

The Anchorage, dating to 1770, is the oldest house in the village. Built by Eliphalet Philbrick, it was later occupied by Capt. Robert Calder, a store owner; Dr. McCrillis; and Tobias Hanson, a tailor. The house was owned for many years by Lt. Comm. James A. Chesley, a man who spent much of his life on the sea, both in the merchant marines and in military service.

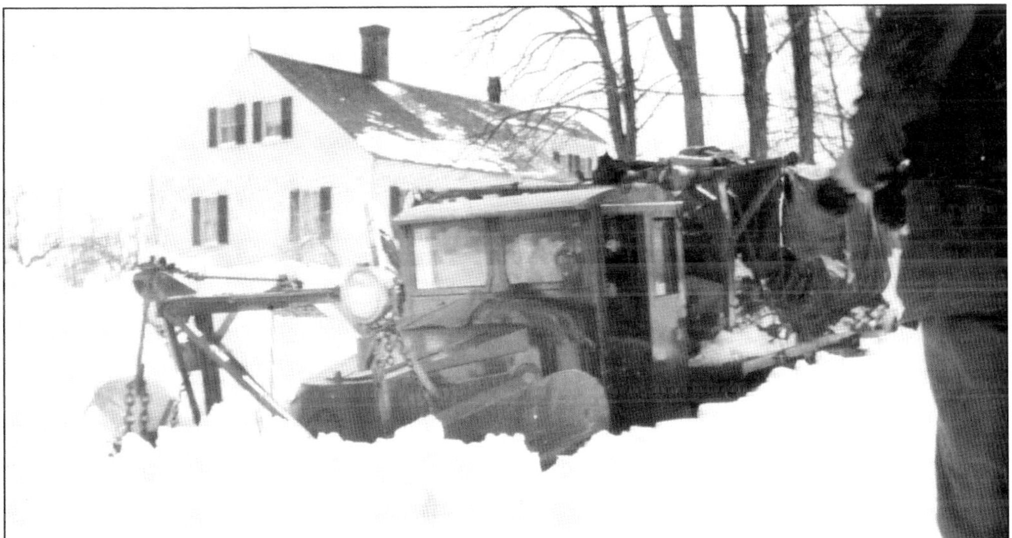

In the 1930s, snow was not plowed until the storm stopped. This large, state-owned plow was sent from town to town to help. One year, it found itself thoroughly stuck in front of the Congregational parsonage on Route 153.

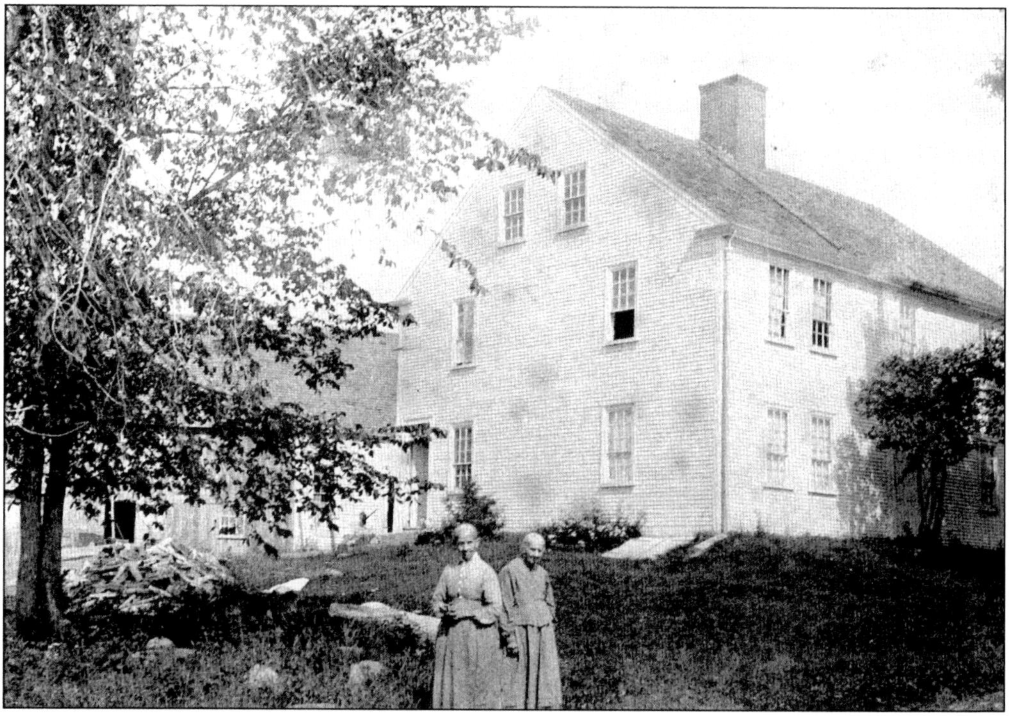

The Timothy Sawyer house was built in 1796 and remained in the family until 1910, with the death of Lucy Maria Sawyer at the age of 101. She lived here with her sister Sarah and her brother Alvah, who was a blacksmith.

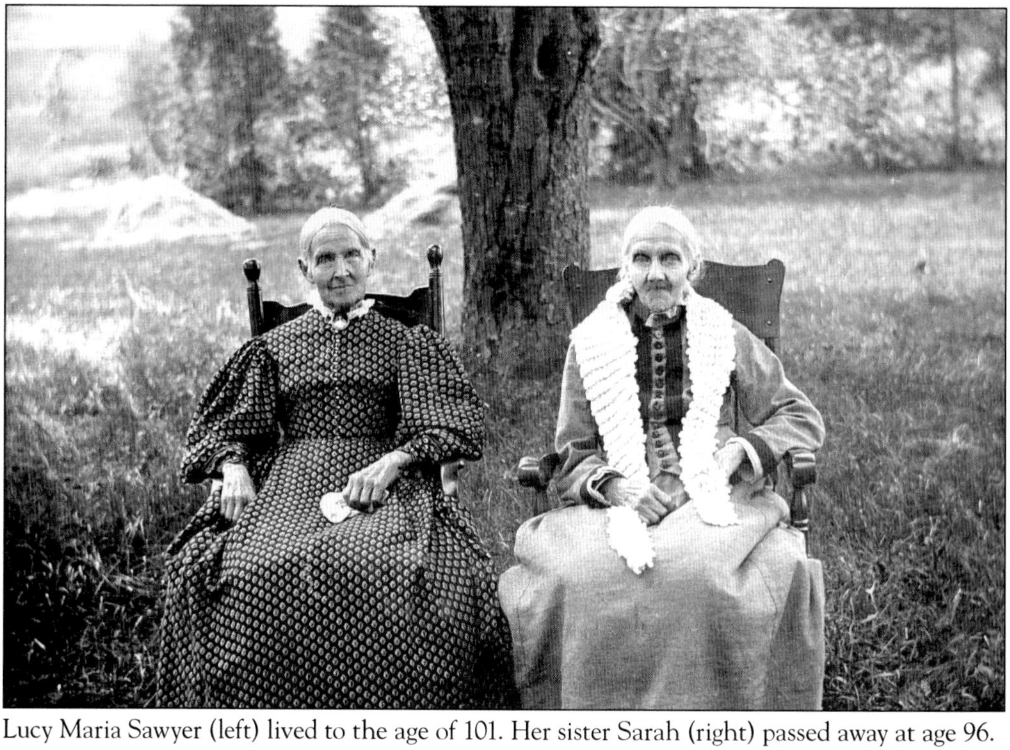

Lucy Maria Sawyer (left) lived to the age of 101. Her sister Sarah (right) passed away at age 96.

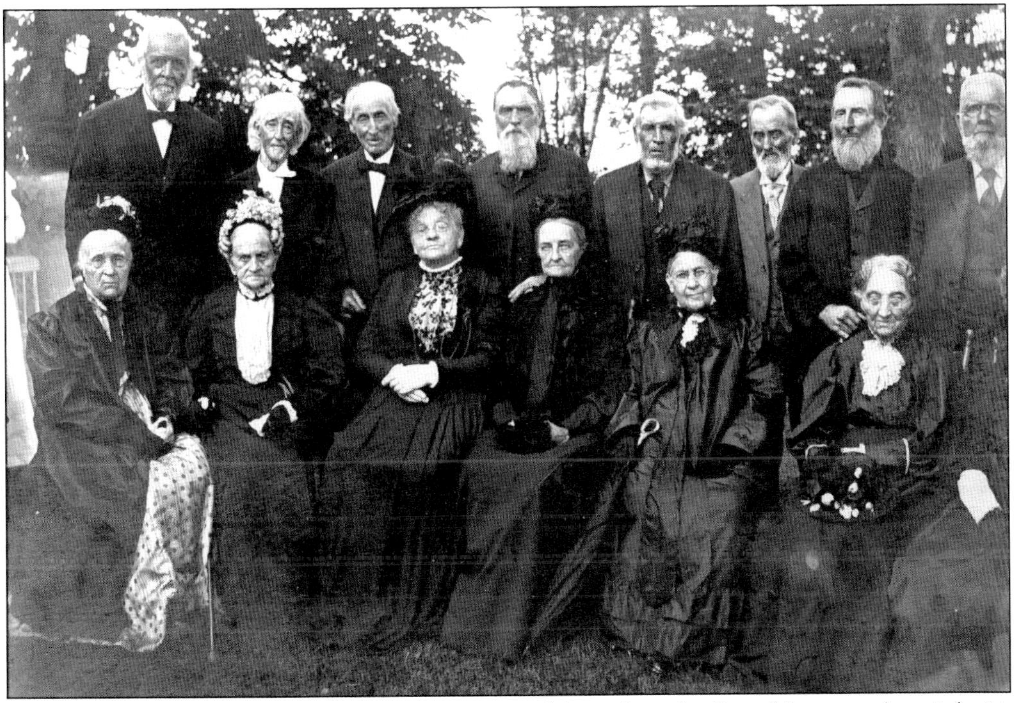

The 100th birthday of Lucy Maria Sawyer was celebrated at the Dow Homestead on July 14, 1909. Pictured on the occasion are the following, from left to right: (first row) Mary Porter Paul, Sarah Beach, Susan Nason, Sarah Maleham, Mrs. Chase, and Susan Lovering; (second row) Dr. Samuel Roberts, Asa Brown, Fred Copp, Jackson Horn, Deacon Satchel Weeks, George Prince Dow, George Gage, and Richard Roberts.

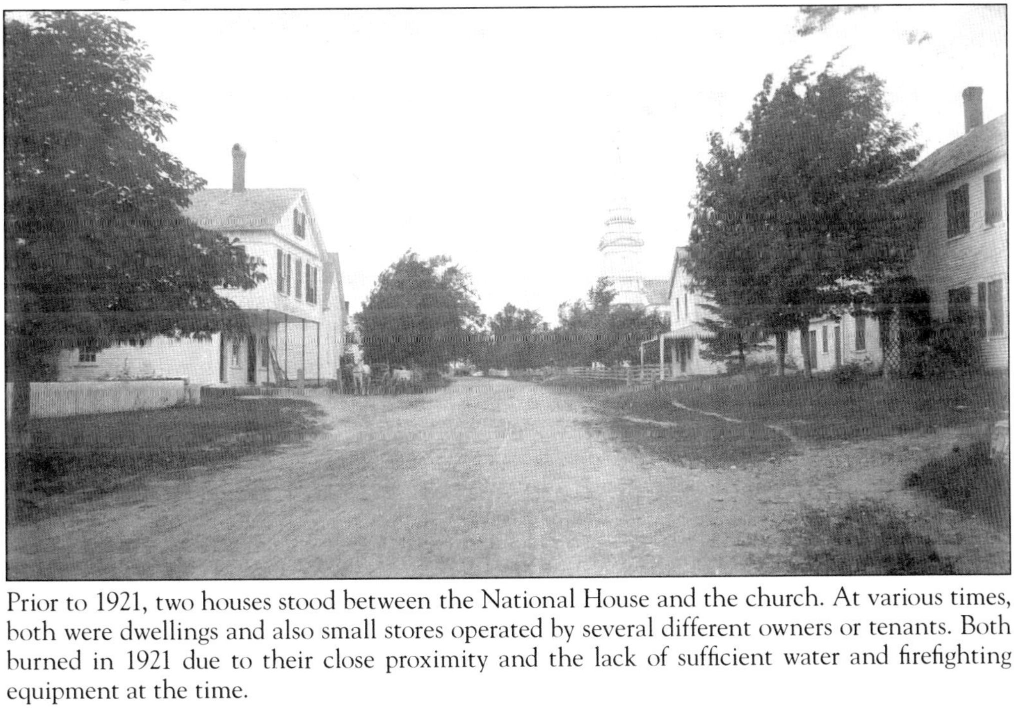

Prior to 1921, two houses stood between the National House and the church. At various times, both were dwellings and also small stores operated by several different owners or tenants. Both burned in 1921 due to their close proximity and the lack of sufficient water and firefighting equipment at the time.

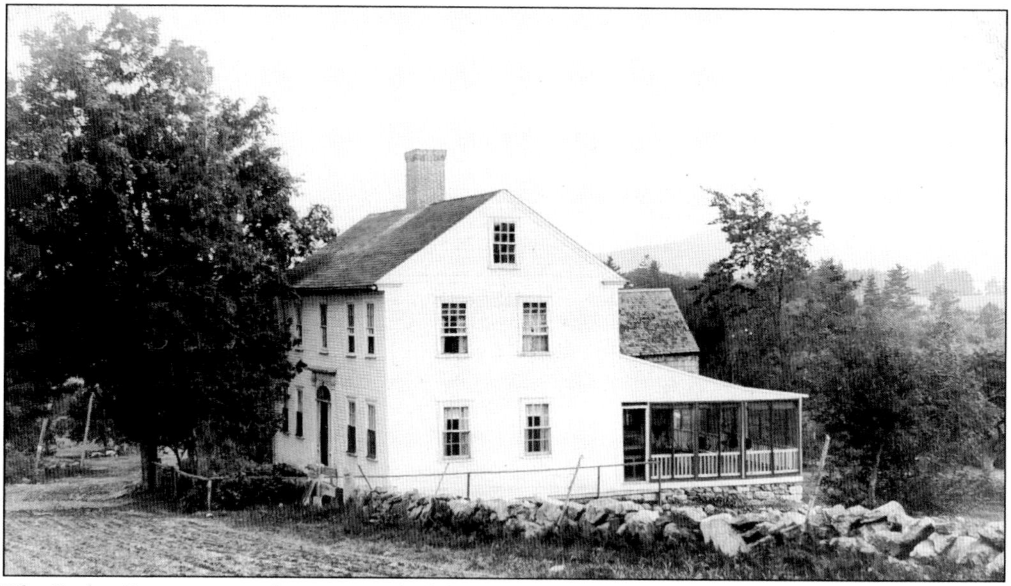

The Barker Parsonage was home to Wakefield's second settled minister. Originally built by Richard Rollins on part of the Rollins farm, the house remains unspoiled, boasting a beehive oven, an arched central chimney, "Indian" (or "comfort") shutters, and a louvered fan over the door.

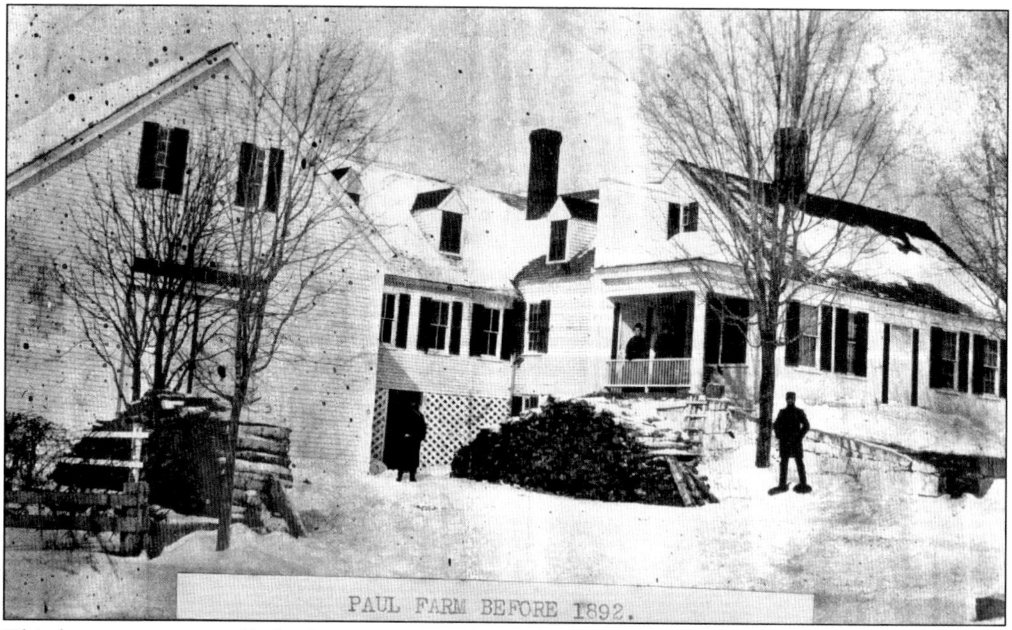

This house was originally built as a cape in the early 1800s. In 1859, Hiram Paul won one-third of the building in a court judgment. He then purchased the other two-thirds and added a second story to accommodate his large family.

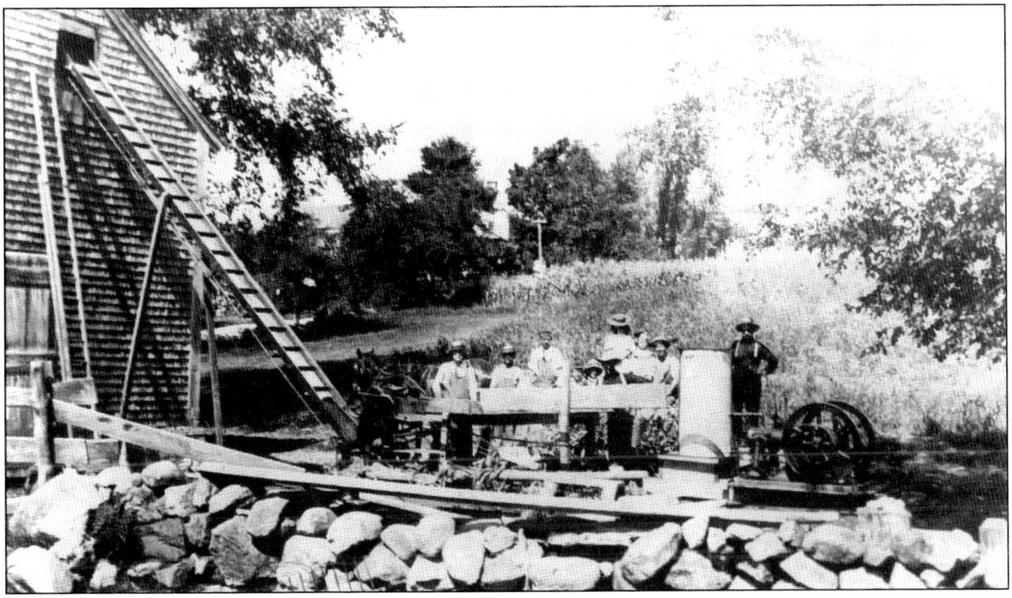

"One lunger" gasoline engines were used to perform many tasks around a farm. This one is operating a stationary corn chopper. The elevator moves the chopped silage up and into the silo behind the Paul farm barn.

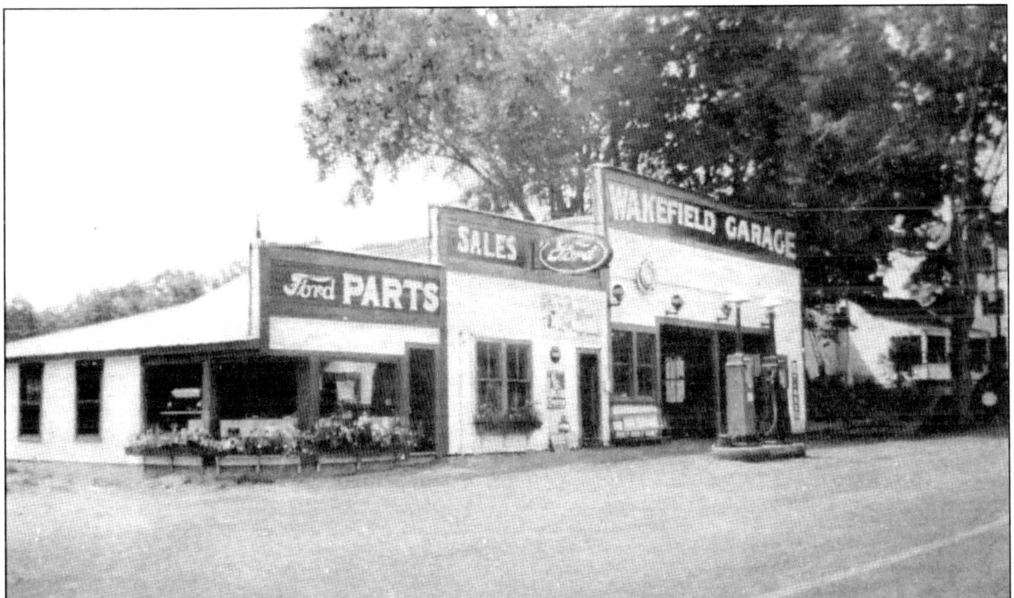

Wakefield Garage was owned and operated by Herbert Kennett for many years, and then by his nephew-in-law Guy Neily. Cars—and gasoline—were cheaper then.

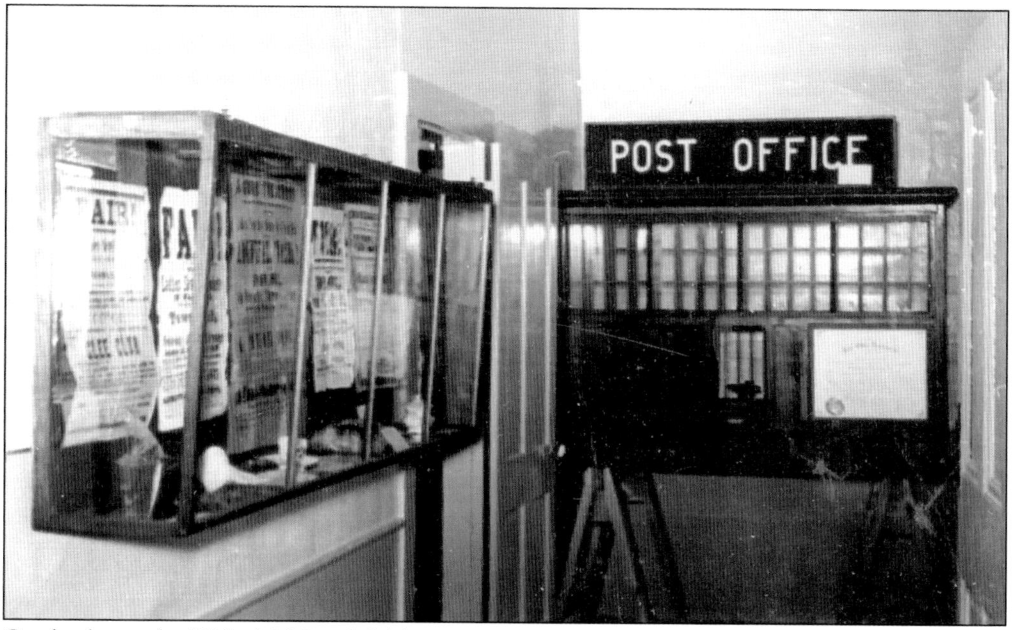

On display at the Wakefield-Brookfield Historical Society is an early Wakefield post office made by Maj. Samuel Smith. Posters in the glass case advertise fairs held in the 1850s by the Ladies Sewing Society, forerunner of the present Parish Helpers group. The historical society, founded in 1938, was originally housed in the old Wakefield Academy room on the second floor of the Congregational church.

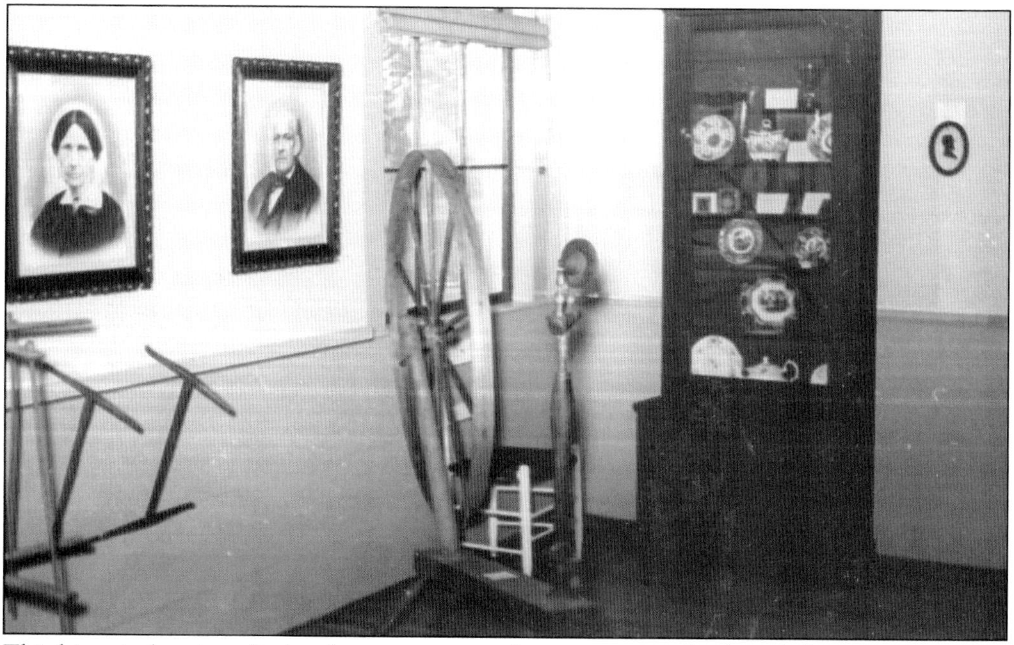

This historical society display shows a yarn winder, a spinning wheel, and chinaware in an old cabinet. The portraits depict Amasa Copp and his wife, who owned much land and many houses and businesses in both Wakefield and Brookfield. The display was produced in 1947, the year the Little Red Schoolhouse became home to the society's collection and meetings.

Two

UNION

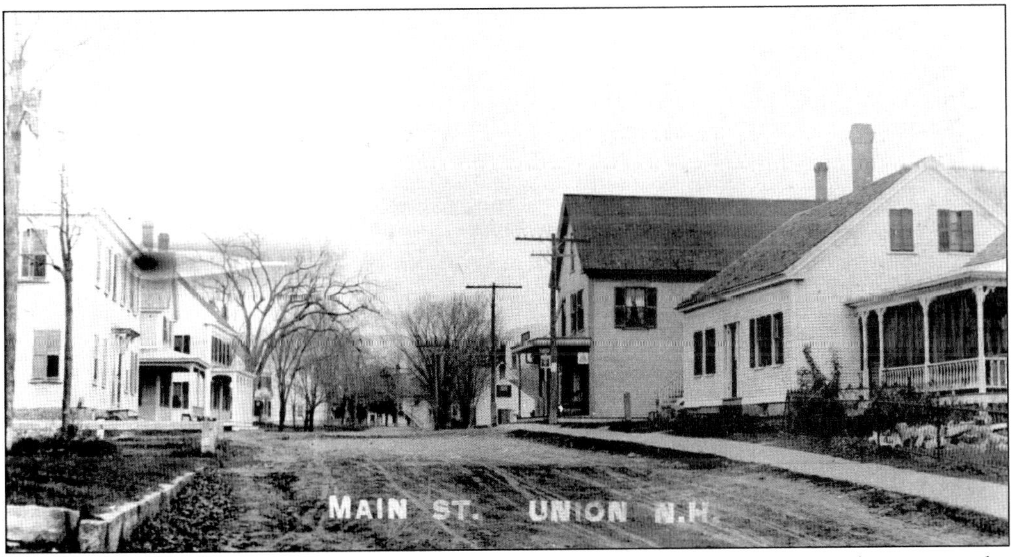

Looking north on Main Street in Union, this view captures William M. Lord's store in the right center.

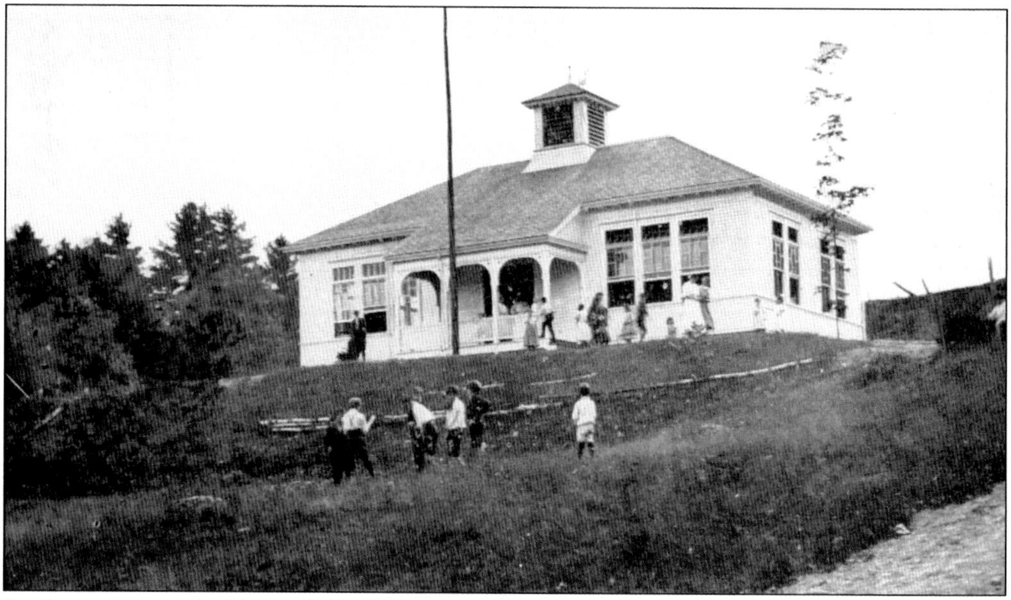

Students pose at the Union School (District 9) in 1910. The schoolhouse, the third one to be built in Union, was constructed in 1903 and is still in use today.

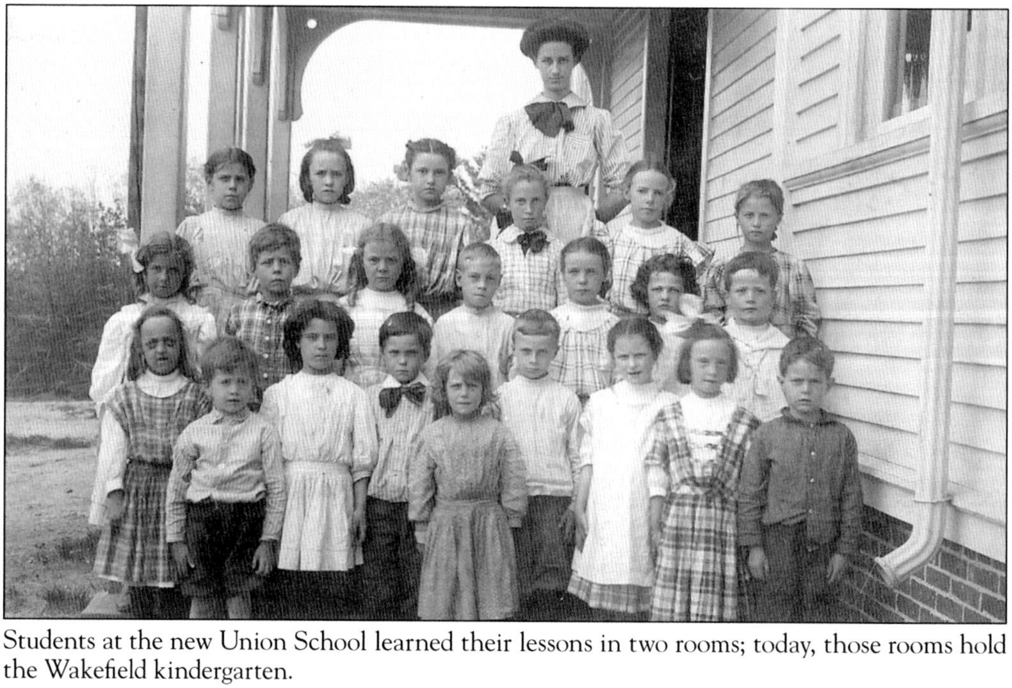

Students at the new Union School learned their lessons in two rooms; today, those rooms hold the Wakefield kindergarten.

The Congregational church in Union was constructed sometime before 1840 and served multiple denominations for decades. The building is said to include portions of the original Wakefield meetinghouse. Different stories have circulated about the "theft" of the meetinghouse, which was rumored to have been removed from its site over the protests of many in the area.

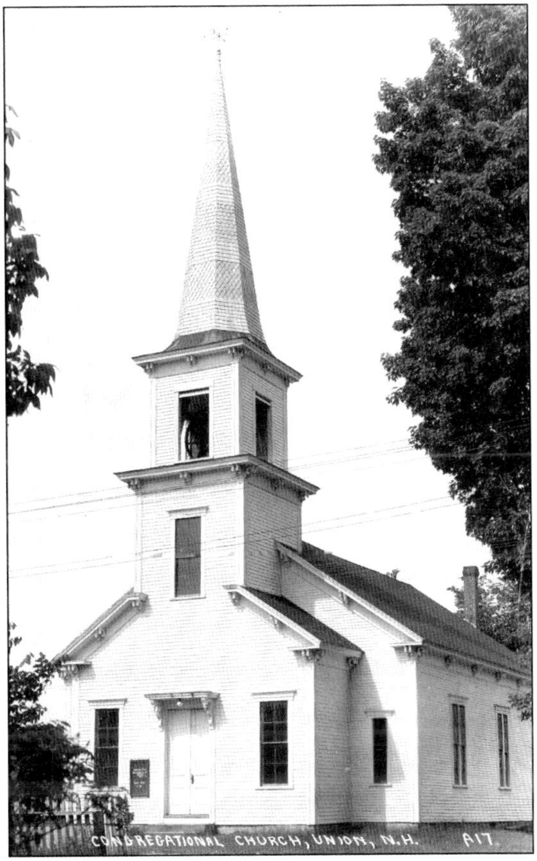

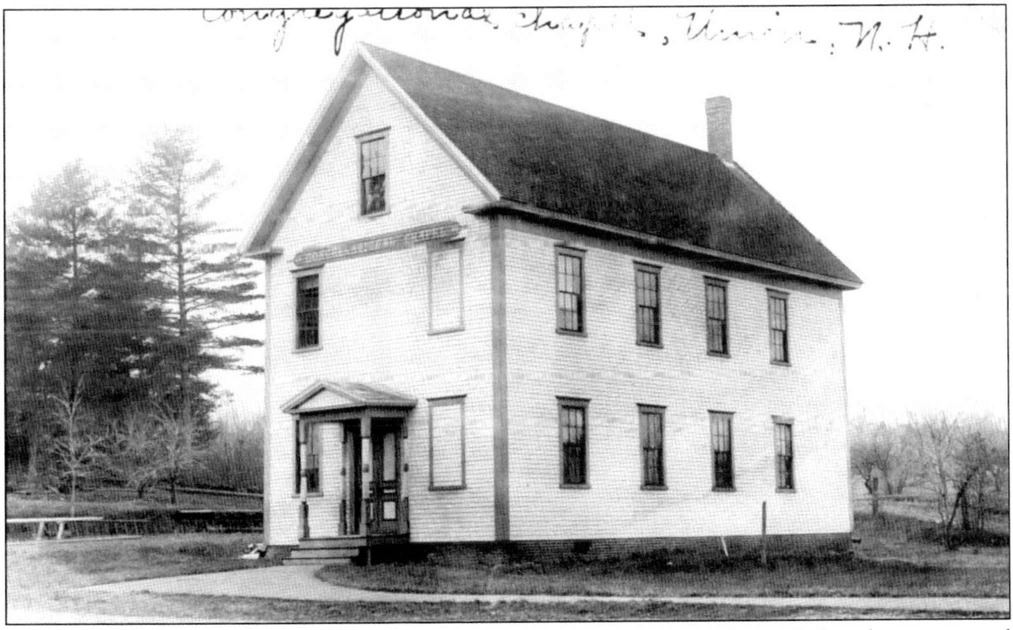

Union's Congregational chapel was built by Frank Drew in 1888. It housed church suppers and activities for many years, and even held the town library for some time.

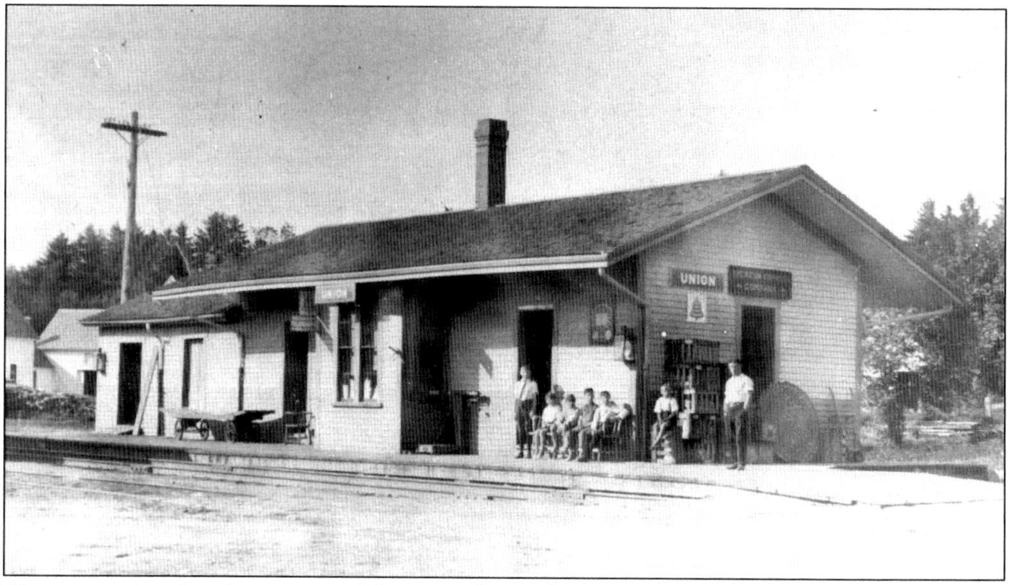

The original railroad station in Union is shown here before 1912. Stagecoaches had been frequenting the village for decades, but the arrival of the Eastern (later Boston and Maine) Railroad in 1854 brought a new rush of activity. Rail and stagecoach traffic bustled through the busy village, as people and goods traveled to and from points farther east, west, and north.

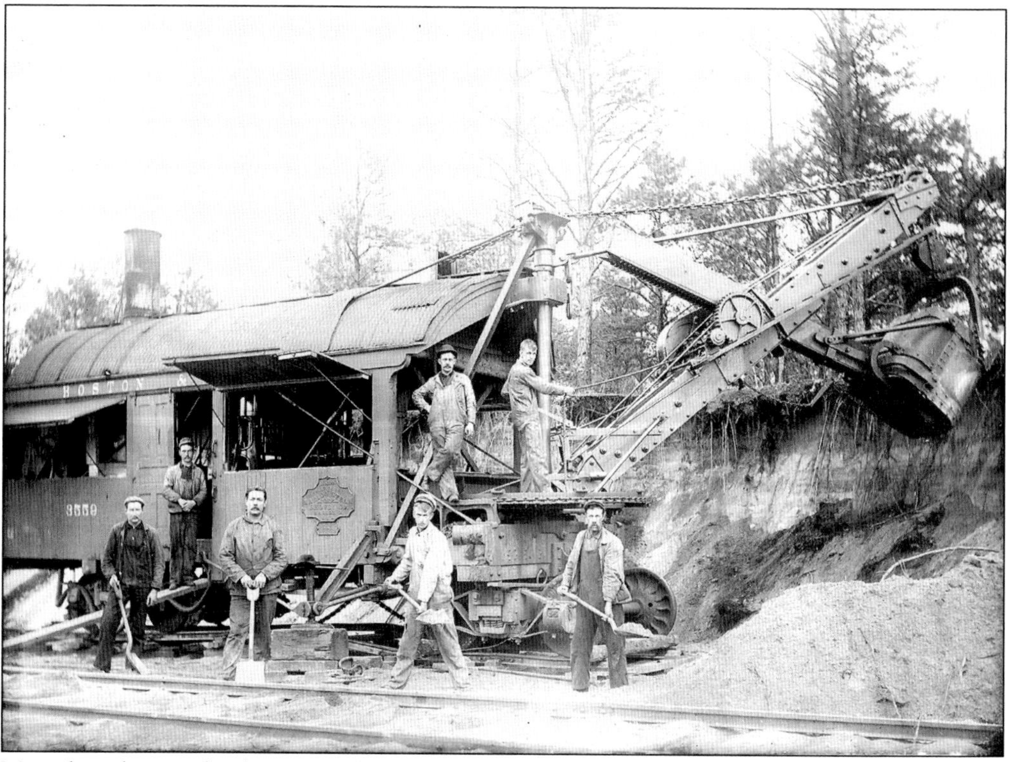

Men clear the way for the new railroad tracks with the help of a train-mounted steam shovel.

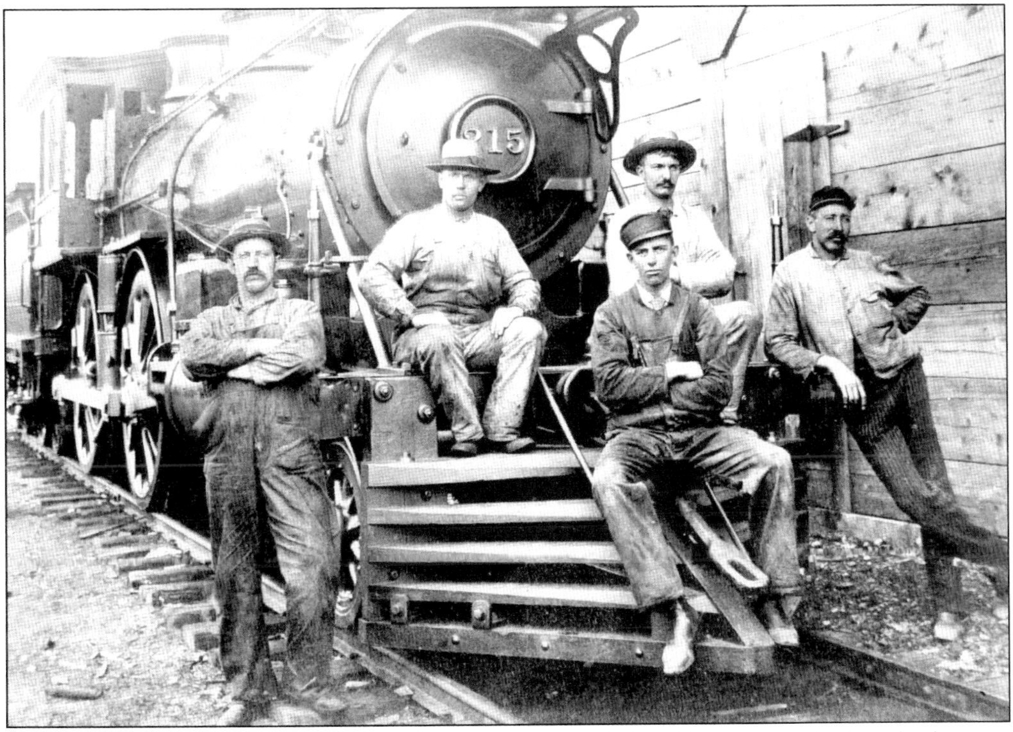

Engine No. 215 is pictured in Union, along with James Tucker, Ernest Campbell, and others.

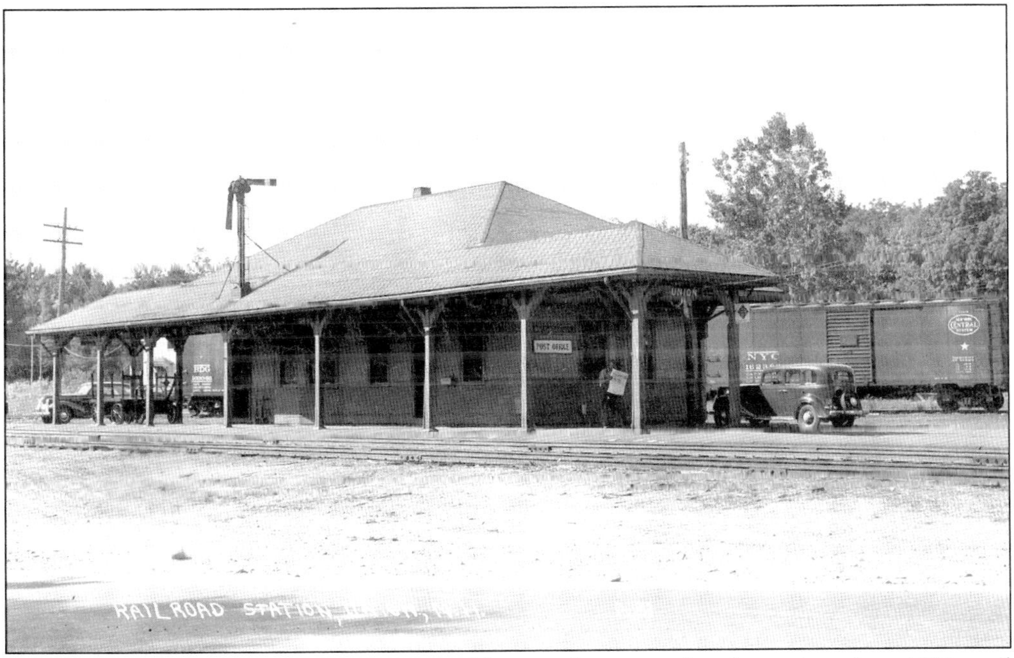

A new station was built in 1912. Union had been a thriving railroad terminus from 1854 until the tracks were again extended north, reaching Sanbornville in 1871. The station closed in 1956; the building became the Union Post Office and then a private home.

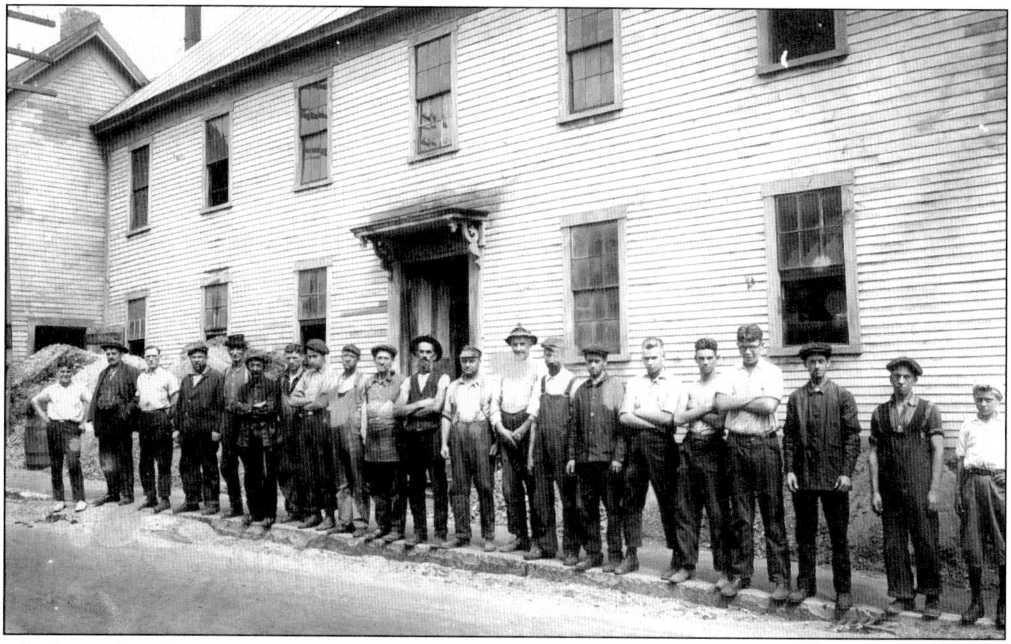

The brass foundry, which made brass fittings and castings, was powered by a water wheel at the Upper Dam. Earlier, it had been a gristmill and an excelsior mill. Once opposite the Masonic temple, the building was torn down in 1940. This photograph includes George Morrison, Pat Shea, Guy Varney, George Kimball, William Wilson, "Tib" Woodman, Walter Kimball, "Let" Hill, Waldo Hill, Ernest Wentworth, and Leon Hill.

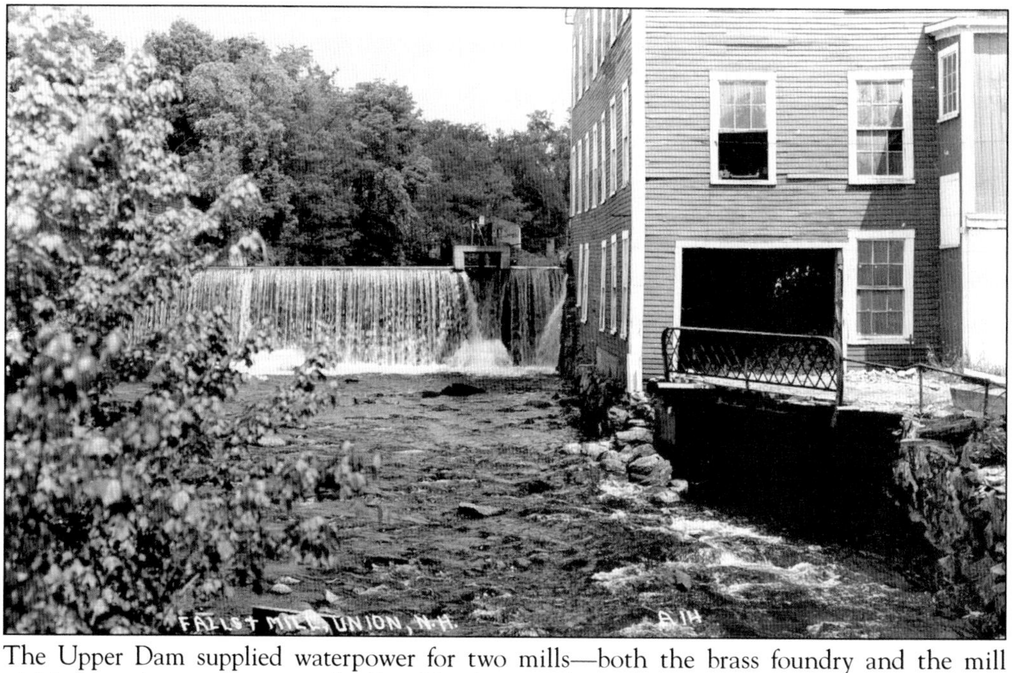

The Upper Dam supplied waterpower for two mills—both the brass foundry and the mill visible here. A sawmill was run by Sam Hutchins in the mid-1800s. At different times, the mill also manufactured car stock for the railroad, excelsior, and when owned by Reuben Sanborn, basket-bottomed chairs.

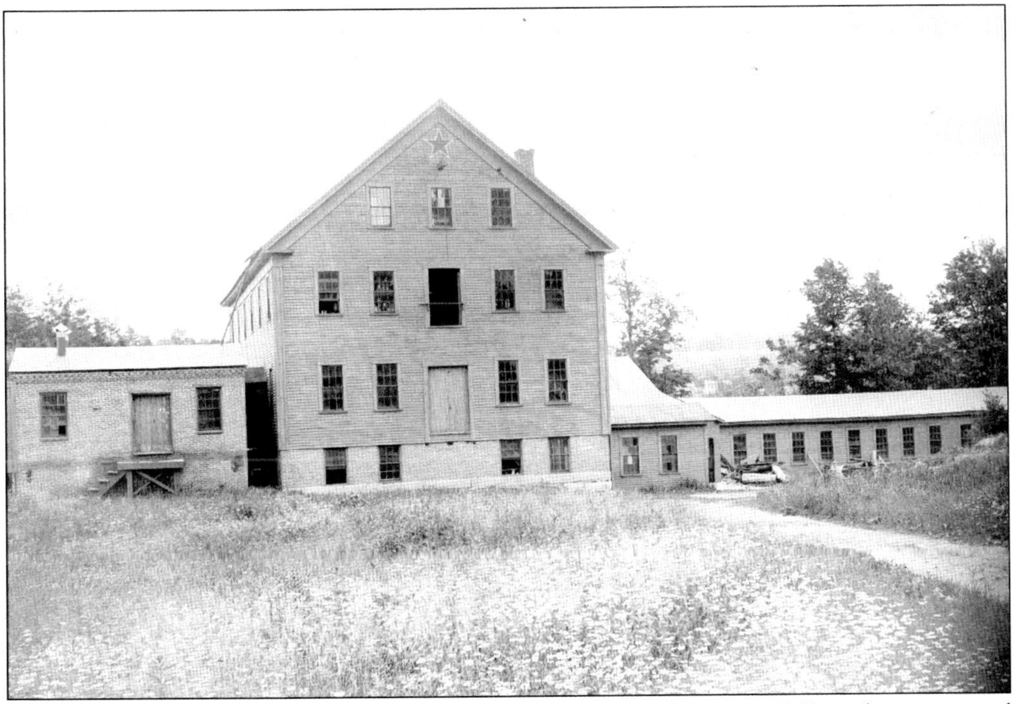

This woolen mill, once off South Main Street, was located on the Lower Falls and was operated by Arthur Taft. The building burned in 1908.

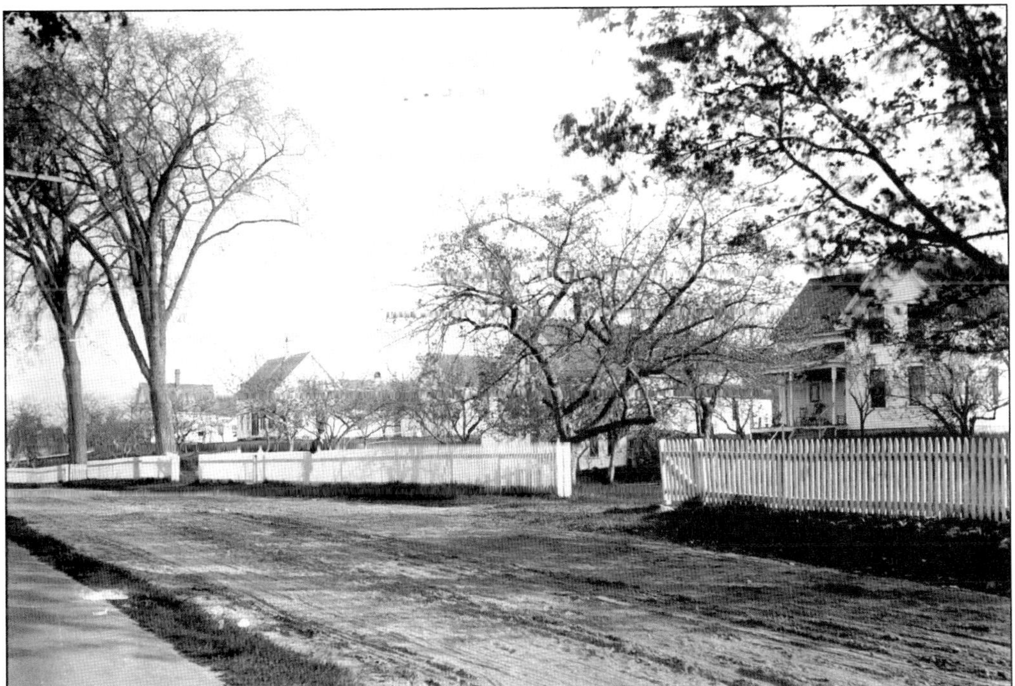

South Main Street in Union is seen in the early 1900s. The house on the far right, built in 1890, is the former parsonage of the Congregational church.

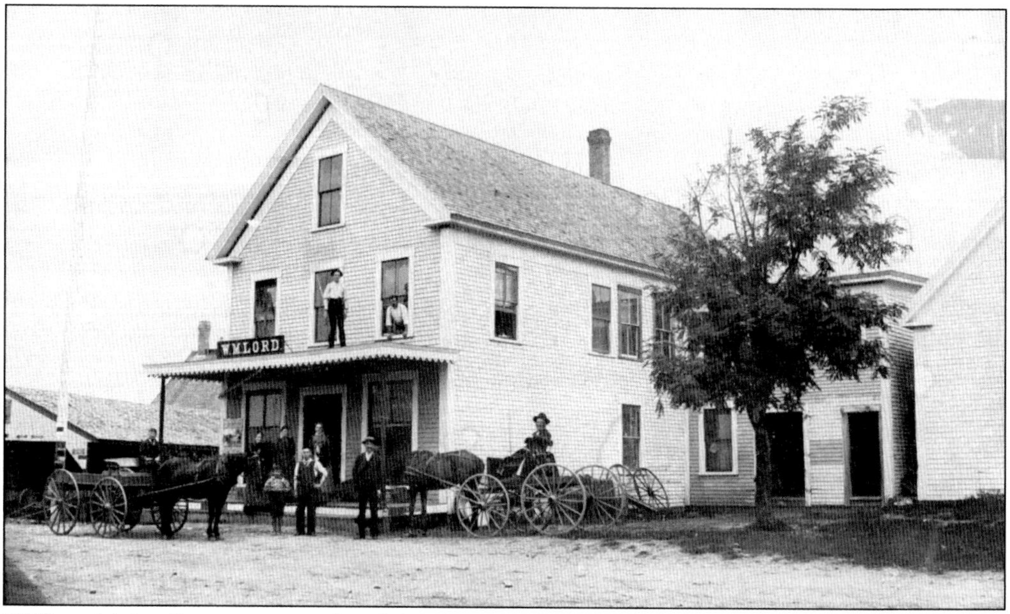

William M. Lord's store, situated on Main Street in Union, is pictured in the early 1900s, before burning in the fire of 1923. A one-story structure rebuilt on the site was bought by Louis Tibbetts and operated as Tibbetts' Country Store from 1945 through 1970.

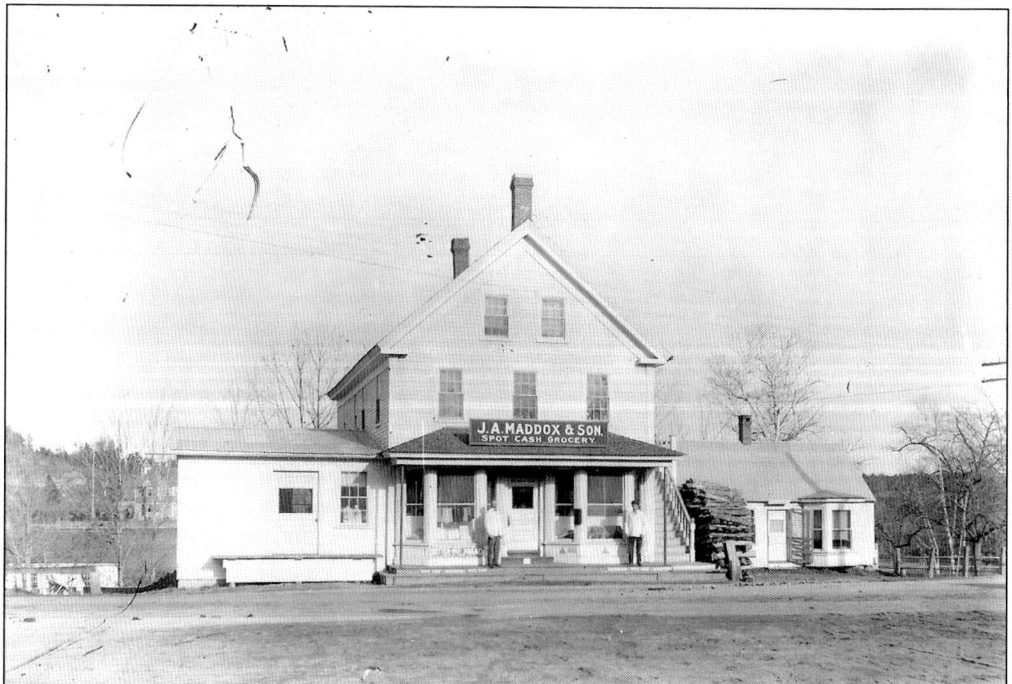

The J. A. Maddox and Son Store was once located in this building on South Main Street in Union. The store had other owners over the years, and at times housed the post office.

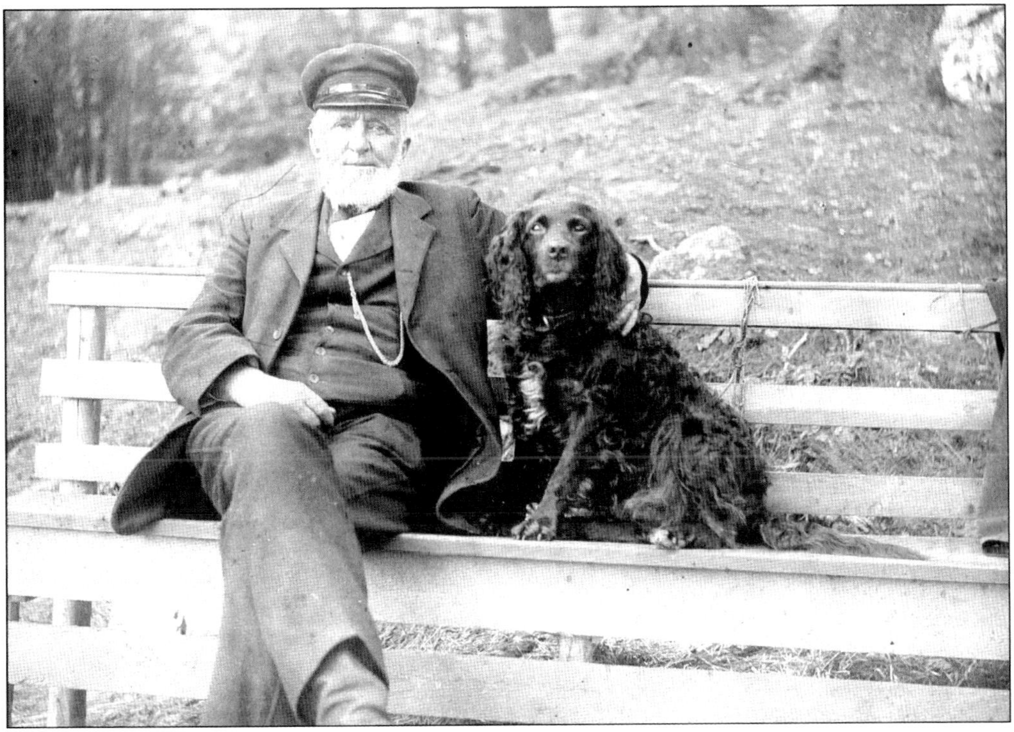

Andrew J. Hayes and his dog Paugus are buried side by side in the Union Cemetery. Paugus's epitaph reads, "A loving dog, a constant friend/ This life perhaps is not his end/ Faithful to every trust and then/ He had more sense than many men."

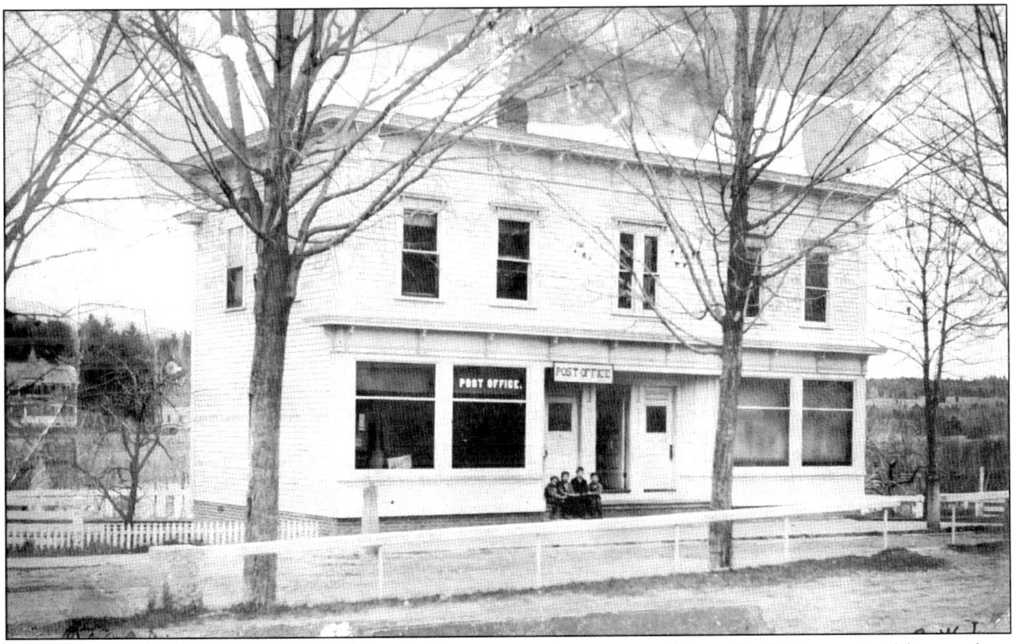

Union's post office opened in 1860 and, like most others, moved from building to building, often changing locations as the postmaster changed. This structure, which is still standing, housed the post office for a time. It later held the Union Village Library, now closed.

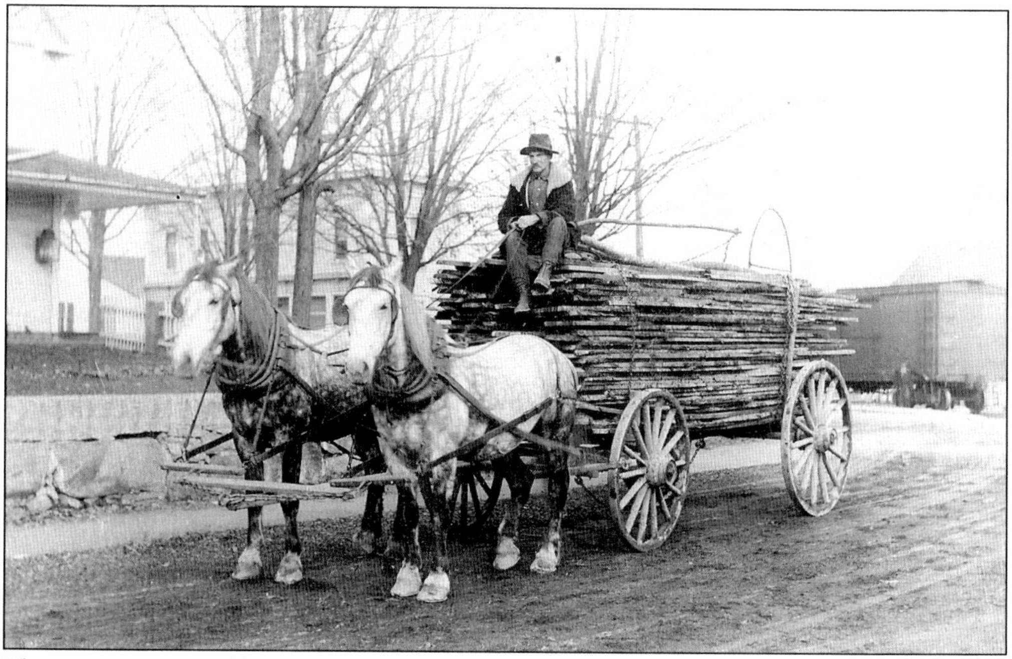

There were innumerable uses for the wood so plentiful in the Wakefield area. Local mills sawed wood into lumber for construction and also produced railroad ties, shingles, furniture, and excelsior. Wood fired the railway engines until replaced by coal, and wood and wood products were shipped out on the trains. In front of the Union Hotel, with the train tracks in the background, this man hauls wood with a horse-drawn cart.

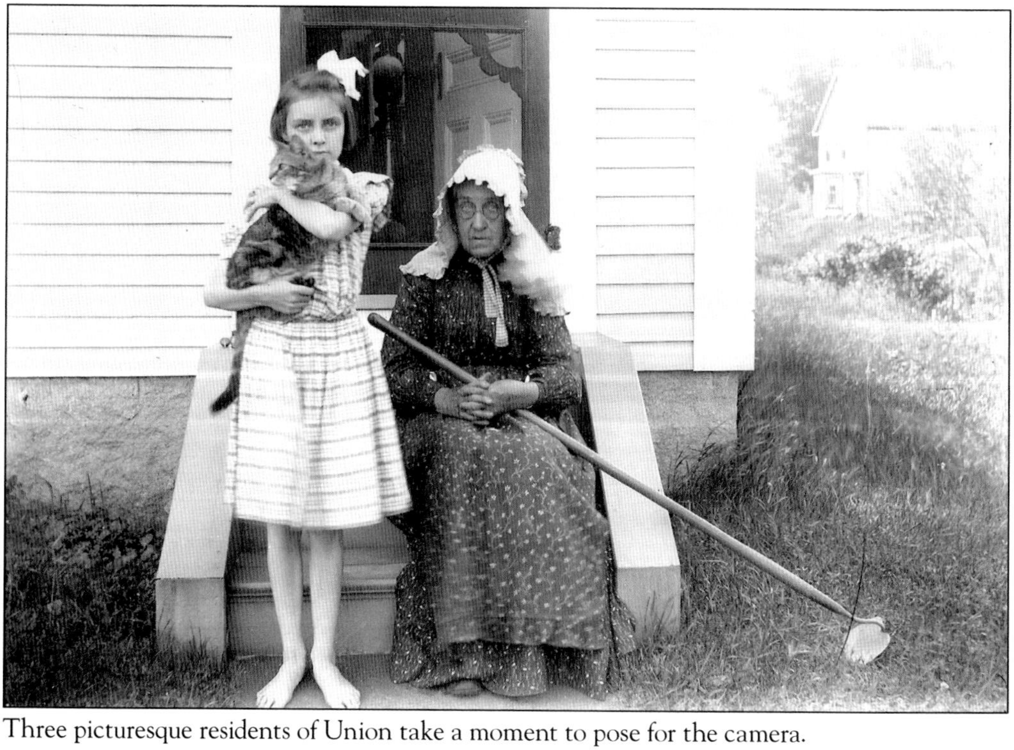

Three picturesque residents of Union take a moment to pose for the camera.

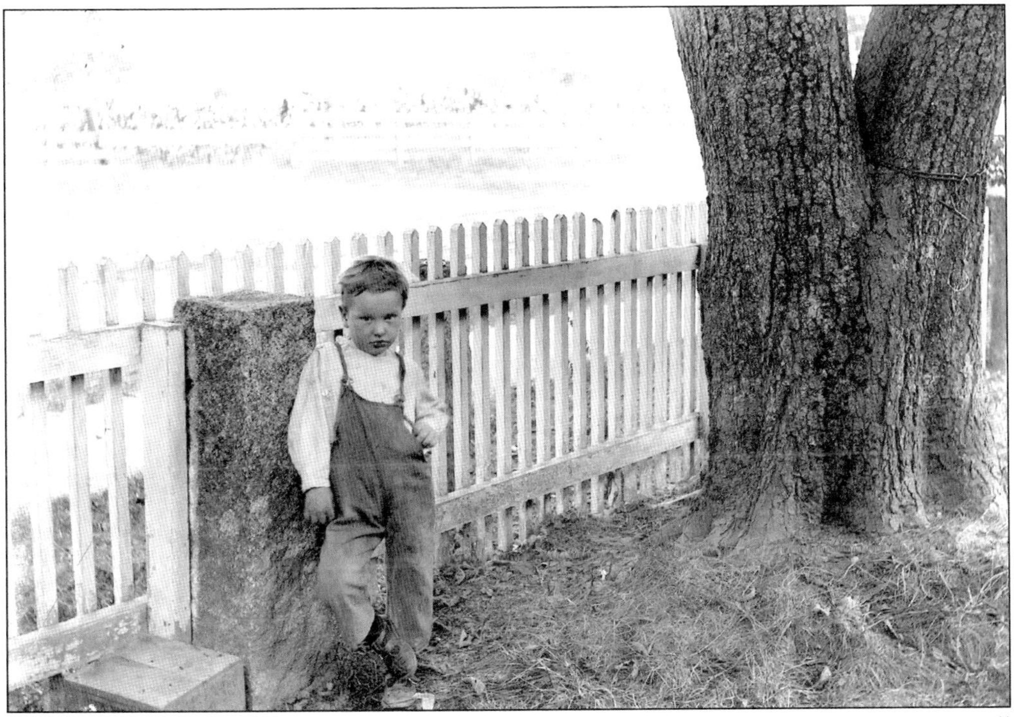

This young resident of Union would have made a good Tom Sawyer. Maybe tomorrow he will recruit some gullible friends to help him paint the picket fence.

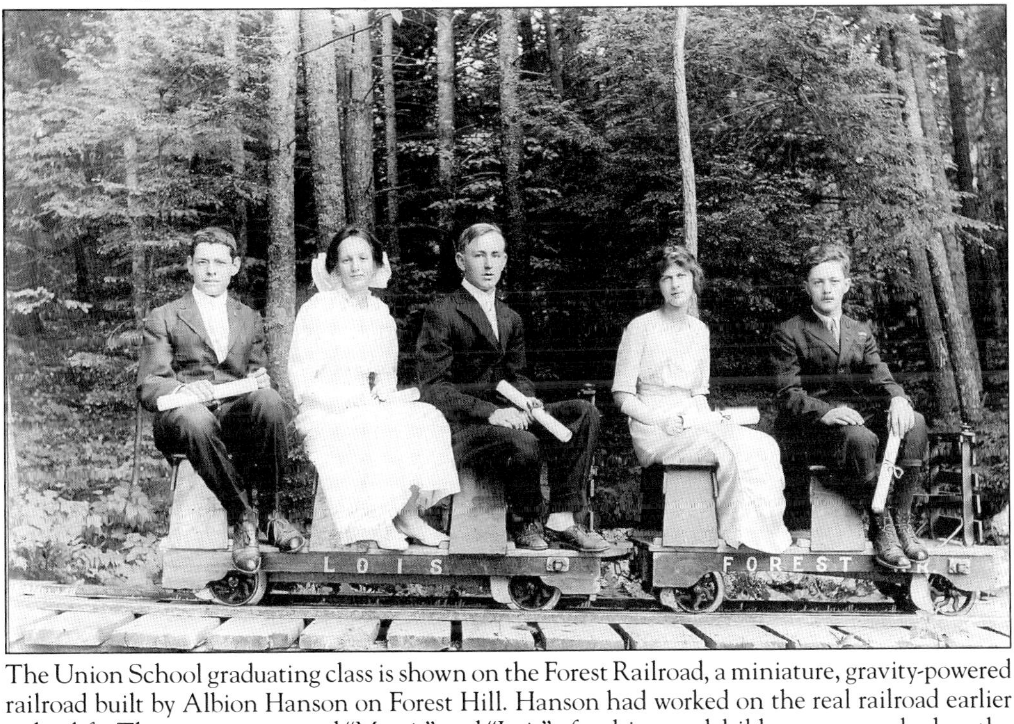

The Union School graduating class is shown on the Forest Railroad, a miniature, gravity-powered railroad built by Albion Hanson on Forest Hill. Hanson had worked on the real railroad earlier in his life. The two cars, named "Morris" and "Lois" after his grandchildren, were pushed up the hill, and then the passengers rode down. Local children were welcome to ride at any time.

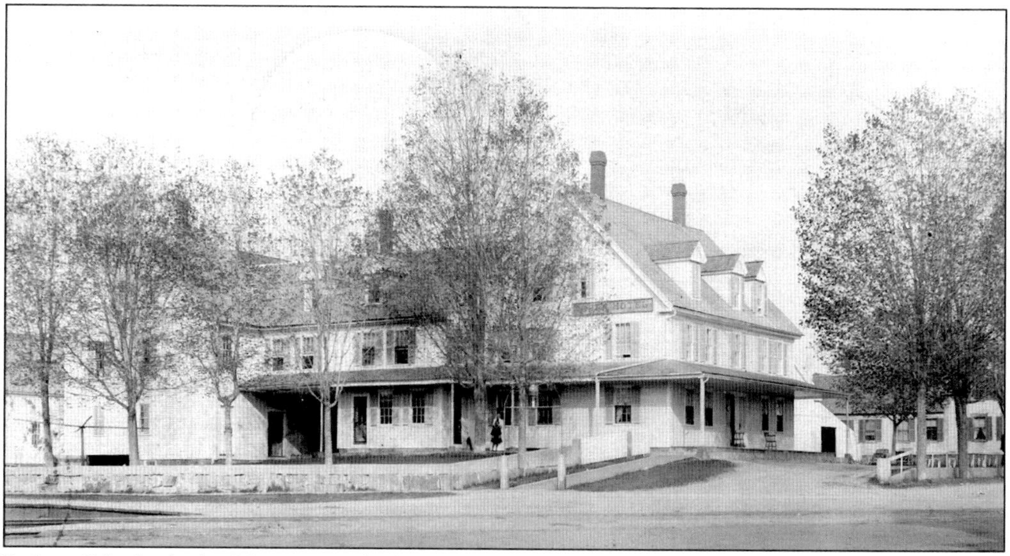

Robert Pike built the Union Hotel, also once known as the Union House and the Red Coach Inn, in the early 1800s. The stagecoach stopped here often, and travelers ate in the elegant dining room. When the railroad came to town, business increased at the already successful inn. A livery stable thrived adjacent to the hotel. Traveling salesmen arrived on the train and then hired horses and wagons at the stable to continue their routes northward.

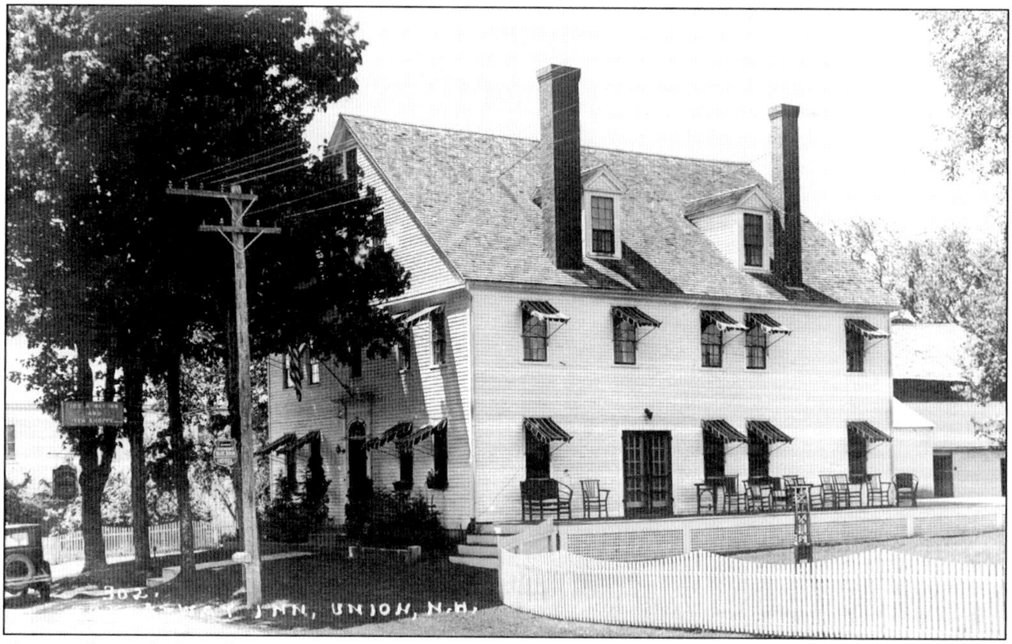

Originally called Hall's Tavern, this longtime inn was later known as Pillsbury Hall and the Tox-A-Way Inn. Joshua Hall received a license to sell liquor here in 1800, and the Hall family provided meals and lodgings to stagecoach and train passengers for many decades. It was reportedly a part of the Underground Railroad, and Henry Ford is said to have stayed here. In the 1940s, the building became a convalescent home owned by Robert Kennison.

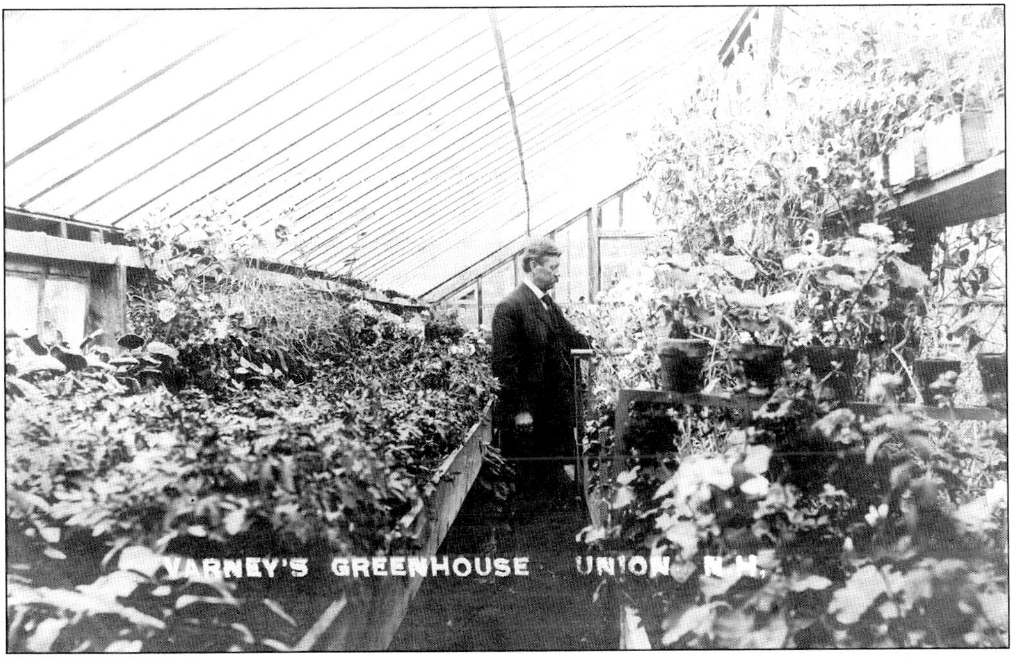

Frank Varney operated two greenhouses in the 1920s and 1930s on the site where the Union Post Office is now located. One year just before Easter, a local woman's car collided with one of the greenhouses and she lost consciousness. Awakening surrounded by lilies, the dazed driver thought that she had died and gone to heaven—literally.

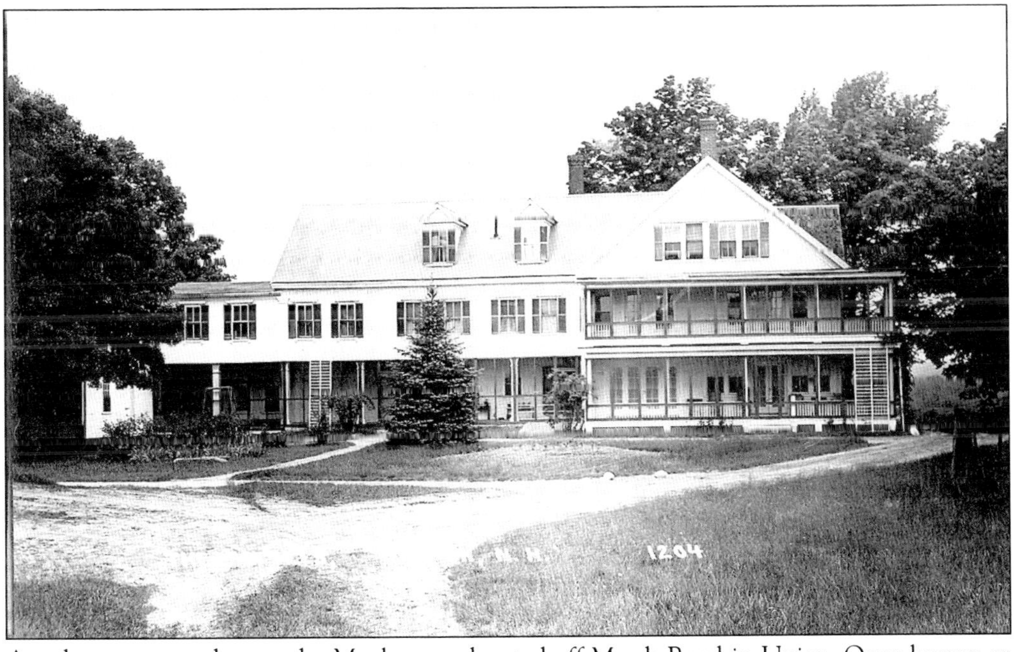

Another area guesthouse, the Maples, was located off Marsh Road in Union. Once known as Maple Ridge, the building was later destroyed by fire.

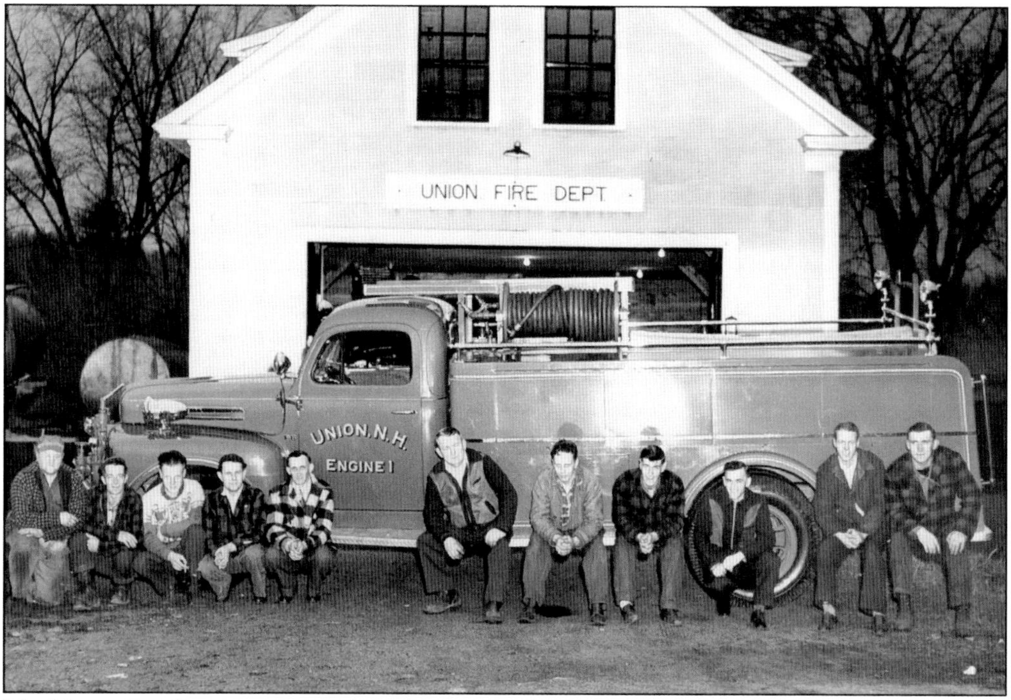

The Union Fire Department purchased a new truck in May 1950. The fire station had been built in 1936.

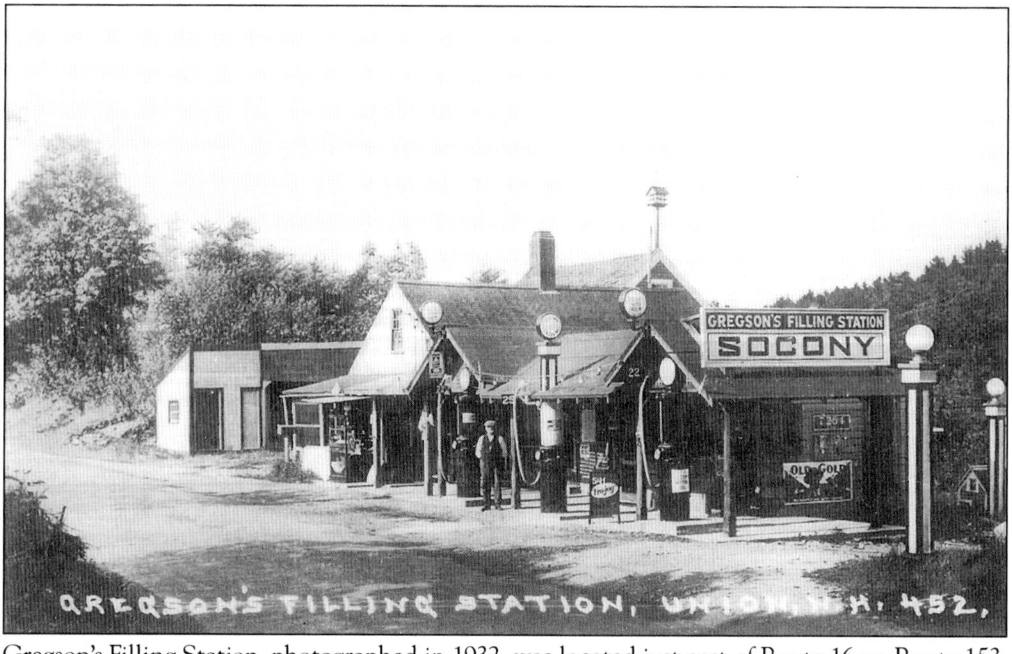

Gregson's Filling Station, photographed in 1932, was located just east of Route 16 on Route 153, next to Union Meadows. A gas station remains on the site today.

Three

SANBORNVILLE

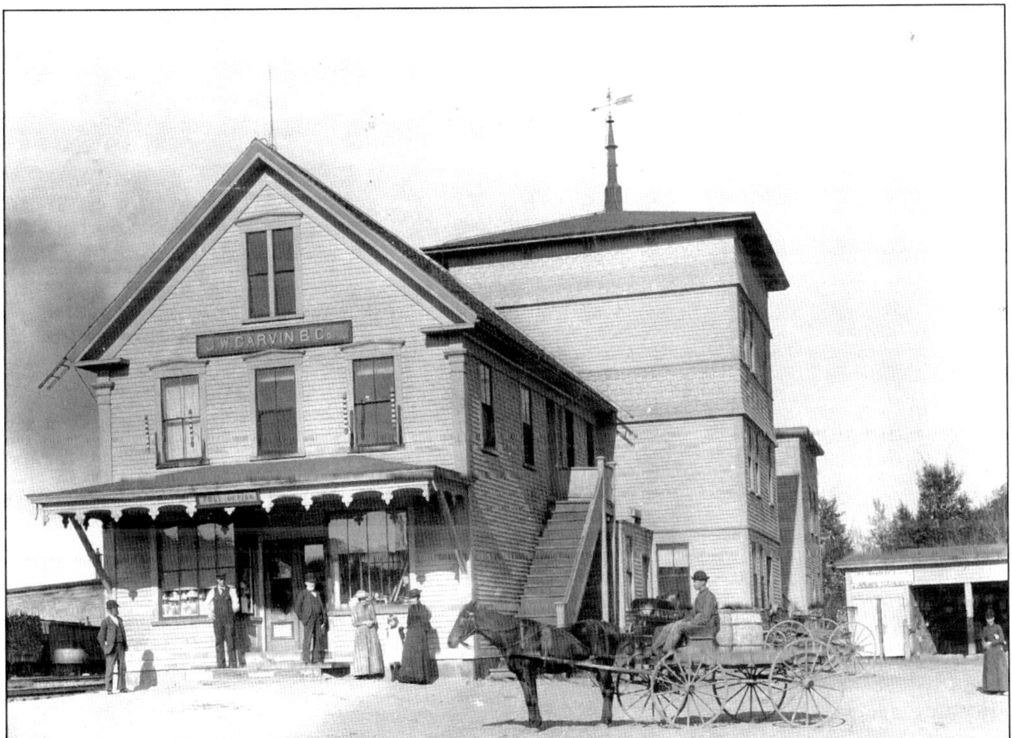

The J. W. Garvin and Company general store, which described itself as "The Oldest Store in Wakefield," was established in 1871, the year the railroad came to Sanbornville (then called Wolfeboro Junction). The building also housed the post office from 1872 until 1909, when the mail facility moved into the town hall. The railroad station stood across from the store on Meadow Street; the tracks are visible on the far left.

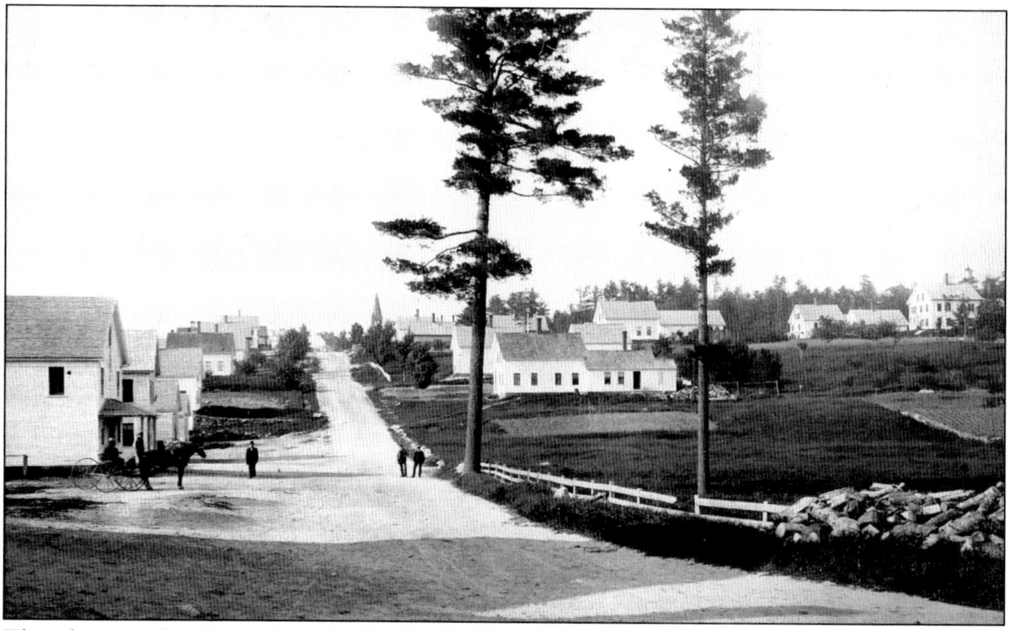

This photograph of High Street in Sanbornville was taken after 1877, when the Episcopal church was completed at the top of the hill, and before 1895, when the town hall was built on the site of the two tall trees. The first four buildings on the left are no longer standing. The first three were shops and the fourth was the Wakefield Free Library.

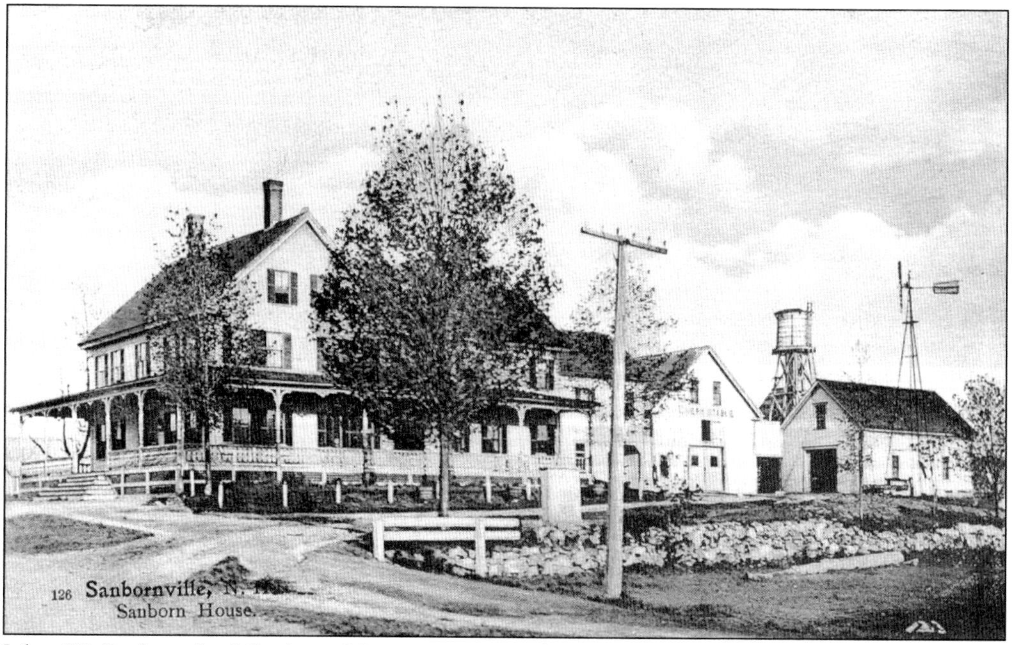

John W. Sanborn had Sanborn House constructed on Meadow Street after the arrival of the railroad. The building provided lodging and also housed public activities from religious and social group meetings to banquets, concerts, and other entertainments. Horses were rented through a livery stable. A long wooden walkway connected the inn with the railroad station, keeping visitors' feet (and skirts) clean.

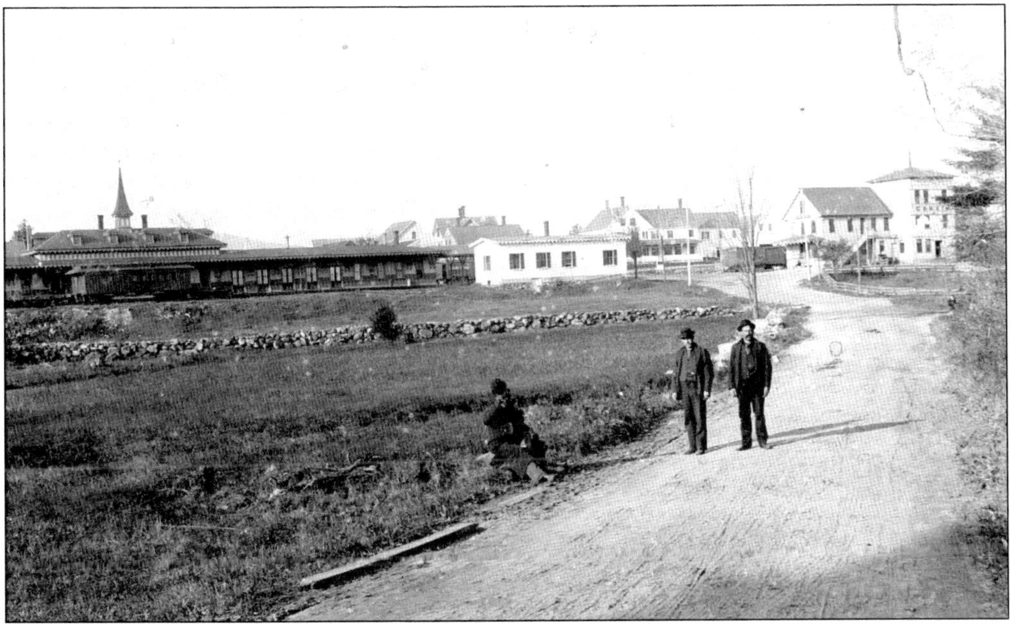

Looking west down Meadow Street in Sanbornville, this view shows the railroad station on the left and J. W. Garvin's store on the right. The small structure in the center, built in 1870, first housed a restaurant next to Garvin's store. Moved across the tracks, in the 1880s it became home to the *Carroll County Pioneer*, which at one point advertised itself as "not the largest paper in the county, but the most wide-a-wake."

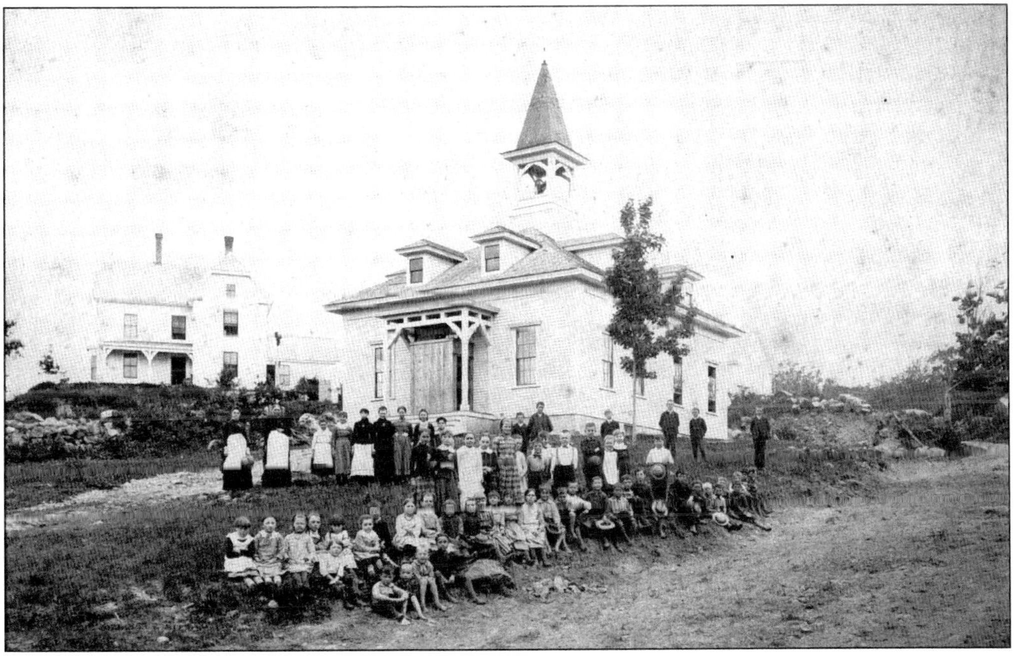

In 1876, the Grammar School was built in Sanbornville, in the newly organized School District 12, to serve the growing population of that area. It was described in a town report as "the best schoolhouse in town." John W. Sanborn supplied the bell. This photograph dates to 1880; a second story was added to the building in 1896.

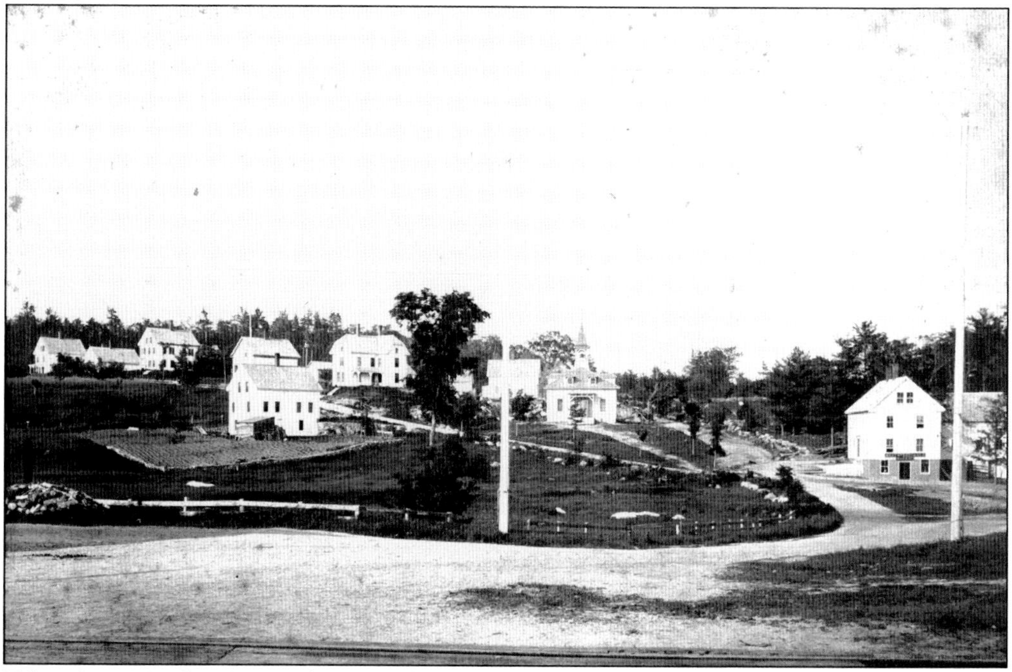

Taken from Meadow Street, this view shows School and Cedar Streets. The Grammar School is near the center of the photograph, which was taken between 1876 and 1896. The large building on the far right bears a sign stating "Meat and Vegetable Market"; the location of the current grocery store on Meadow Street in Sanbornville is not far from this site.

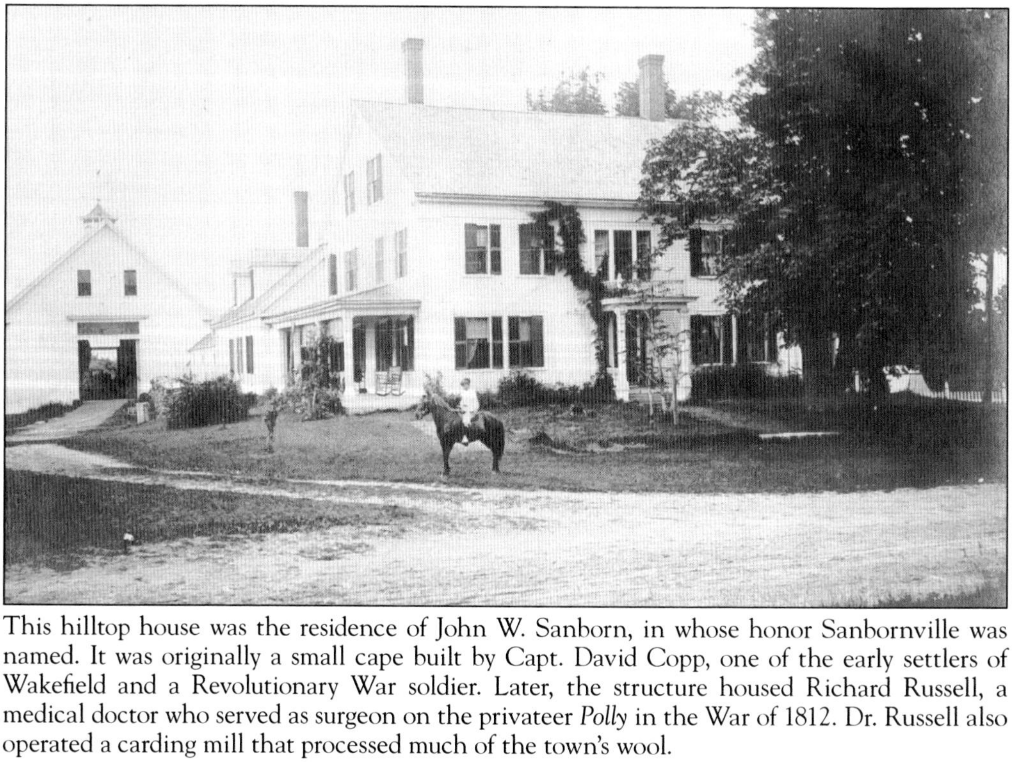

This hilltop house was the residence of John W. Sanborn, in whose honor Sanbornville was named. It was originally a small cape built by Capt. David Copp, one of the early settlers of Wakefield and a Revolutionary War soldier. Later, the structure housed Richard Russell, a medical doctor who served as surgeon on the privateer *Polly* in the War of 1812. Dr. Russell also operated a carding mill that processed much of the town's wool.

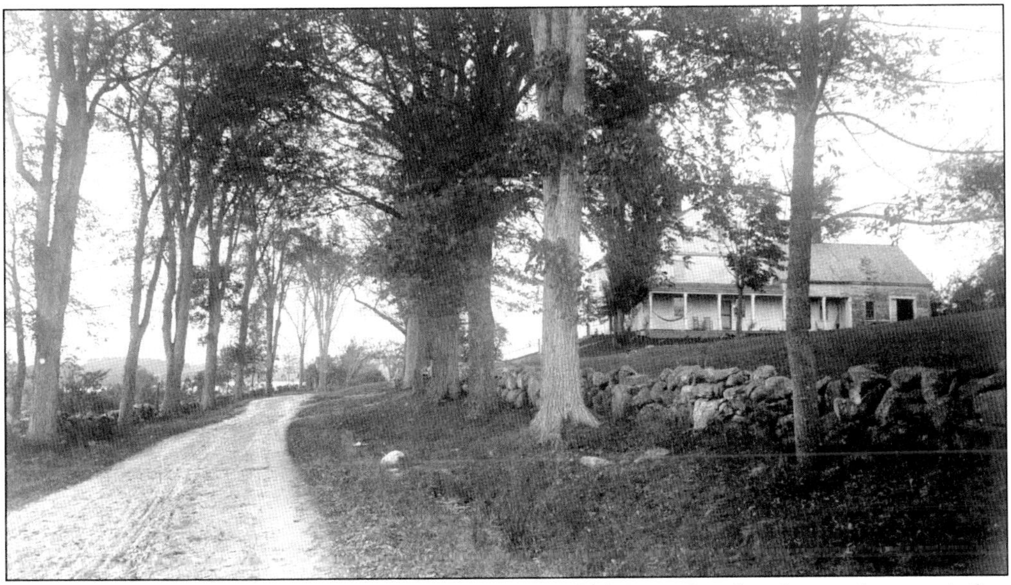

The Asa Piper Parsonage was built on what is now Old Stage Road to house the town's first permanent minister, who settled in Wakefield in 1785. Reverend Piper's salary included some labor and materials for the construction of the house, as well as 45 pounds in money and 35 pounds in "Country produce" (corn, rye, beef, and pork). The town's original church stood where the Lovell Lake Cemetery is now located.

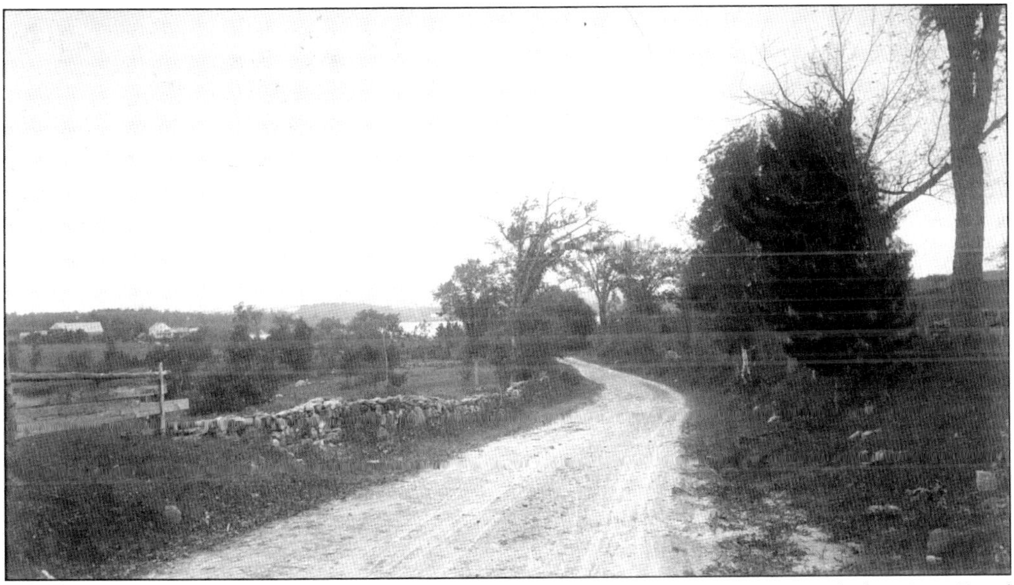

One of the earliest roads in the area, Old Stage Road has had several names, including Post Road and Piper Ridge Road, but its current appellation recalls the route's early use by stagecoaches. The stagecoaches traveled from Dover to Conway, stopping in Wakefield at the Old Maids Tavern (so called because it was operated by two spinster sisters) and at the National House in Wakefield Corner. Lovell Lake is visible in the distance.

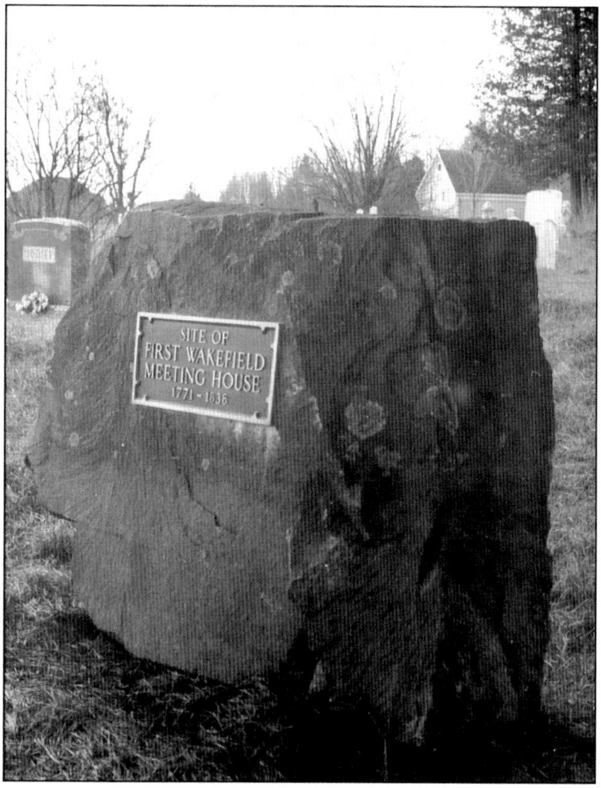

This stone at the Lovell Lake Cemetery on Route 109 marks the site of Wakefield's original meetinghouse. Built in 1771, the meetinghouse combined the functions of town hall and church. However, after the construction of a new church and separate town hall in Wakefield Corner in the early 1800s, the building fell into disuse. It is said to have been moved to Union and eventually incorporated into the Congregational church.

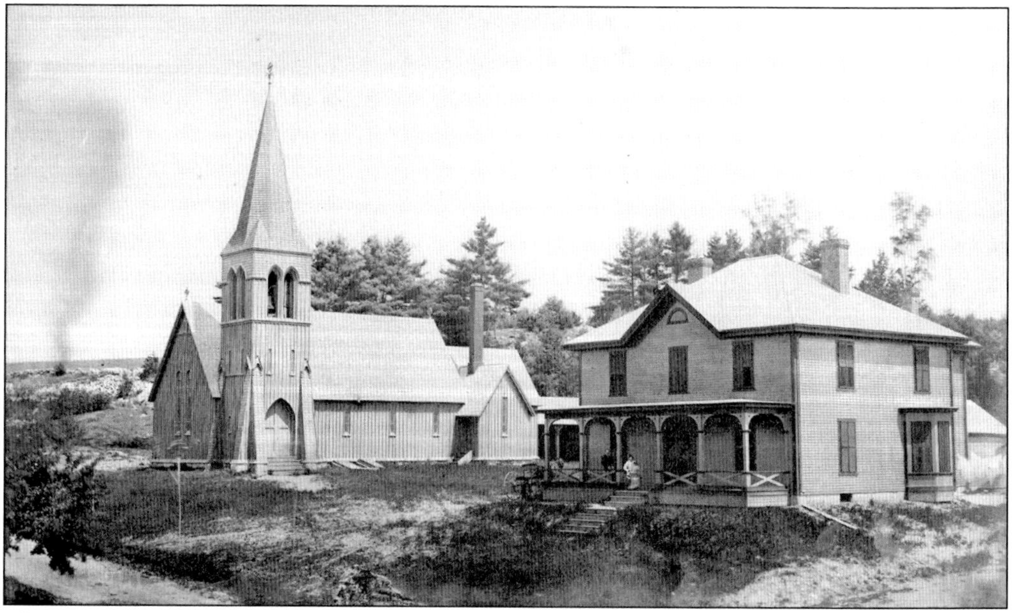

The Church of St. John the Baptist was built on High Street in 1876. The land and $100 were offered for the use of any religious institution by John W. Sanborn, who was trying to develop the village of Wolfeboro Junction (later Sanbornville). The prominent Dow family led the movement to construct an Episcopal church on the site. The building is one of only four Carpenter Gothic churches in the country. The rectory was added in 1880.

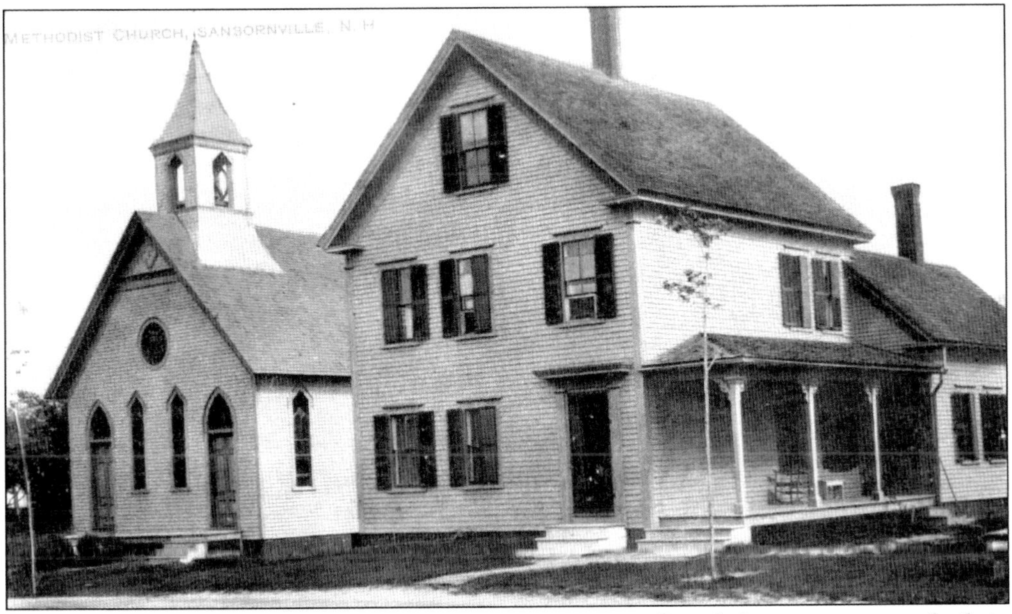

The Methodist church was erected on Meadow Street in 1887, and the parsonage was built in 1892. Prior to the construction of the church, Methodists in Sanbornville had been holding meetings in a variety of buildings, including the Grammar School, the Dow Academy building, and the Sanborn House. This photograph was taken in 1919.

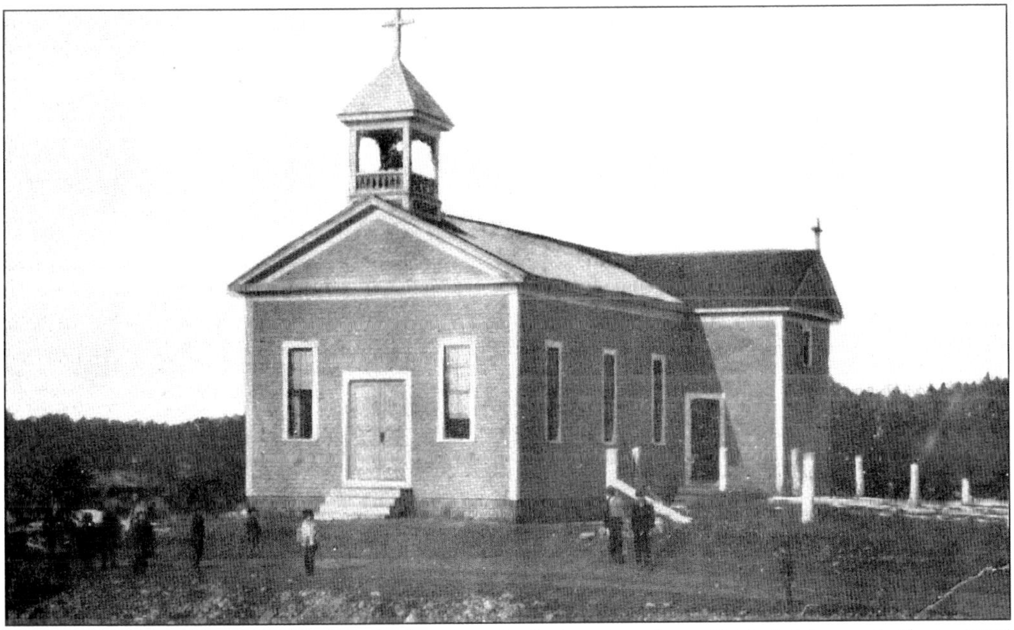

The original St. Anthony's Chapel, the first Catholic church in Wakefield, was built in 1895 on St. Anthony's Road. This area on the west side of town was settled by families from Quebec and known as French Town. Originally, the church was a mission of St. Leo's Church in Gonic; however, it became an independent parish in 1908. The chapel burned in 1909 and was replaced by the current church on Meadow Street.

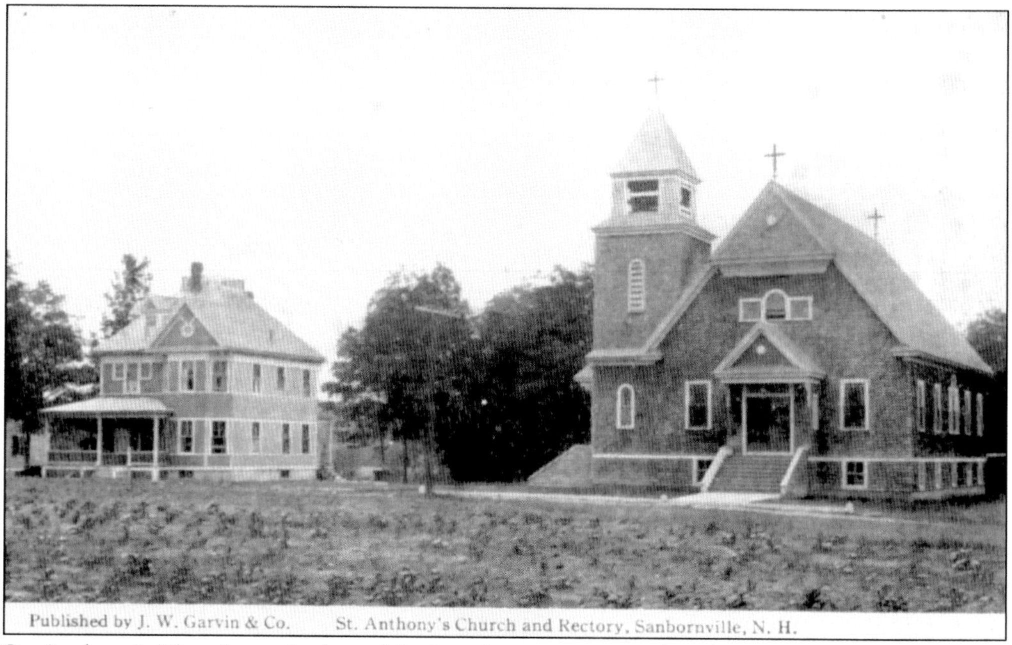

St. Anthony's Church was built on Meadow Street in 1909, after the first Catholic chapel was destroyed by fire. Both the church and the adjacent rectory have been remodeled since they were built; an early photograph shows that the exterior of the church was once green.

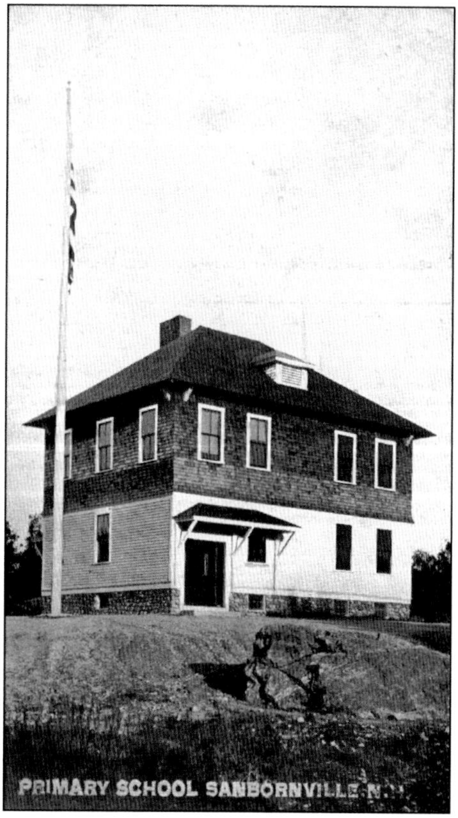

The Sanbornville Primary School, built in 1905, was in use for approximately 50 years. The first and second grades were housed on the ground floor, while the third and fourth grades met on the second floor.

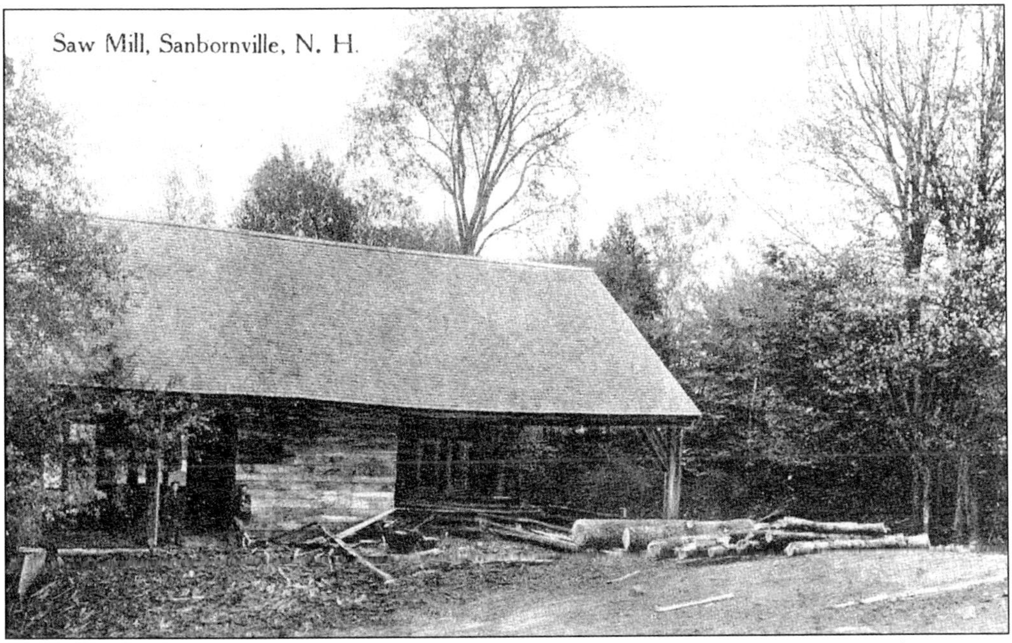

This sawmill, pictured in 1904, was owned by John W. Sanborn and located on Meadow Street, just below the current St. Anthony's Church. Sawed boards were stored where the rectory now stands, and local boys swam in the millpond. At one time, railroad ties were cut at the mill, which was torn down in 1941.

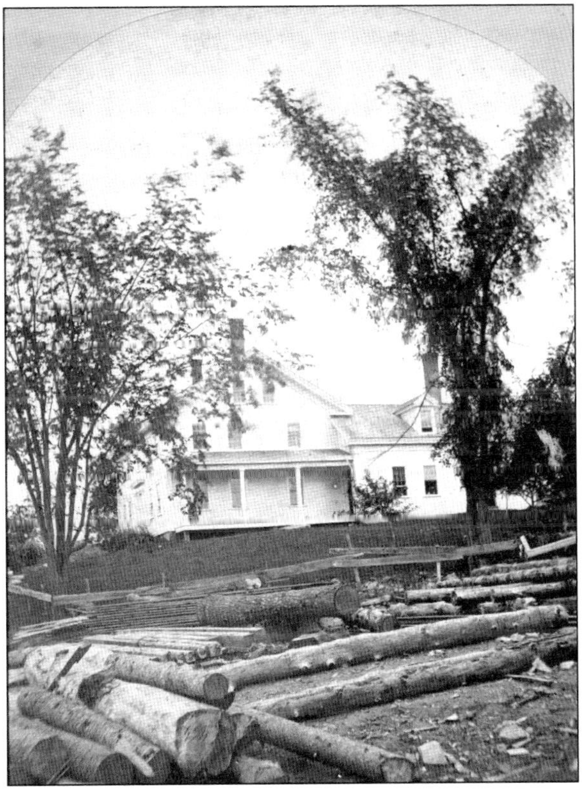

Originally owned by Capt. David Copp, the old sawmill at the outlet of Lovell Lake was one of the oldest mills in Wakefield. Many gristmills, fulling and carding mills, and sawmills were powered by the town's numerous waterways. Most of the mills, like this one, are no longer standing. The Wayside Inn, in the background, is said to be the second oldest building in Sanbornville.

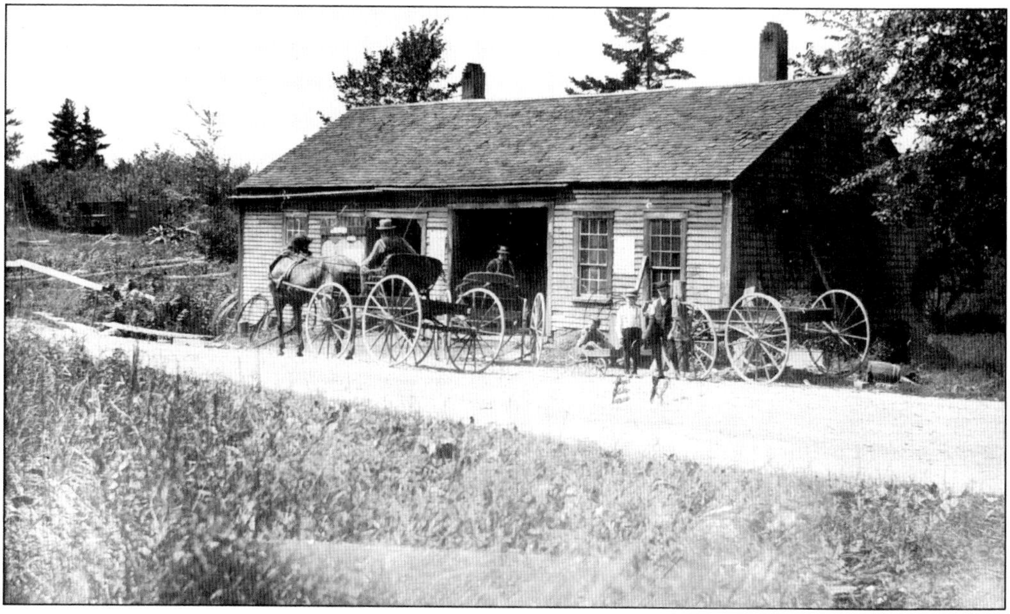

The blacksmith shop across the road from the Wayside Inn was operated by J. Runnells, who also owned the inn. Keeping pace with current modes of transportation, the building later became a gas station and then an automobile repair shop, which it remains to this day.

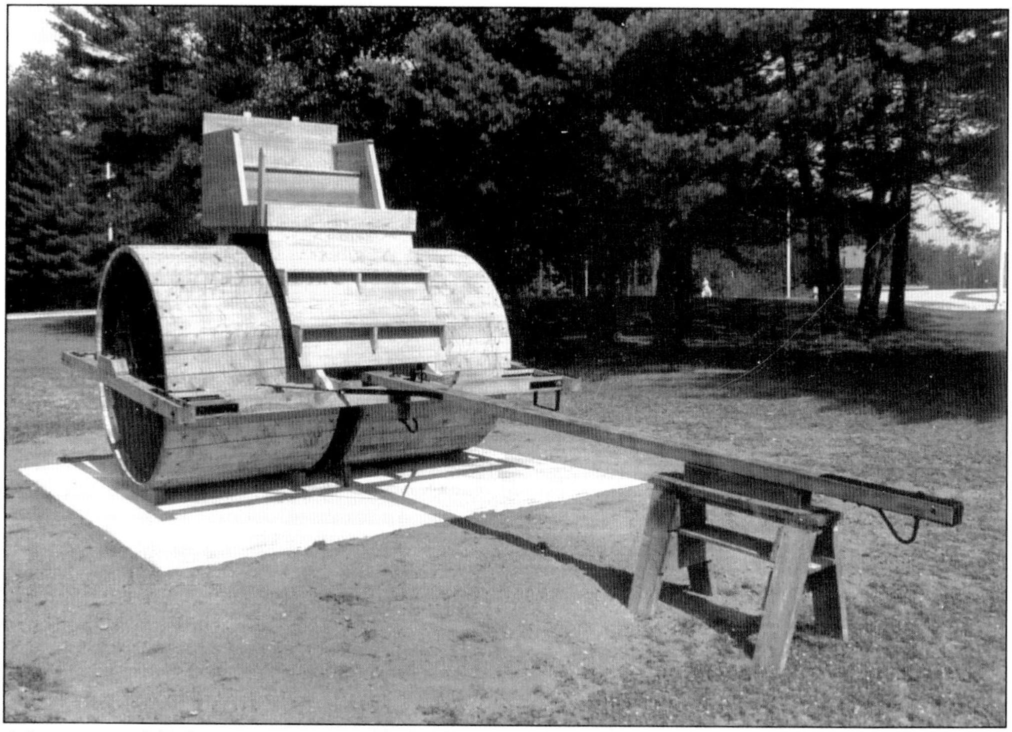

After a snowfall, horses or oxen pulled a heavy wooden roller down the roads to compact the snow and make it passable for sleighs. In 1926, the town of Wakefield purchased this wooden snow roller for $300. William Twombley donated it to the department of transportation in 1990, and it is now displayed in front of the department's building in Concord.

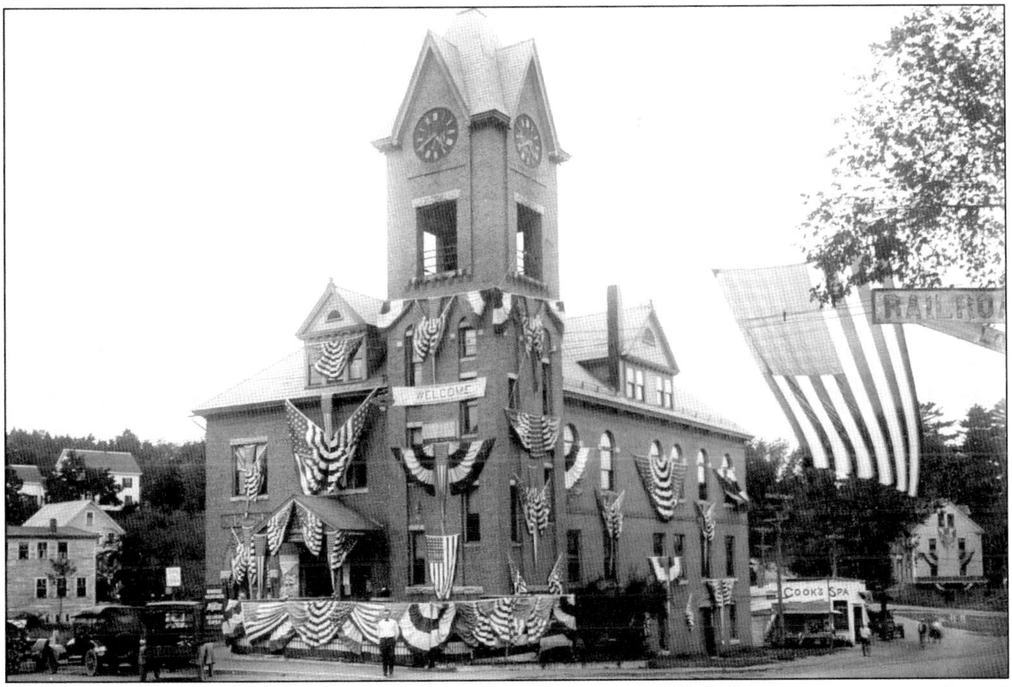

The town hall is decorated for Old Home Day in 1922. Many buildings in town were draped with bunting for the day and were flying the American flag. The Cook's Spa building, which no longer exists, stands behind the town hall on the right.

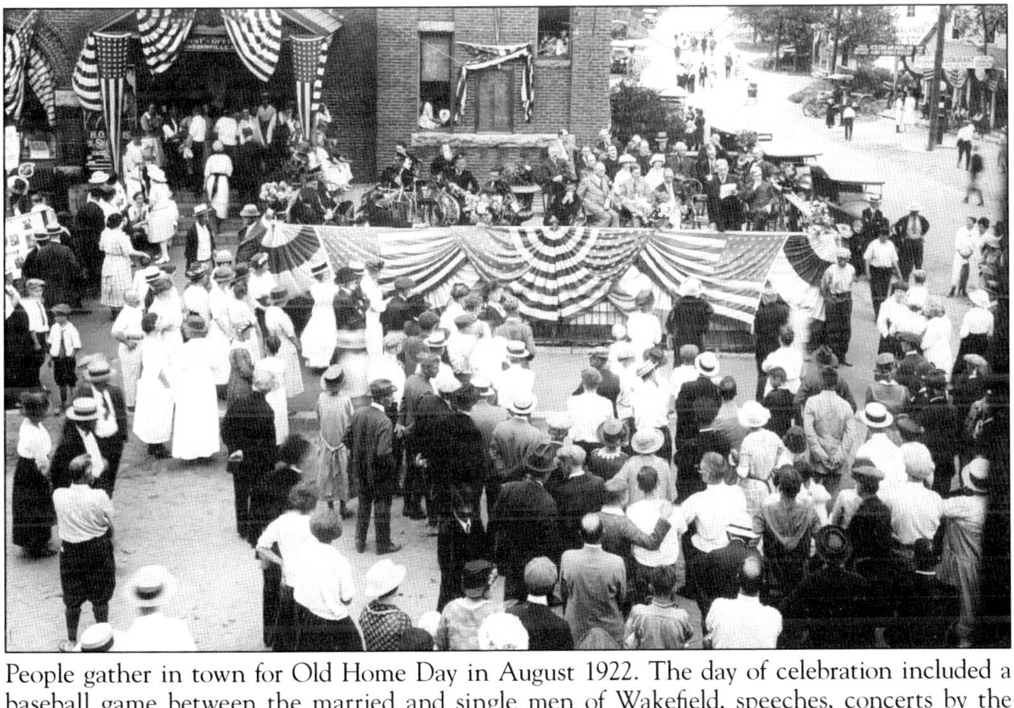

People gather in town for Old Home Day in August 1922. The day of celebration included a baseball game between the married and single men of Wakefield, speeches, concerts by the Rochester City Band, and fireworks, as well as the dedication of the World War I Honor Roll on the side of the town hall.

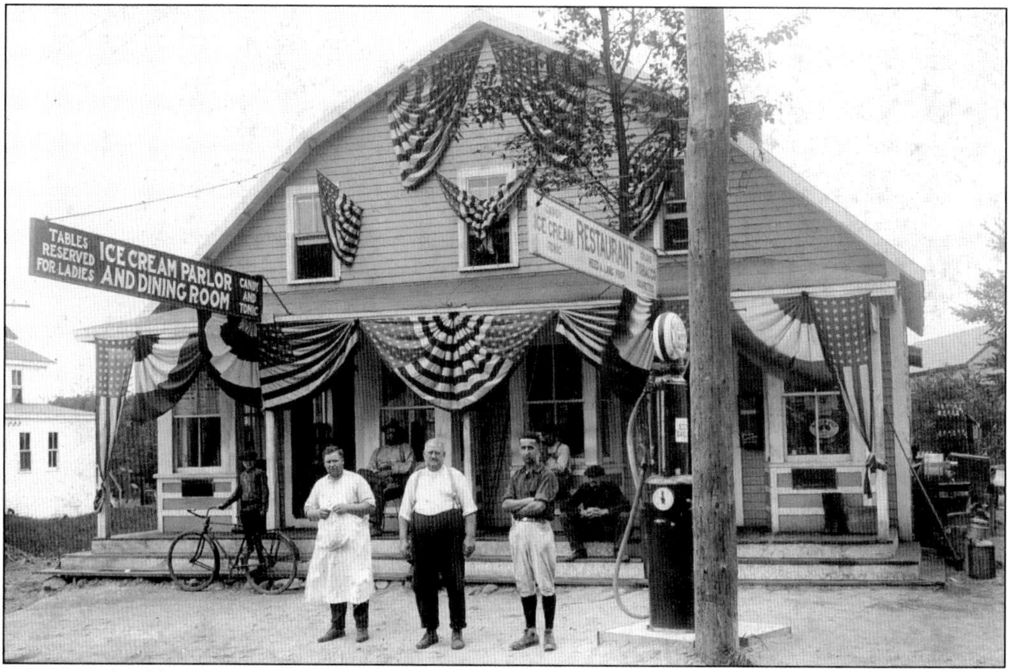

Like most buildings in town, Lang's Restaurant is bedecked with bunting for Old Home Day in 1922. Included in the photograph are Frank Clark, proprietor Reed Lang, and Walter Wentworth, as well as P. Jenness by the window, and Eli Adjutant on the step. The structure was located across from the town hall and, at a later date, was Fifield's Market. It no longer stands.

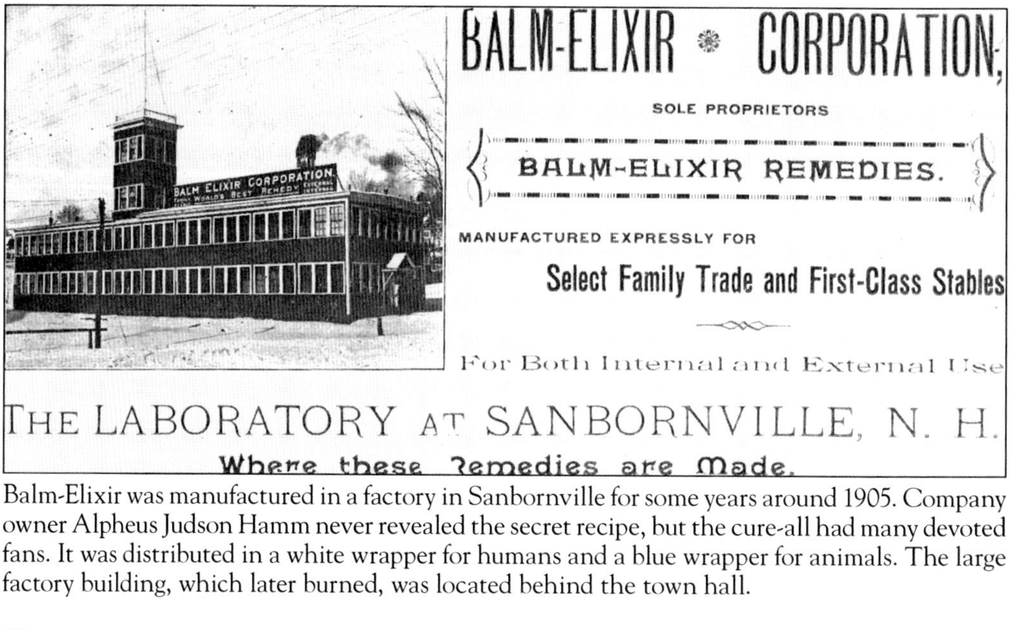

Balm-Elixir was manufactured in a factory in Sanbornville for some years around 1905. Company owner Alpheus Judson Hamm never revealed the secret recipe, but the cure-all had many devoted fans. It was distributed in a white wrapper for humans and a blue wrapper for animals. The large factory building, which later burned, was located behind the town hall.

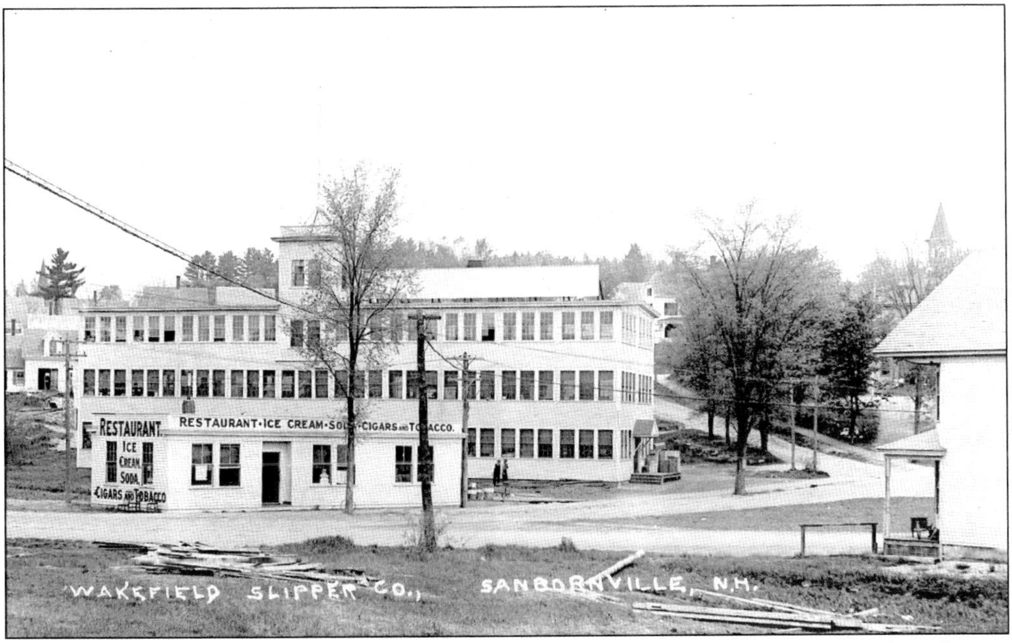

The Wakefield Slipper Company added a third story when it took over the Balm-Elixir factory building. The Bickum Shoe Company was the next occupant of the structure, which burned in 1922. Cook's Spa, later named Sarah's Spa, stands in the foreground of the photograph; it remained in place after the factory was destroyed.

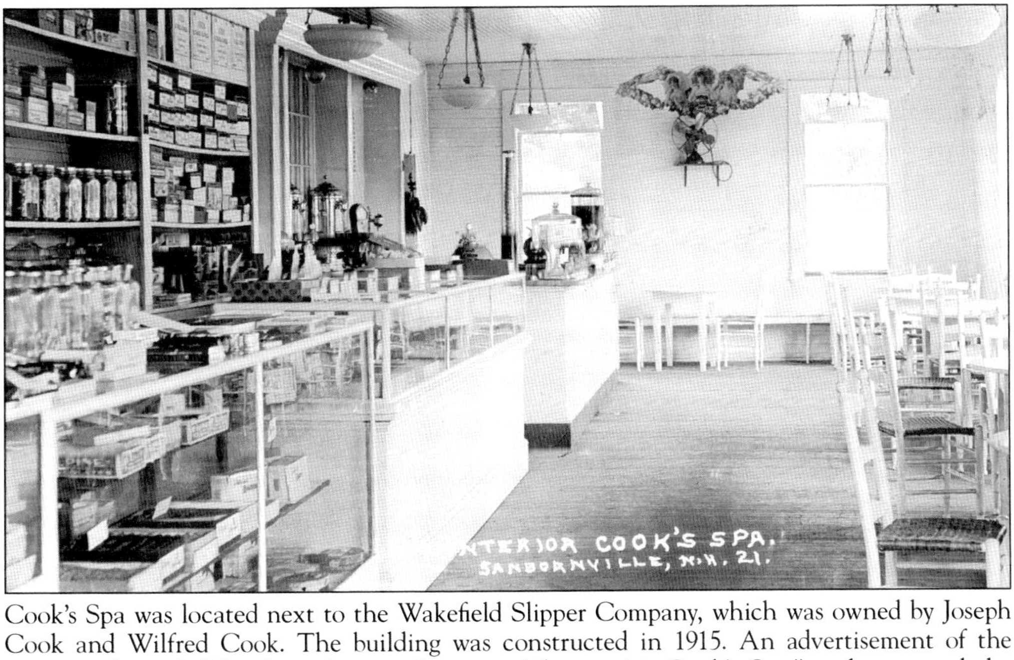

Cook's Spa was located next to the Wakefield Slipper Company, which was owned by Joseph Cook and Wilfred Cook. The building was constructed in 1915. An advertisement of the time proclaimed, "You haven't seen the town 'til you visit Cook's Spa," and promoted the establishment's "Ice Cream, Soda, Tonic, Lunches, Candy and Tobacco."

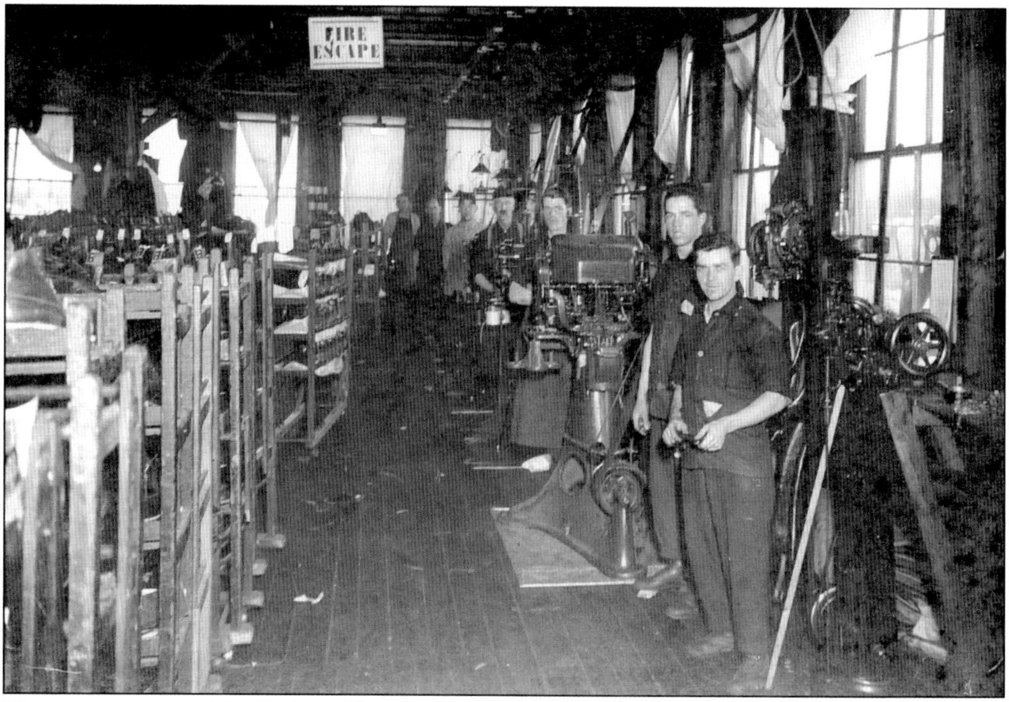

This interior view of the Bickum Shoe Company shows finished shoes on racks, as well as workers and machinery. Shoe making was a much more industrial process at this time than when cobbler Freeman Pike made shoes by hand from wooden lasts in Wakefield Corner.

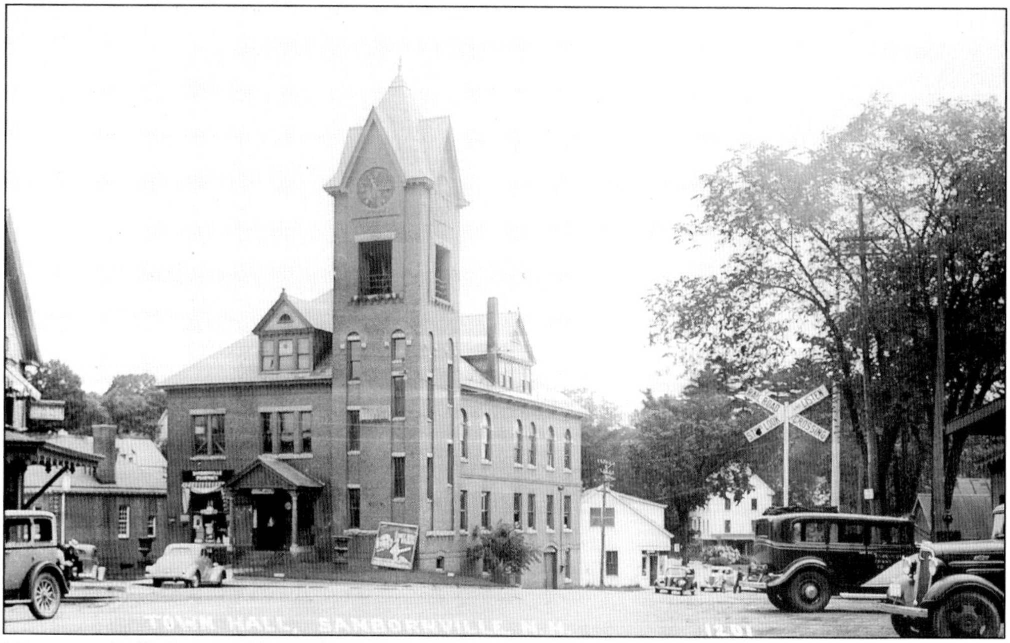

The town hall, designed by architect A. T. Ramsdell, was built in 1895. The first floor contained rooms intended for offices, a bank, a store, and a banquet hall with kitchen. The second floor housed the meeting hall, which is now the Opera House. In this photograph, note the poster for a movie shown in the Opera House, and the pharmacy that was once on the first floor.

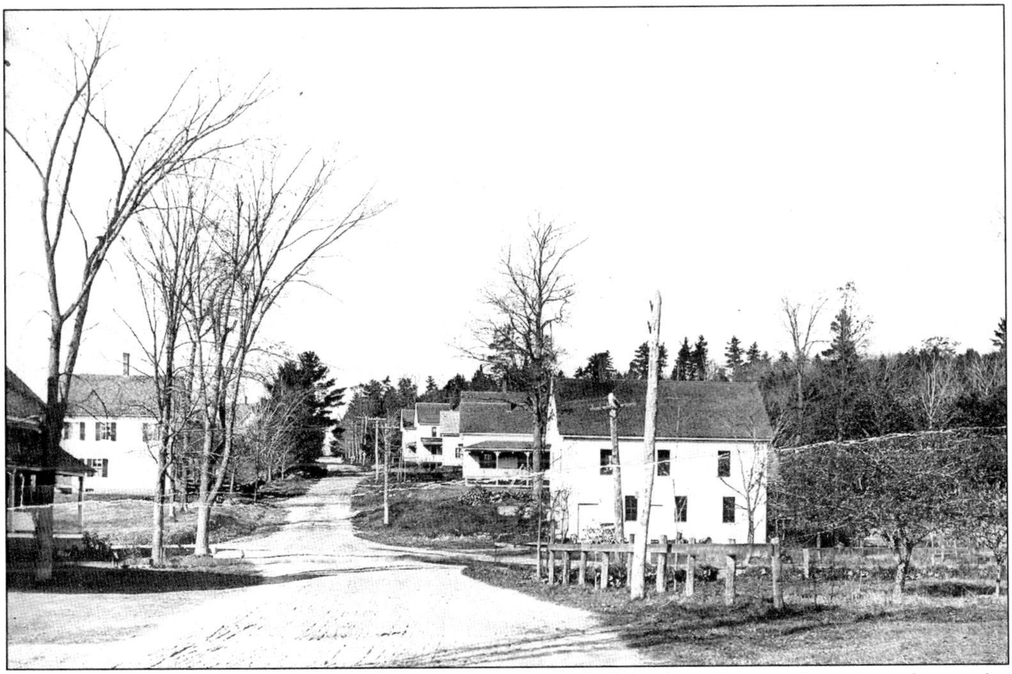

Looking north up Route 153 at the intersection with Meadow Street, this view shows the creamery that would be remodeled into the Lovell Lake House on the right. The creamery processed about 350 pounds of butter per day in the late 19th century.

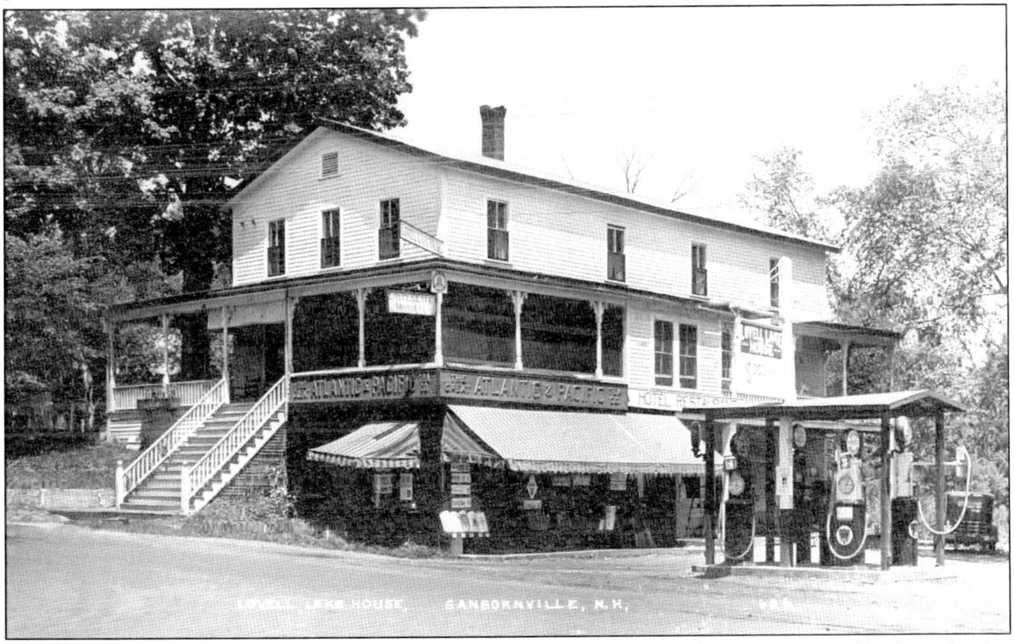

Photographed in 1922, the Lovell Lake House was opened to the public in 1914 by Charles B. Thoms, who had remodeled the old creamery previously on the site. It advertised "Good Rooms with Bath" and provided gasoline pumps and a restaurant. The building also housed the Great Atlantic and Pacific Tea Company (A&P), a small grocery store. The building would later become the Poor People's Pub.

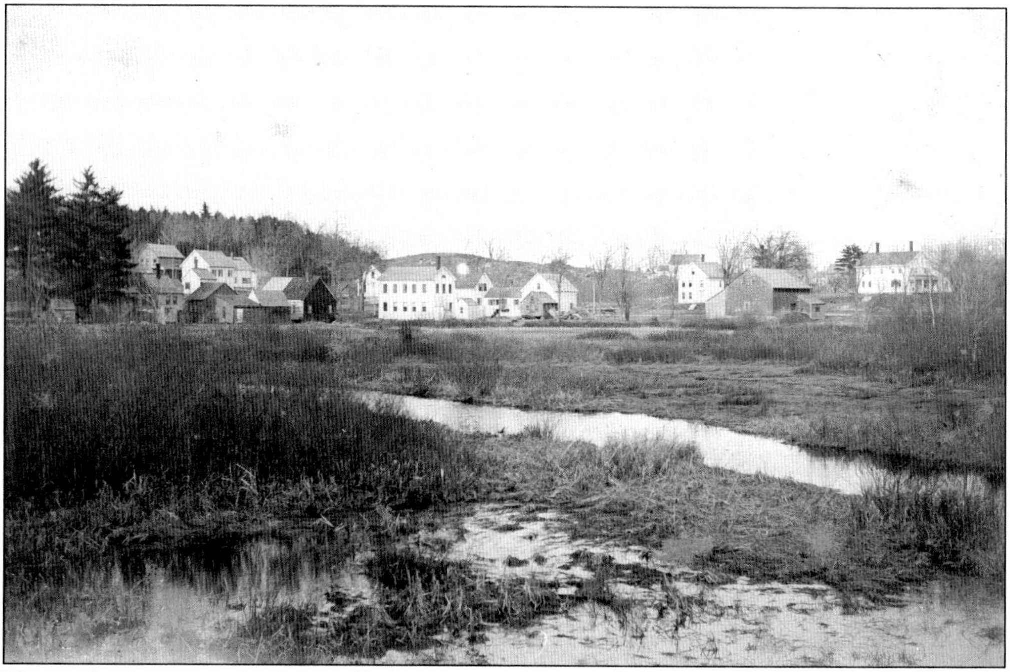

The wetlands just south of the village gave Meadow Street its name. The Wayside Inn can be seen on the far right, and the Dow Academy building near the center. Josiah Dow, a wealthy merchant, founded Dow Academy in 1815. Originally located near the Dow Homestead, the building was moved in 1886 to its current location in Sanbornville.

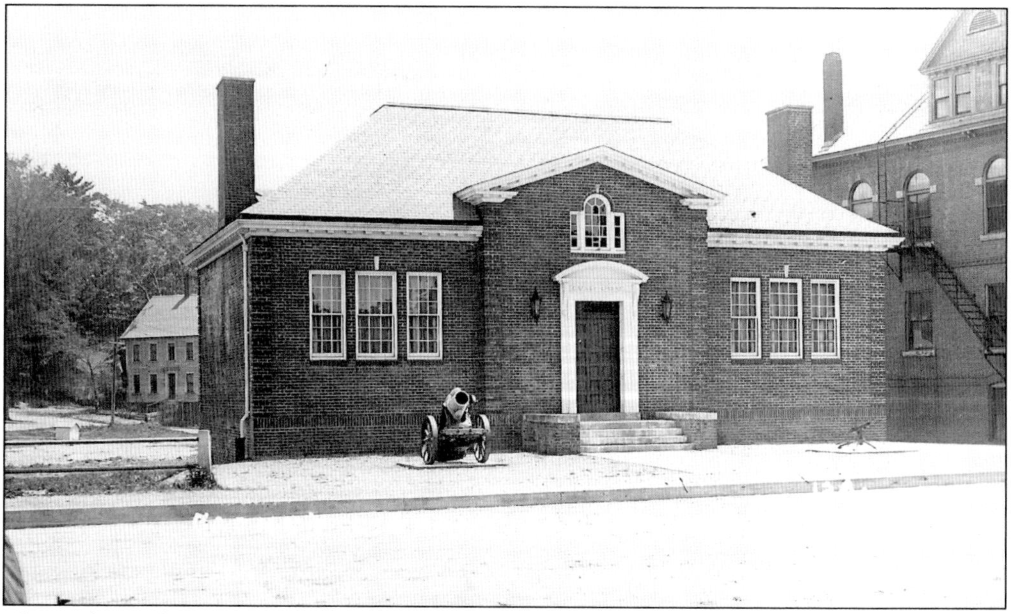

The Gafney Library, dedicated in 1925, was named for Charles B. Gafney, a lawyer and judge from Rochester who was a friend of John W. Sanborn. In his will, Gafney left $5,000 to establish a library for Carroll County. The original library in Sanbornville, founded in 1882, was located in a small building on High Street; it was closed in 1925, and the books were given to the Gafney Library.

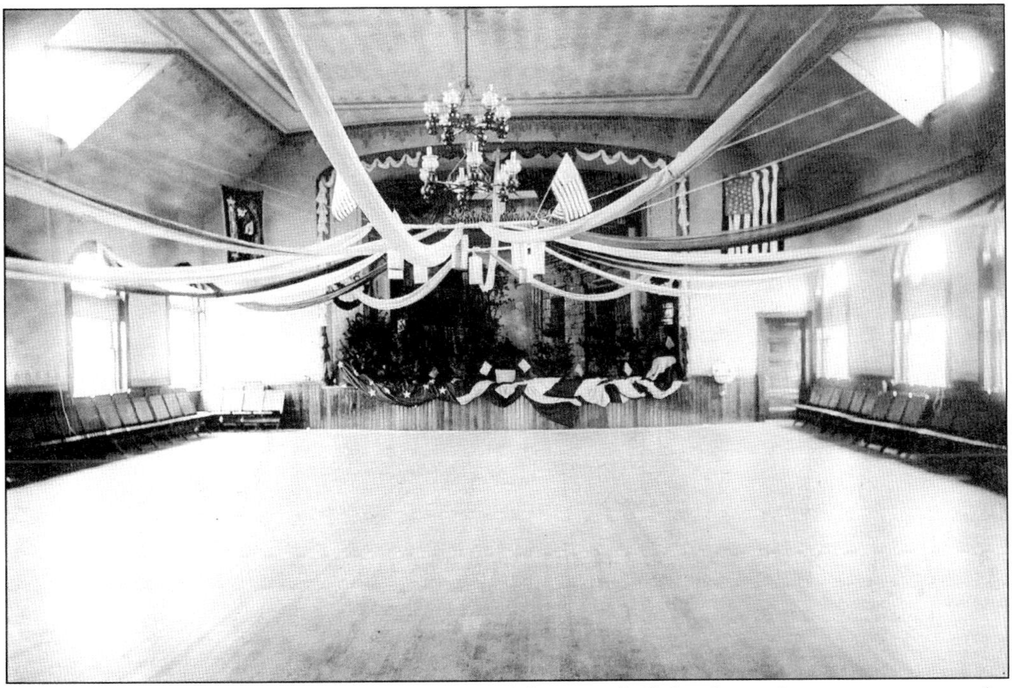

The Opera House, occupying the second floor of the town hall, has hosted many events over the years, including meetings, plays, dances, movies, concerts, and variety shows. It remains in use today, as do the old chairs visible along the sides of the room.

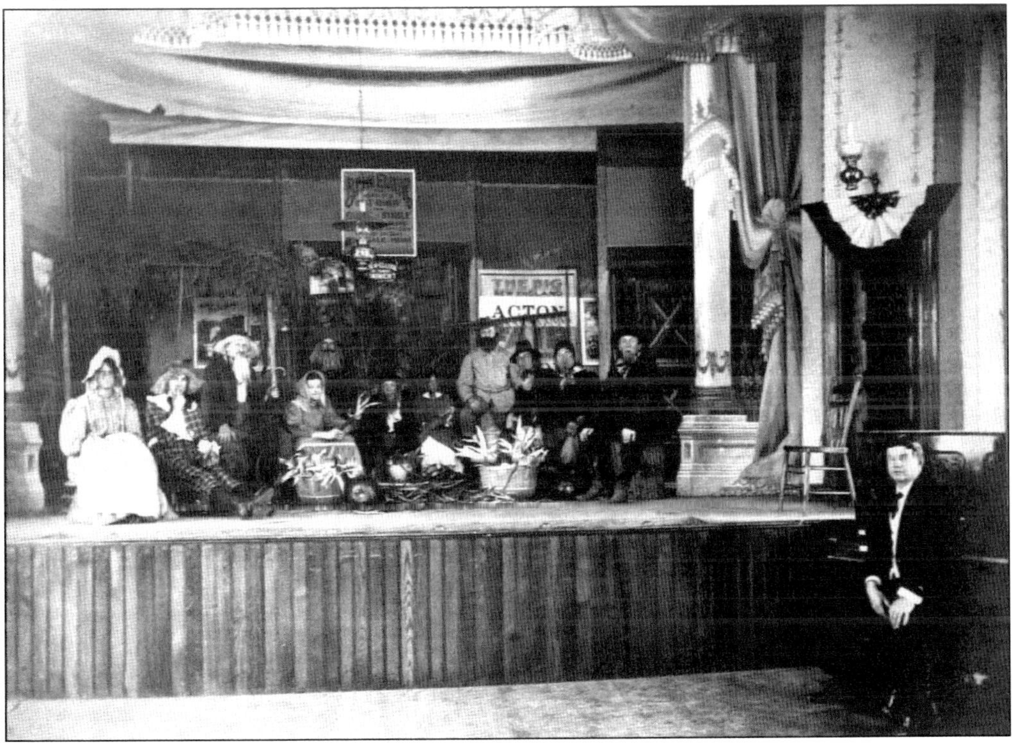

Townspeople perform in an early theatrical event in the Opera House.

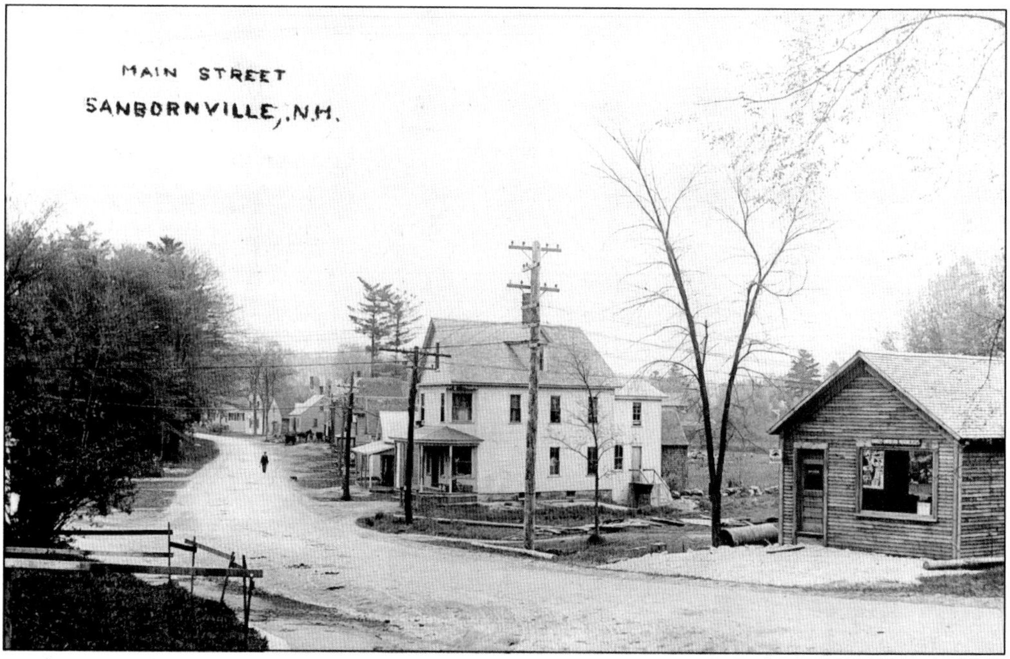

Looking east down Meadow Street (once Main Street), this view reveals that the telephone has come to town. The New England Telephone and Telegraph Company was authorized to begin installing poles and wire in 1896. The small dark building on the far right was the telephone office, housing the operators who asked "number, please" before the introduction of dial phones in 1950.

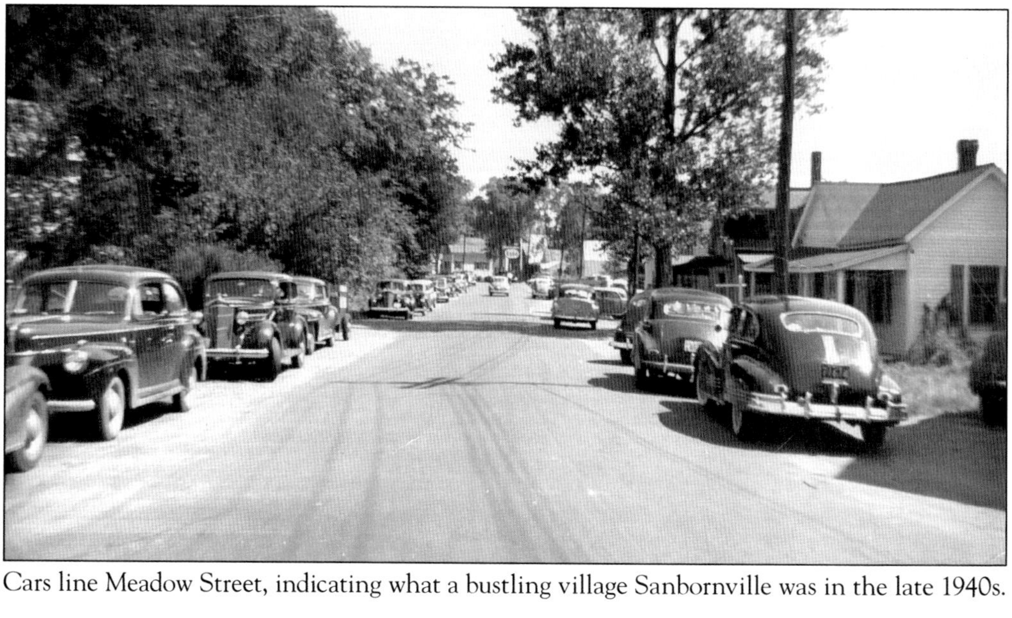

Cars line Meadow Street, indicating what a bustling village Sanbornville was in the late 1940s.

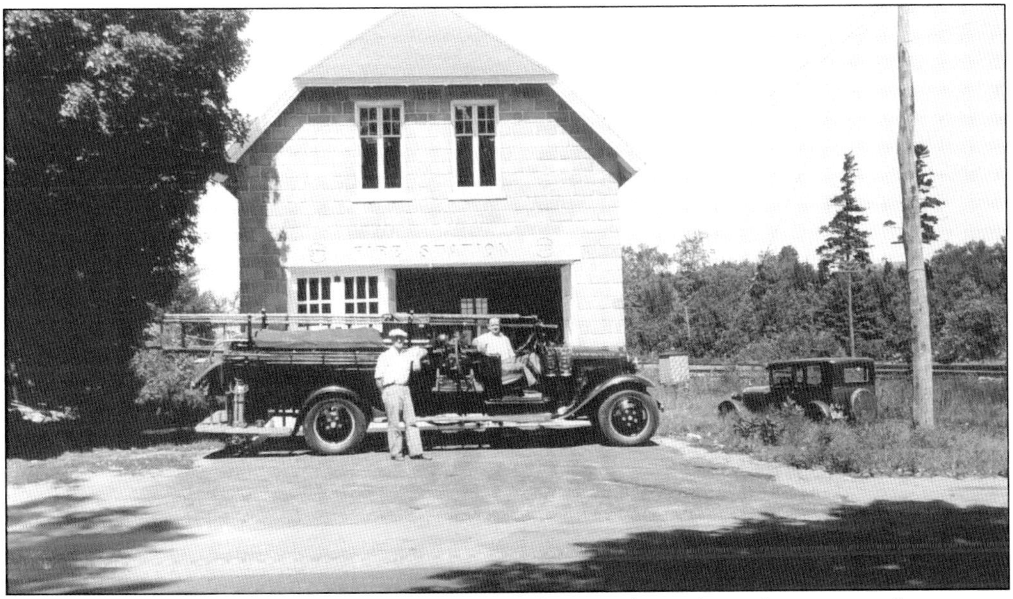

As seen here in 1936, the building that currently houses the parks and recreation department and the Wakefield Food Pantry once served as the firehouse. A Works Progress Administration project, it was constructed with cement blocks that workers made on site in 1935.

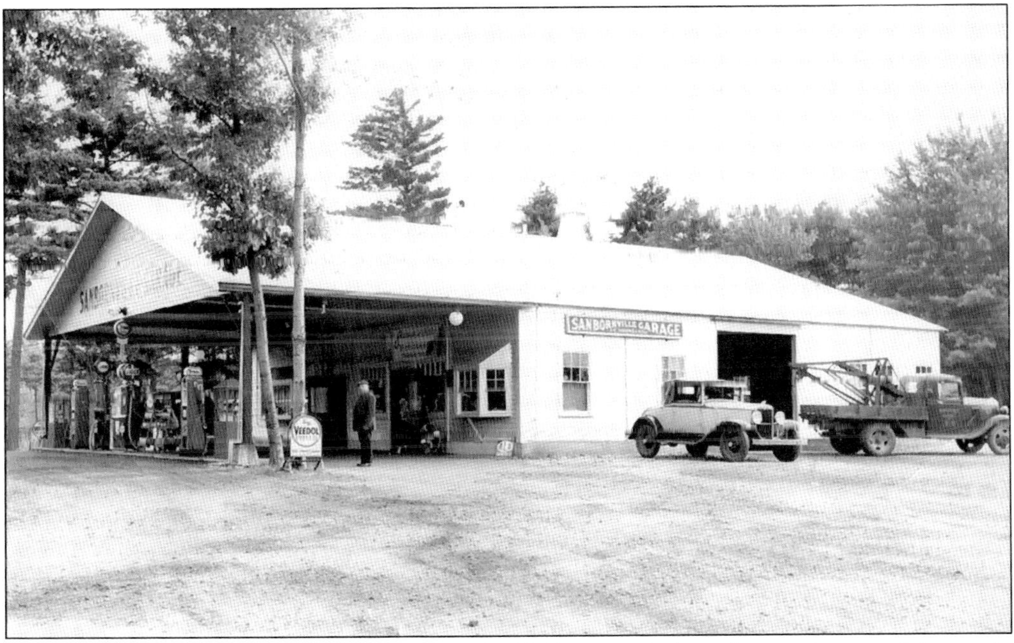

The Sanbornville Garage, photographed in the 1940s, provided gasoline and automobile repair. The Public Safety Building now stands on this site.

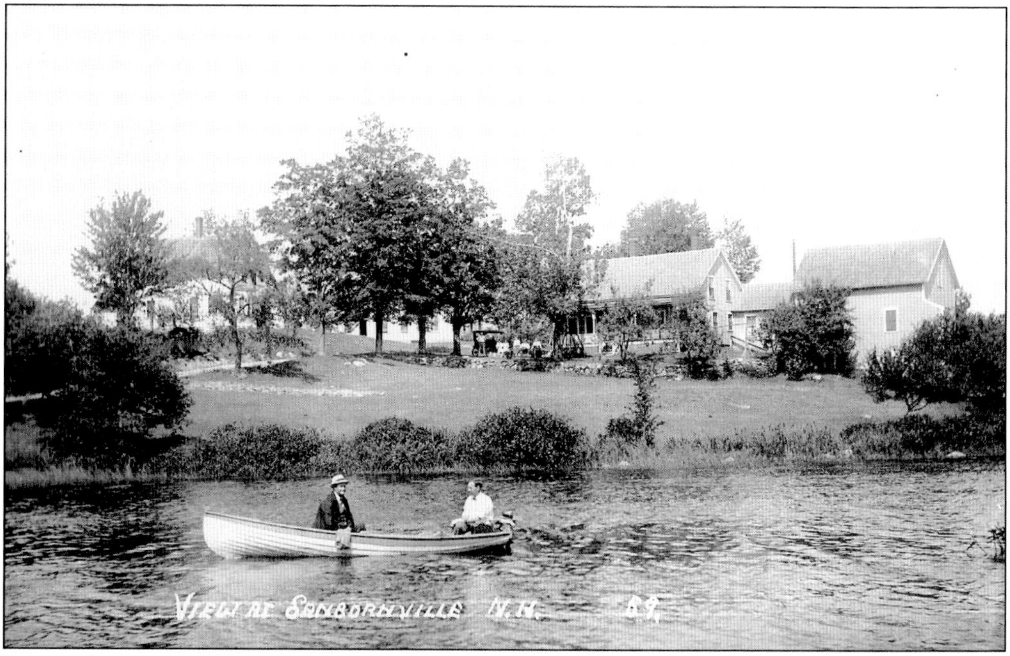

Boaters have enjoyed the beauty of Wakefield's many lakes for decades. This view of Lovell Lake shows Witchtrot Road in the background. Many summer visitors traveled here by train, staying in local inns and boardinghouses, to appreciate peaceful country moments such as this one.

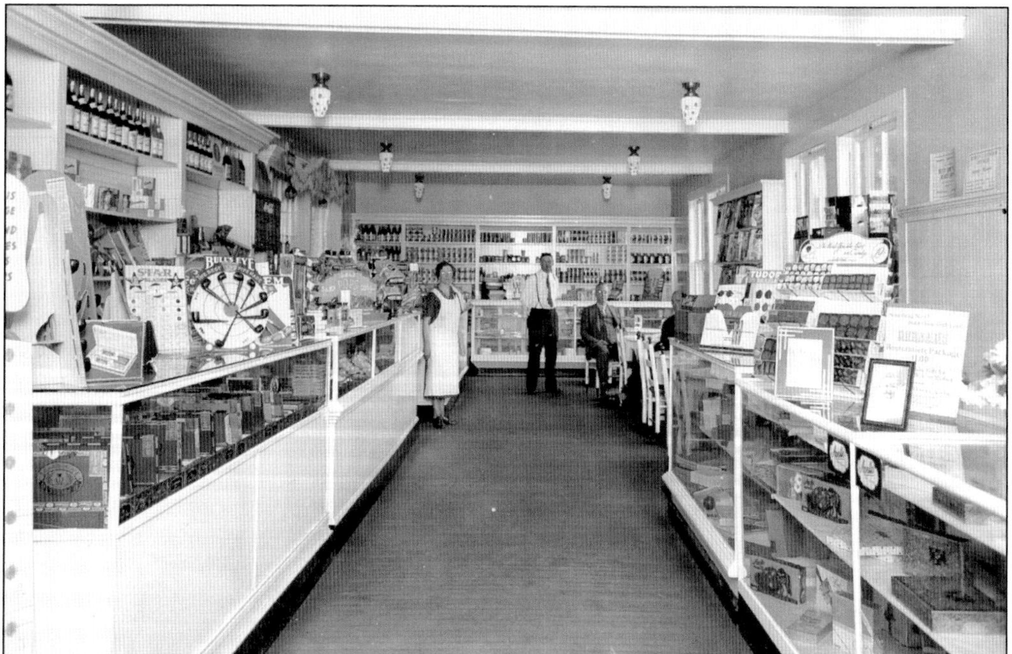

Sarah and Ernest Hamilton operated Sarah's Spa, on Meadow Street behind the town hall, in the building that had previously housed Cook's Spa. The shop offered ice cream, sodas, sandwiches, candy, and tobacco. A customer could also buy beer to take out, but not to drink on the premises.

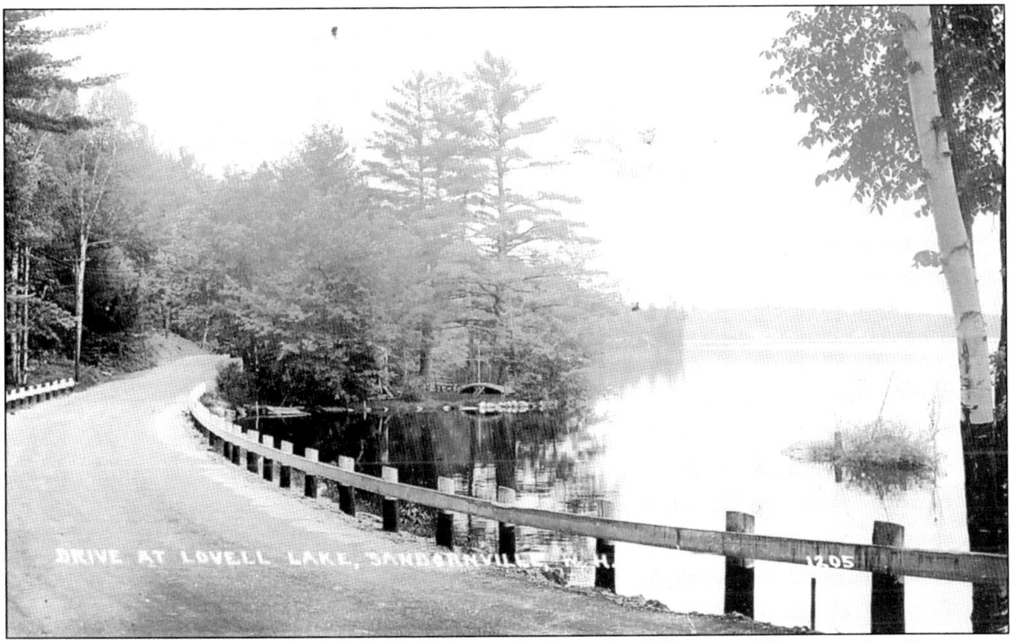

This photograph shows Route 109 along Lovell Lake in an earlier—and less populated—time.

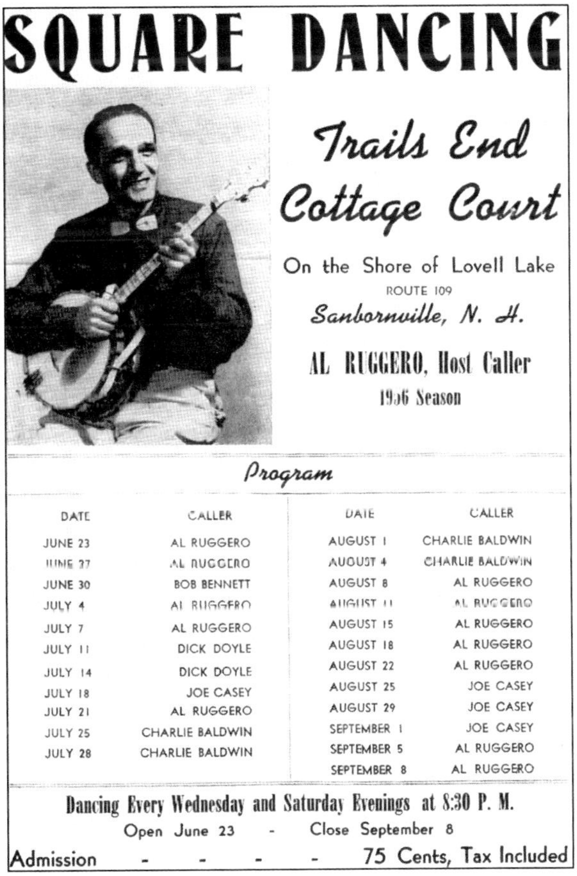

Trail's End, located near the town end of Lovell Lake, was a popular vacation destination through much of the 20th century. The recreation hall hosted square dances for many years.

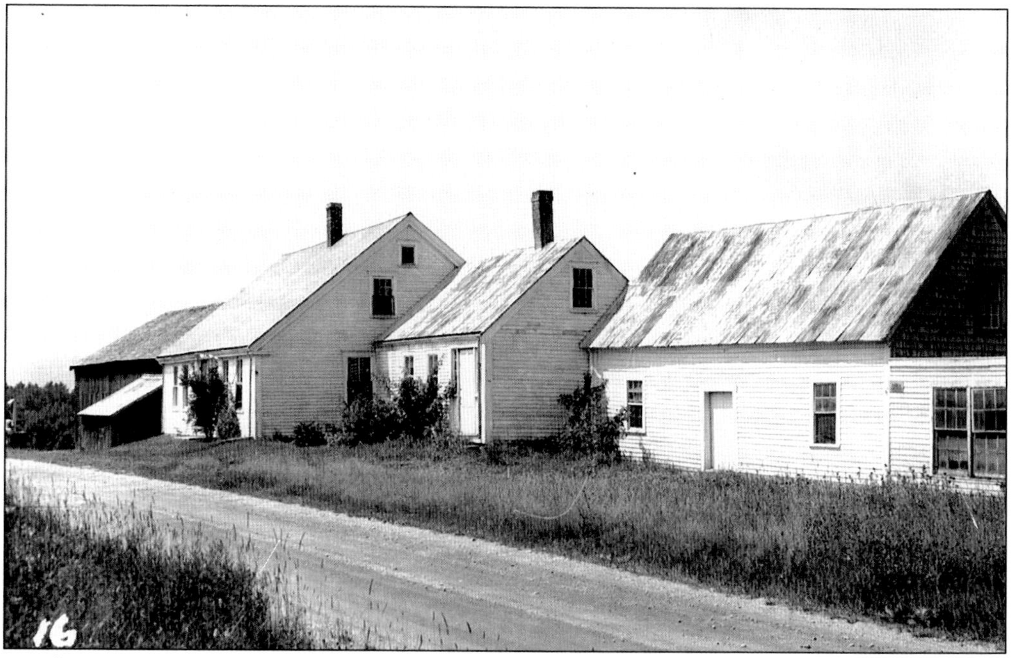

Witchtrot Farm, just over a mile from town on Witchtrot Road, was Daniel Hall's homestead in the late 1700s. Daniel and Patience's daughter Hannah married John Sanborn, and they were the grandparents of John W. Sanborn. This farm is wonderfully representative of all the farms that were established in the early years on what was then called Hall's Road. Others survive, but like this one, are no longer farmed.

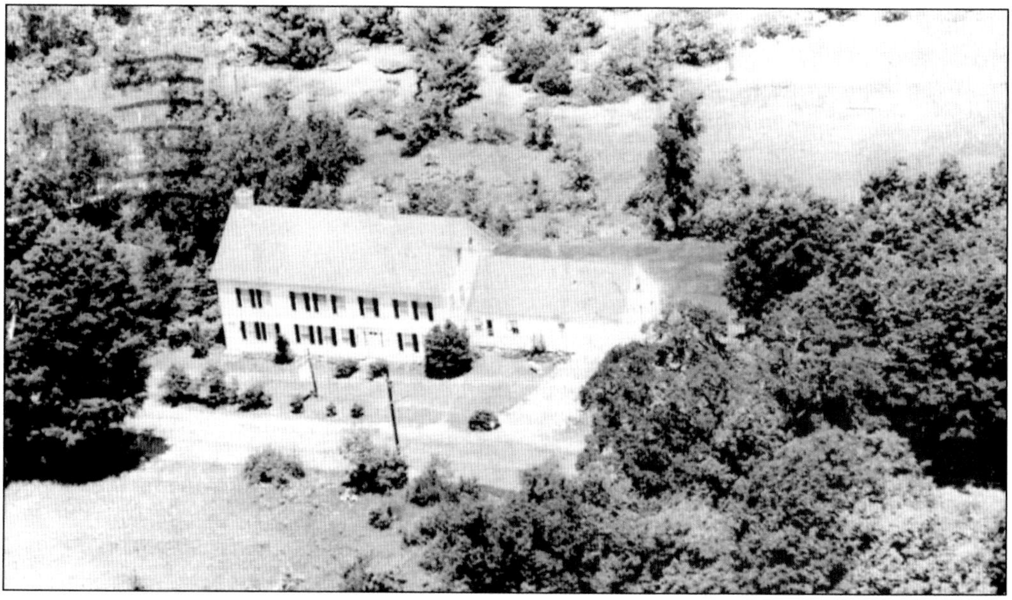

Built in 1772, Pod Auger Manor eventually became the home of Edwin and Hélène Geauque (pronounced Jay-Oak). From the 1940s through the 1960s, the Geauques operated Wake-Brook House, a small publishing company. They reprinted select books whose copyrights had expired and bound them by hand with cloth covers. They produced approximately 1,000 copies of five to eight different books each year.

Four

The Railroad and Ice Industries

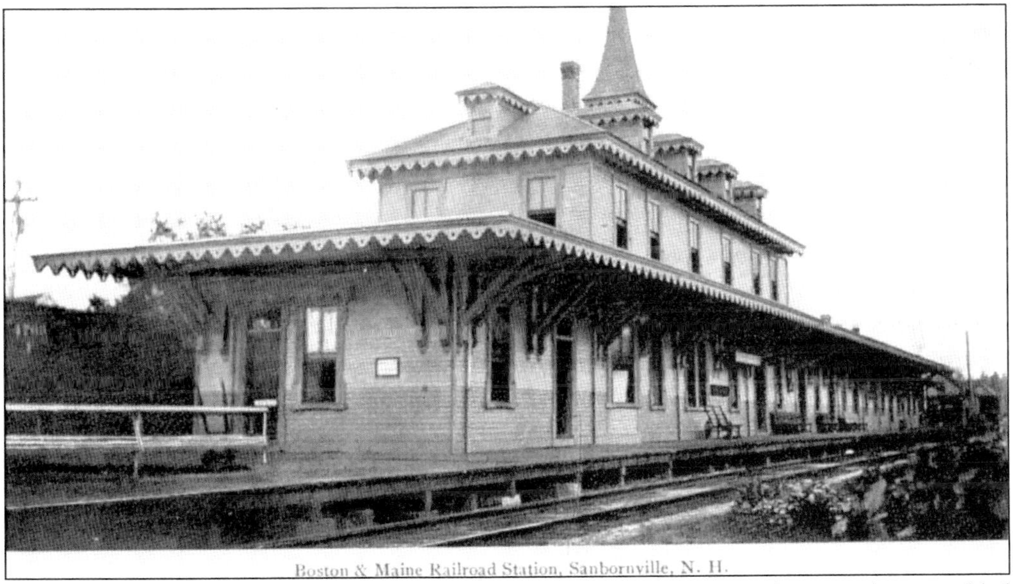

The Sanbornville railroad station was originally a one-story building. The second story, added in 1900, contained offices such as that of John W. Sanborn.

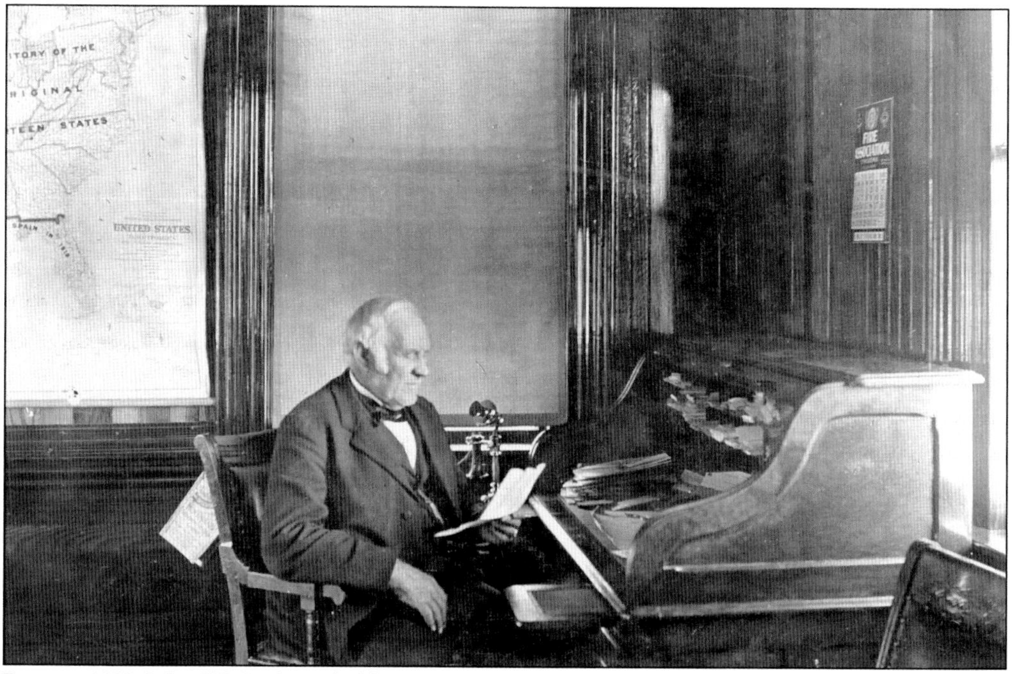

Born in 1822, John W. Sanborn held many positions in his life, including teacher, bank president, and politician. It was through his association with the Boston and Maine Railroad, however, that he most directly affected Wolfeboro Junction, the part of Wakefield that would be renamed in his honor in 1895. Sanborn served as superintendent of the Northern Division of the railroad and eventually as general manager of the entire Boston and Maine Railroad.

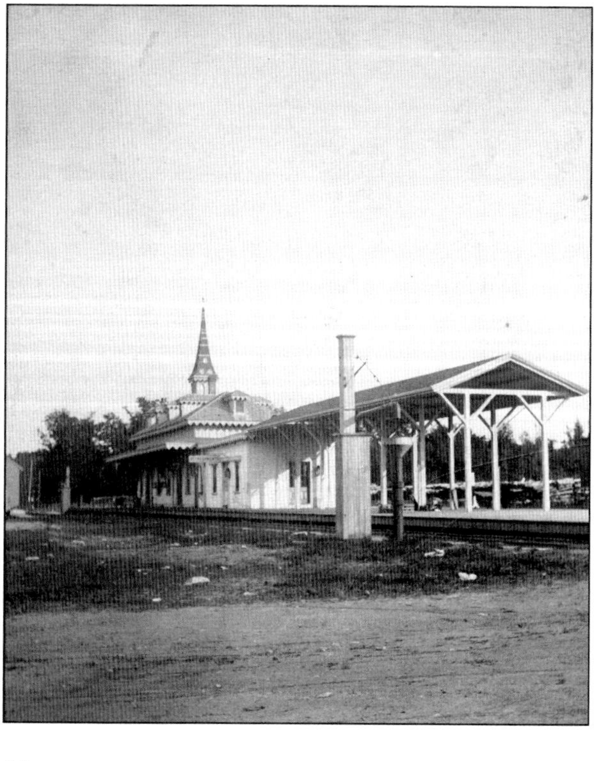

The first railroad station in Sanbornville was a small building, which was soon moved to Cotton Valley. A larger station replaced it to accommodate increasing demand. John W. Sanborn was instrumental in bringing the railroad's carpenter, machine, and car shops to Sanbornville. People and businesses followed, and the village soon became the economic center of Wakefield.

An 1872 wood-burning engine is on the tracks in Sanbornville in 1885. J. W. Garvin's general store, appearing in the background, was established in 1871 when the railroad came to town.

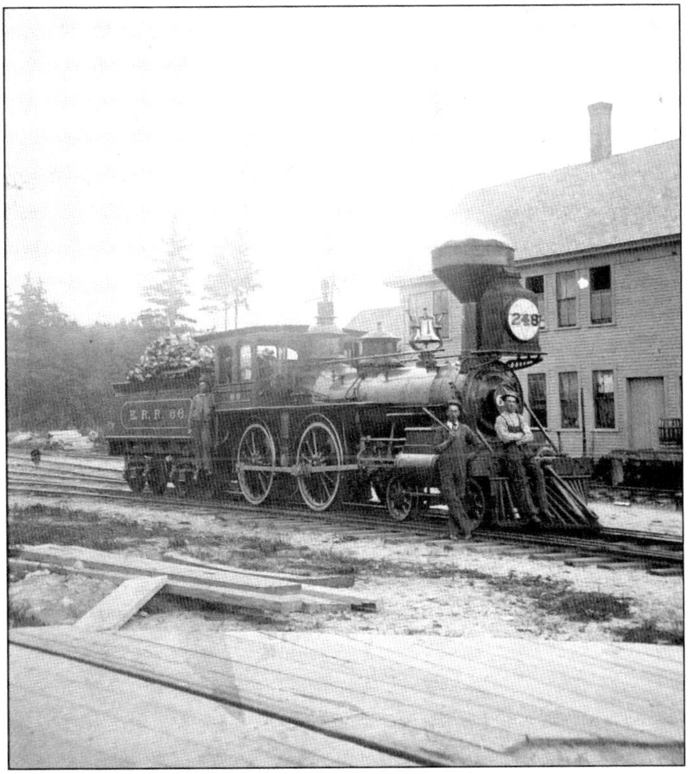

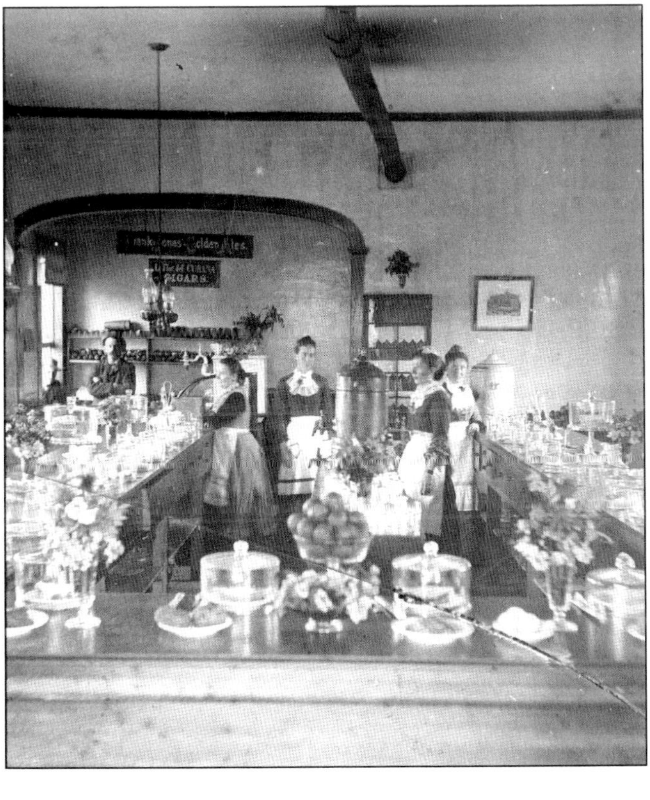

The first restaurant at the Sanbornville railroad station is pictured in 1881. The eatery was initially quite small but grew with the expansion of the station building. In time, it was replaced by the G. W. Armstrong Restaurant, which seated about 150 people in the main dining room.

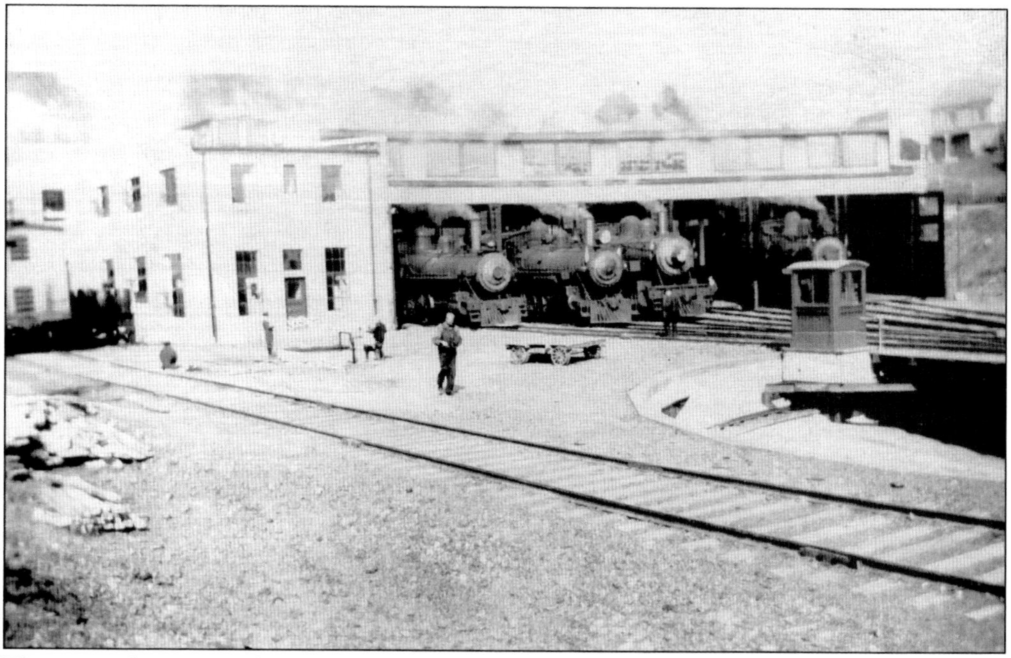

The engine house, seen here in 1885, accommodated eight engines. The roundtable, which still exists in Turntable Park, allowed an engine to be turned in a circle so that it could run in the opposite direction.

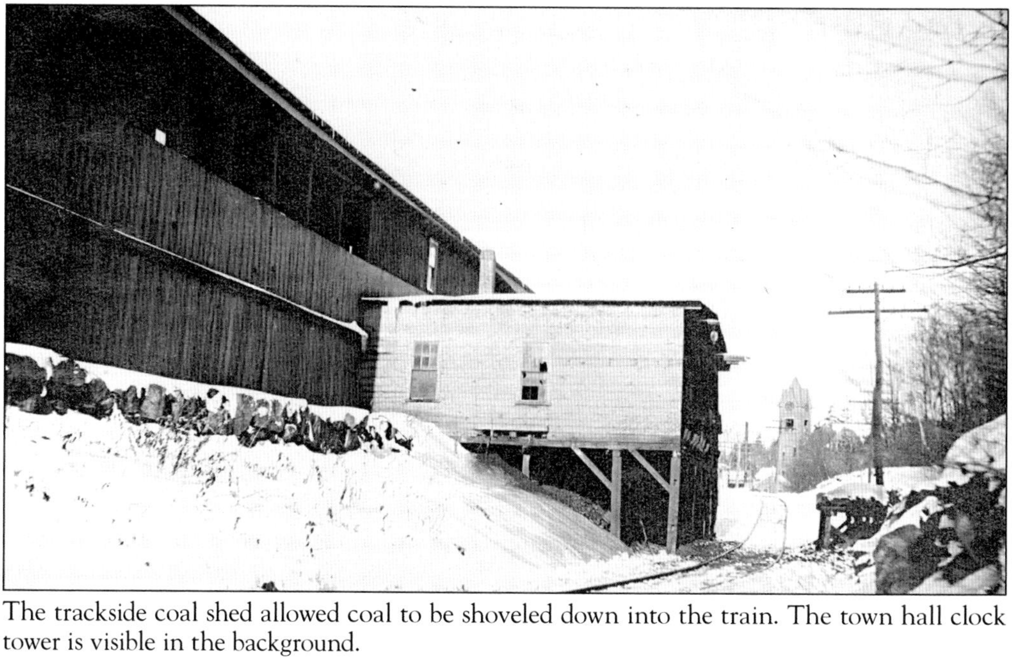

The trackside coal shed allowed coal to be shoveled down into the train. The town hall clock tower is visible in the background.

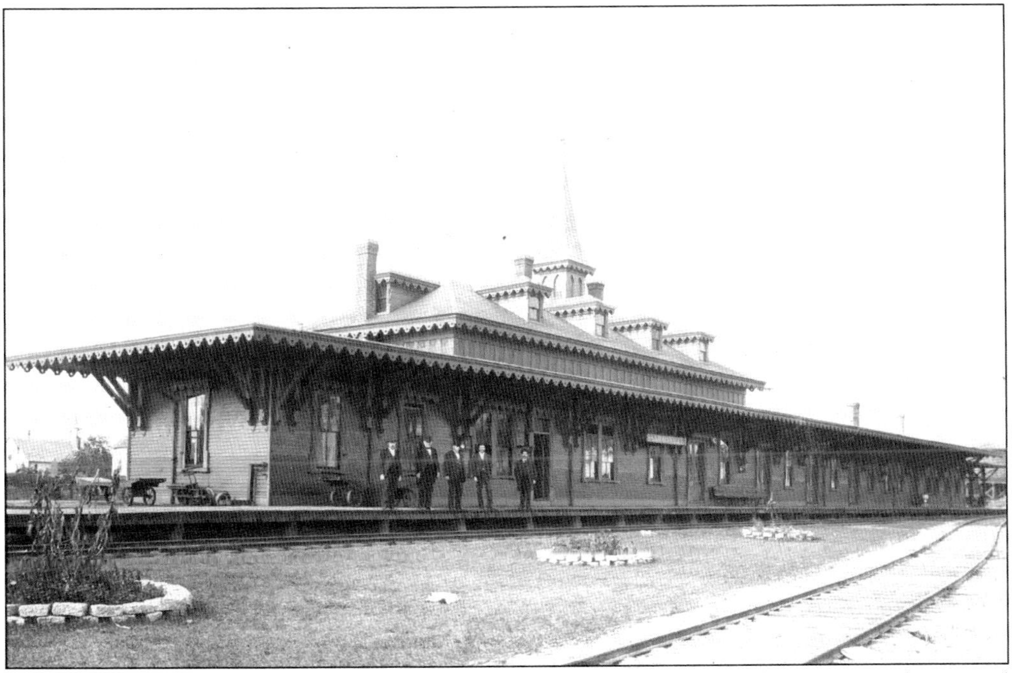

The second Sanbornville railroad station, as seen in 1895, still had only one story; the second story was not added until 1900. This photograph includes, from left to right, George Smith, John W. Sanborn, Wesley Abbott, Wilbur Knight, and George S. Dorr.

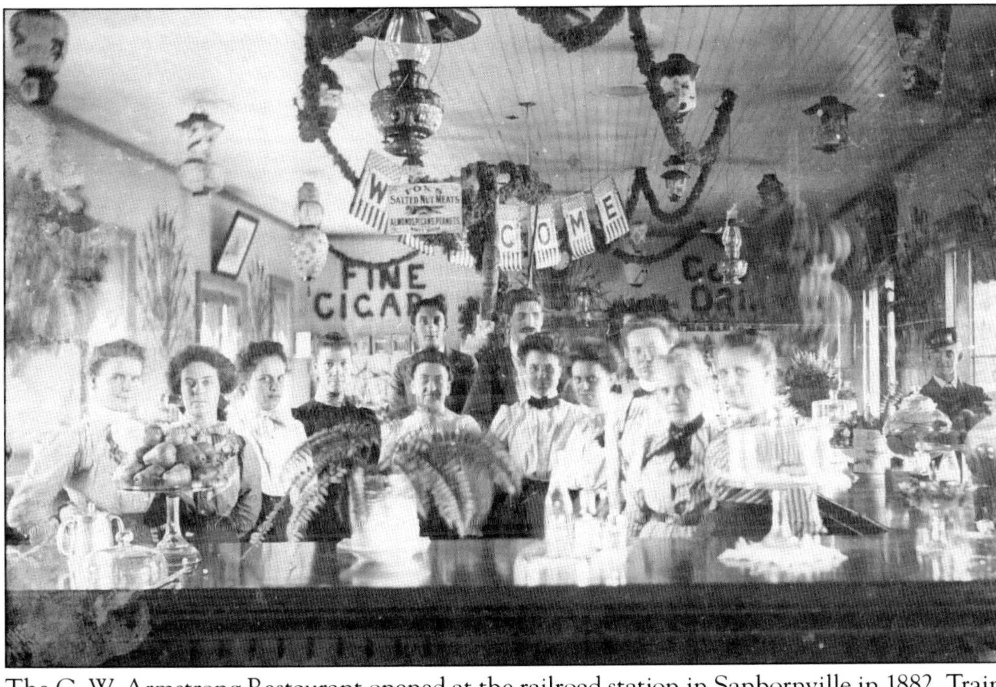

The G. W. Armstrong Restaurant opened at the railroad station in Sanbornville in 1882. Trains stopped here for a half-hour, allowing passengers to eat a quick lunch. Pictured here in 1900 are A. F. Graves, Clayton Smith, Annie Fellows, Carrie Knight, Nettie Fellows, Katie Foley, Grace Ouellette, Clara Robinson, Annie Hanson, Ruth Garland, Mary Ahearn, and Edina Downs.

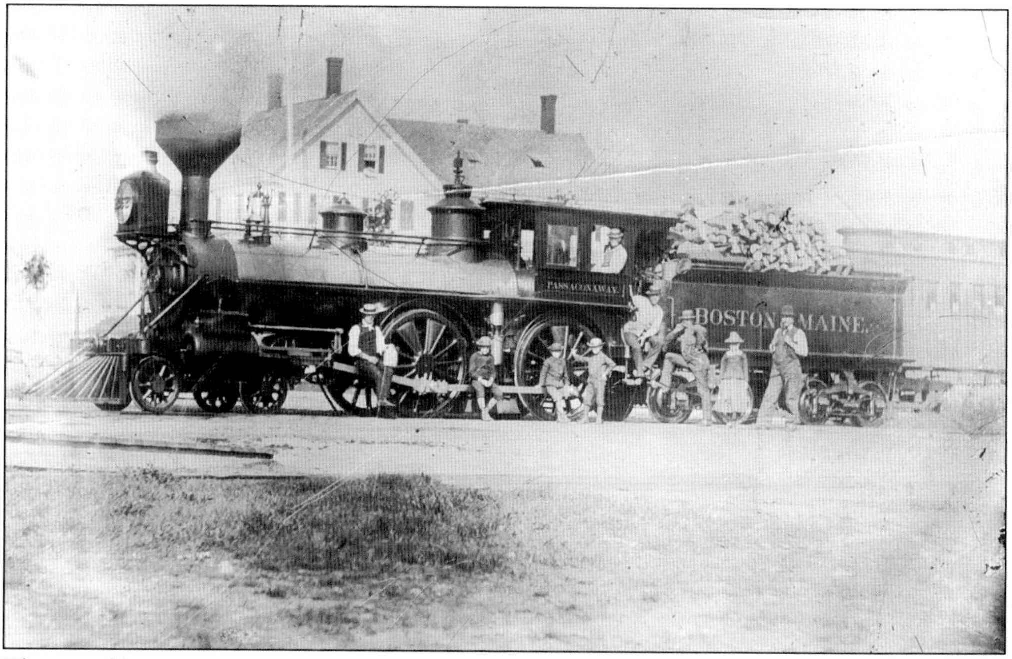

This wood-burning engine (No. 262) of the Boston and Maine Railroad is seen in Sanbornville, with the Sanborn house in the background. The image includes Willis Hanson (third boy from the front of the engine) and Charles E. Randall (with a foot on the step). Note the load of wood, great quantities of which were burned by the engines.

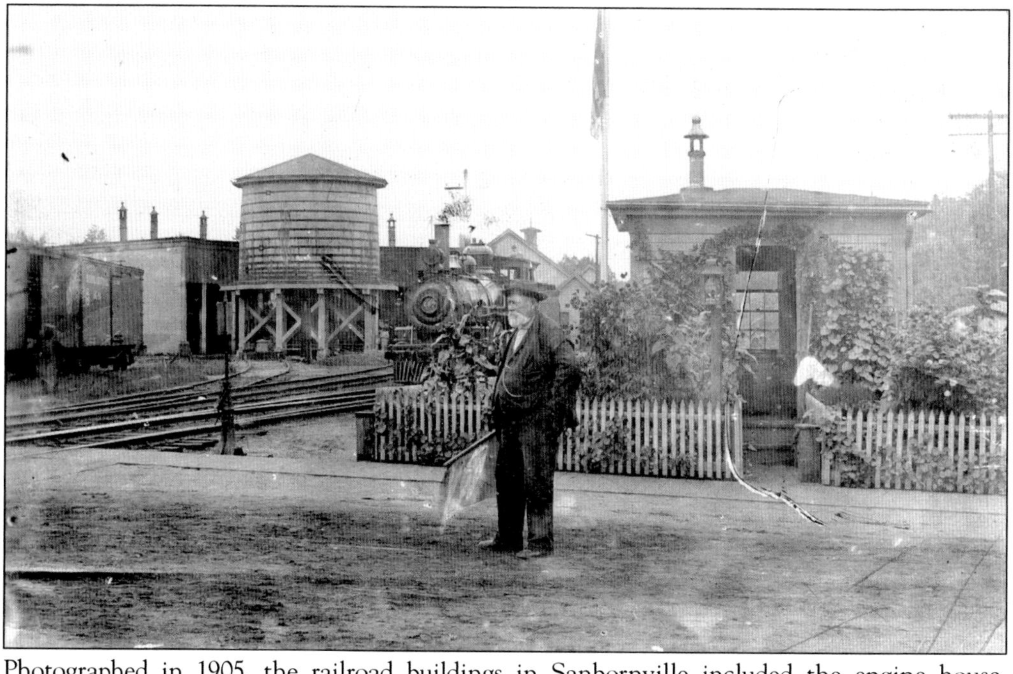

Photographed in 1905, the railroad buildings in Sanbornville included the engine house, carpenter shop, water tower, and flag station. The flag station, with its flourishing garden, was located next to the J. W. Garvin store and between two railroad tracks. One track went to Conway, and one to Wolfeboro. Flagman Ivory Rice is also pictured.

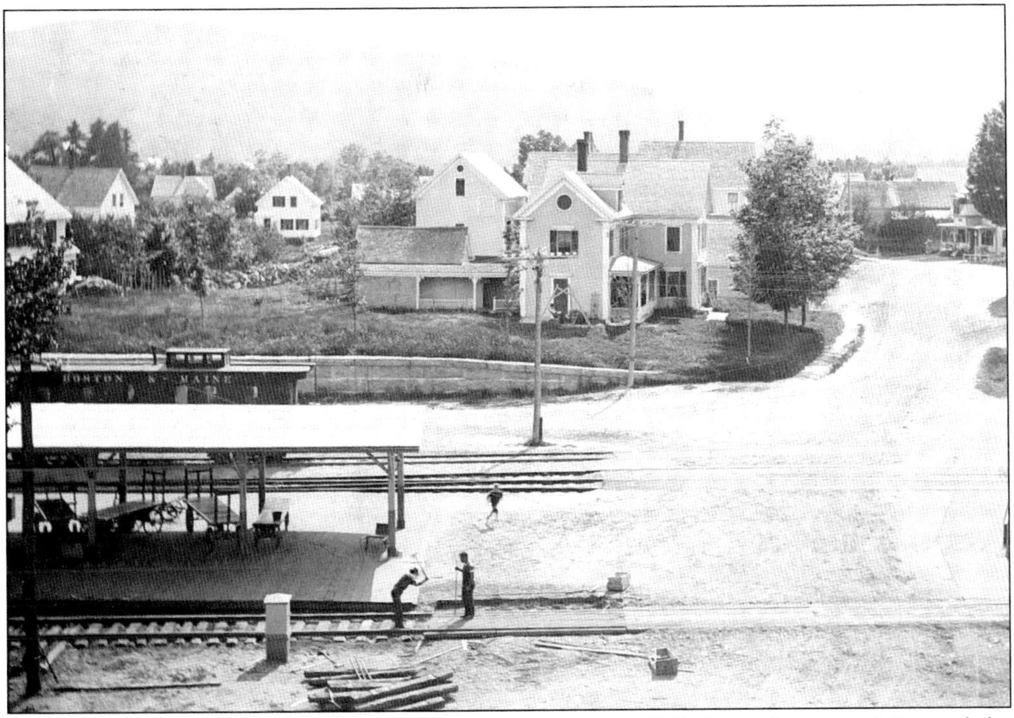

Men work on the railroad tracks in this image taken in 1902 from the second floor of the recently built town hall. Several sets of tracks crossed Meadow Street at this time.

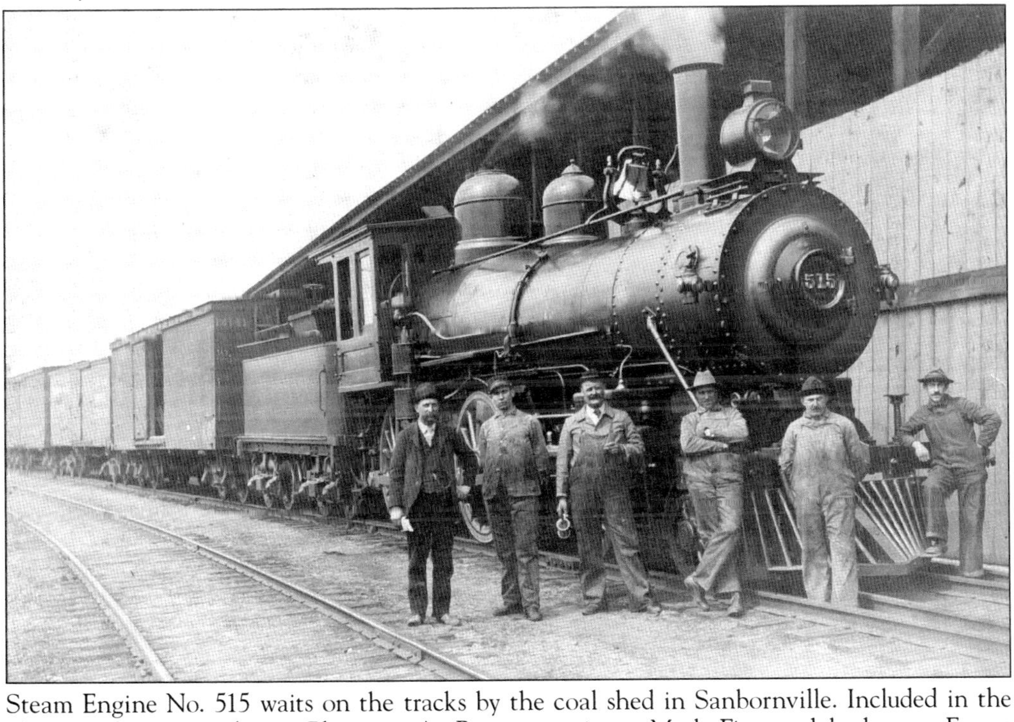

Steam Engine No. 515 waits on the tracks by the coal shed in Sanbornville. Included in the photograph are conductor Plummer A. Brown, engineer Mark Fitz, and brakemen Ernest Campbell and Charles Cheney.

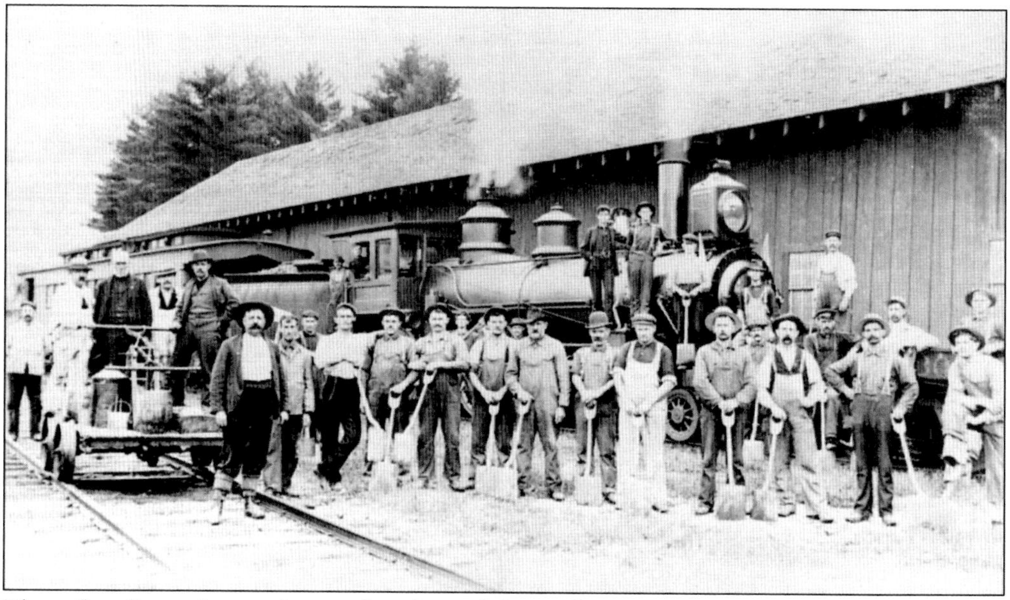

The railroad's car shop and paint shop burned down along with the engine house in 1911. The Boston and Maine Railroad rebuilt the shops in Dover, and an important industry disappeared from the village center.

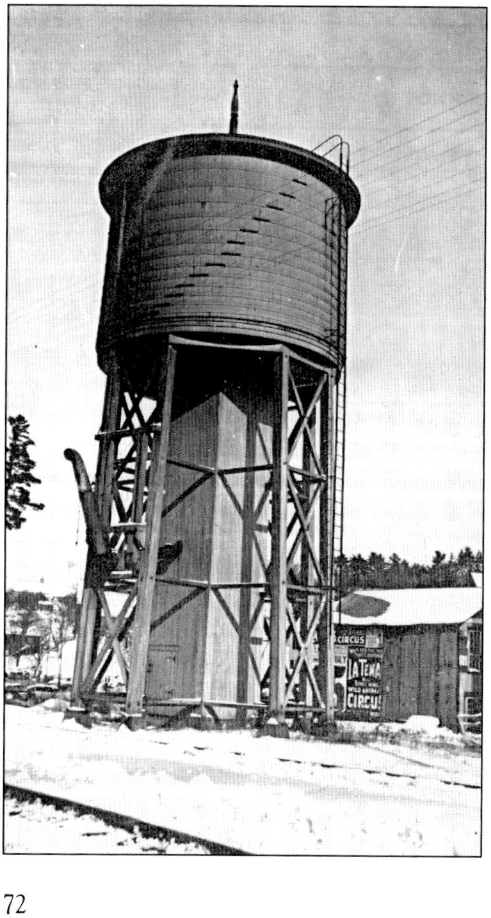

The 50,000-gallon water tank, located behind the Garvin building, is pictured in 1914.

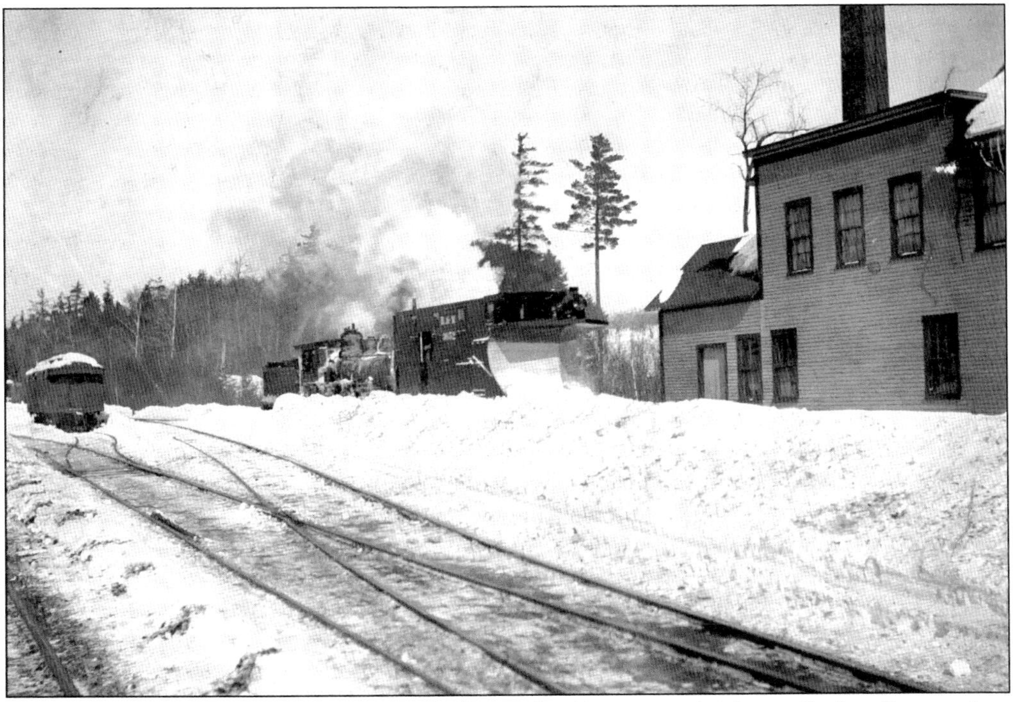

The snowplow, shown in 1908, was built at the Boston and Maine Railroad's car shop in Sanbornville.

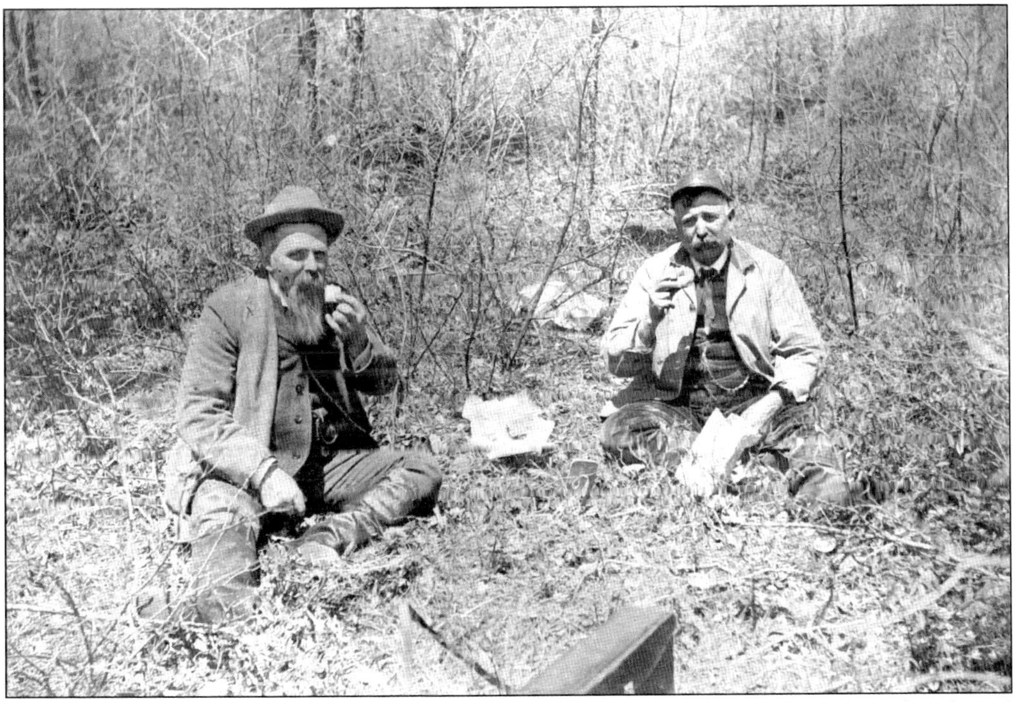

William F. Sanborn (left), assistant superintendent of the Boston and Maine Railroad, and conductor Plummer A. Brown enjoy a picnic. Sanborn was known affectionately as "Billy Goat."

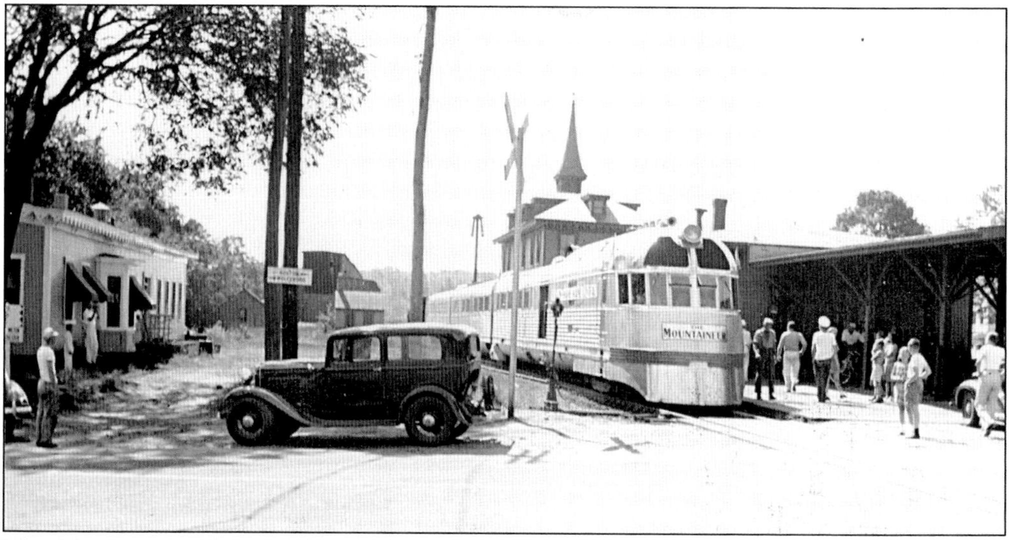

The *Mountaineer*, photographed in 1944, traveled from Boston to Bethlehem and Littleton. Sanbornville was its first stop after leaving Boston.

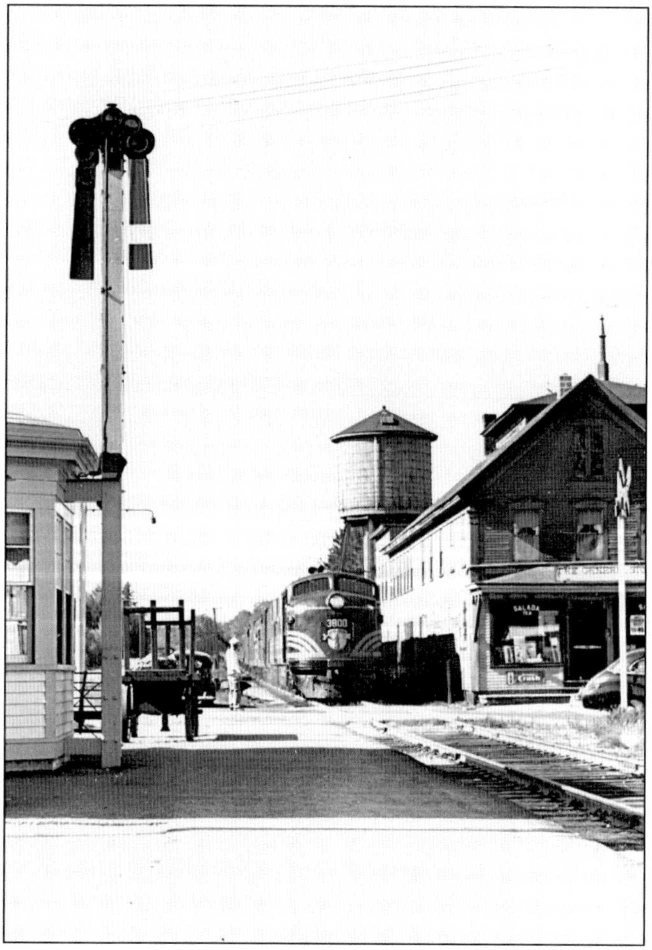

This 1954 view, depicting a diesel engine and the water tower, shows how the trains and station area have changed since the early days of steam engines. Passenger service to Sanbornville ended in 1961, and now the tracks are used only to transport gravel from Ossipee.

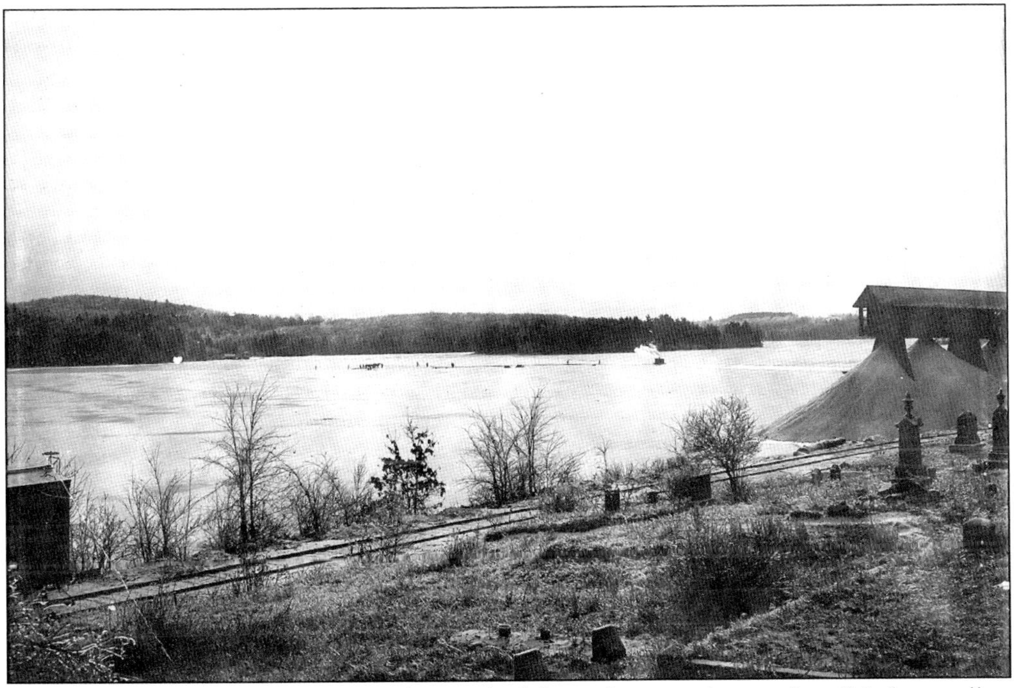

Prior to 1880, a spur of railroad tracks was laid from the main line to Lovell Lake to allow transportation of ice taken from the lake. The tracks were near the Lovell Lake Cemetery.

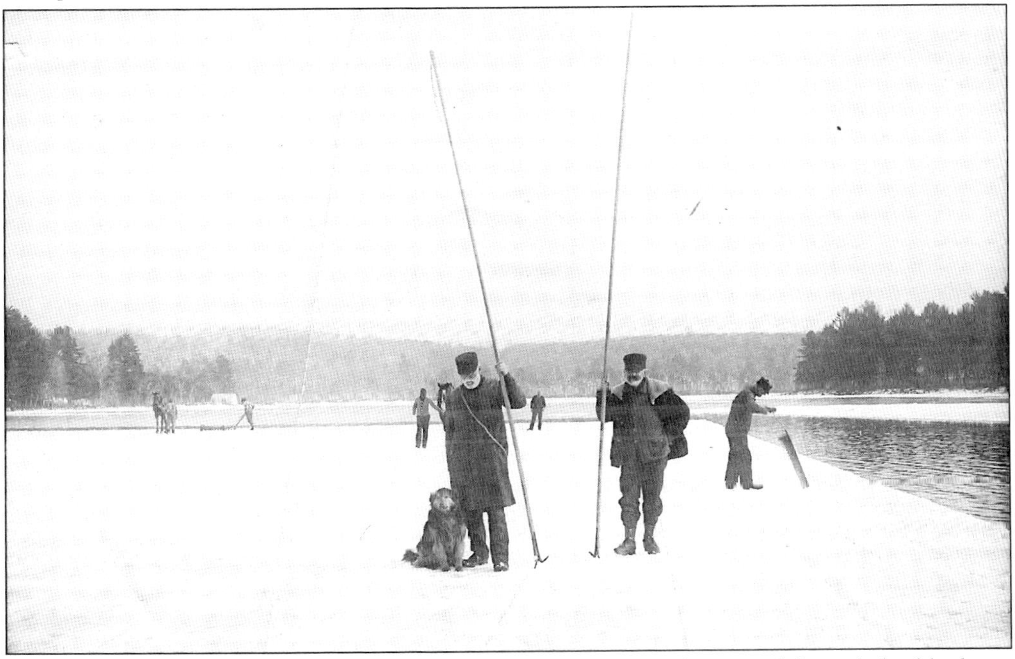

In the early days of ice harvesting, men cut the ice with handsaws and floated the blocks to shore with long ice hooks. The men had special boots with steel spikes to keep them from slipping. Eventually, a whole industry of ice tools and machinery developed, including plows, markers, saws, planers, cutters, chisels, forks, bars, skids, scrapers, scales, hooks, tongs, grapples, and measuring irons, all of which had many varieties for different uses.

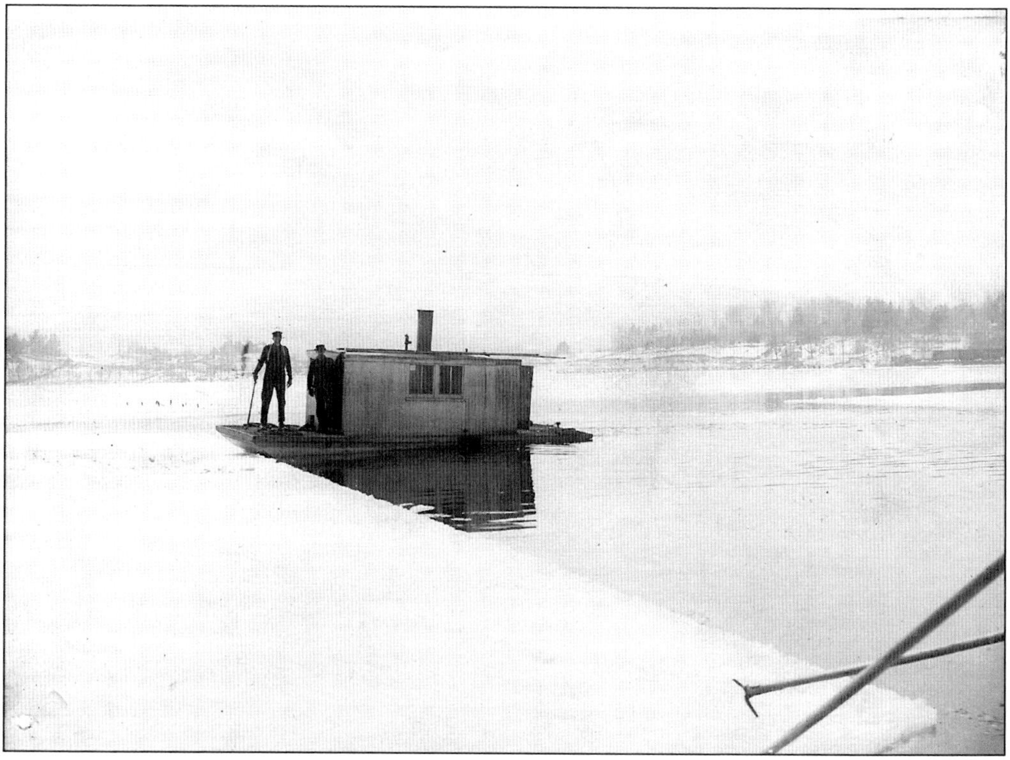

In the 19th century, New England towns with ponds often had a vibrant ice industry, employing many farmers in the winter. In the 1880s, Lovell Lake became the center of the industry in town, eventually producing 25 to 30 railroad cars of ice per day. At the height of the business, in 1919, 119,000 tons of ice were taken from the lake. The boat shown here helped move the ice blocks to shore.

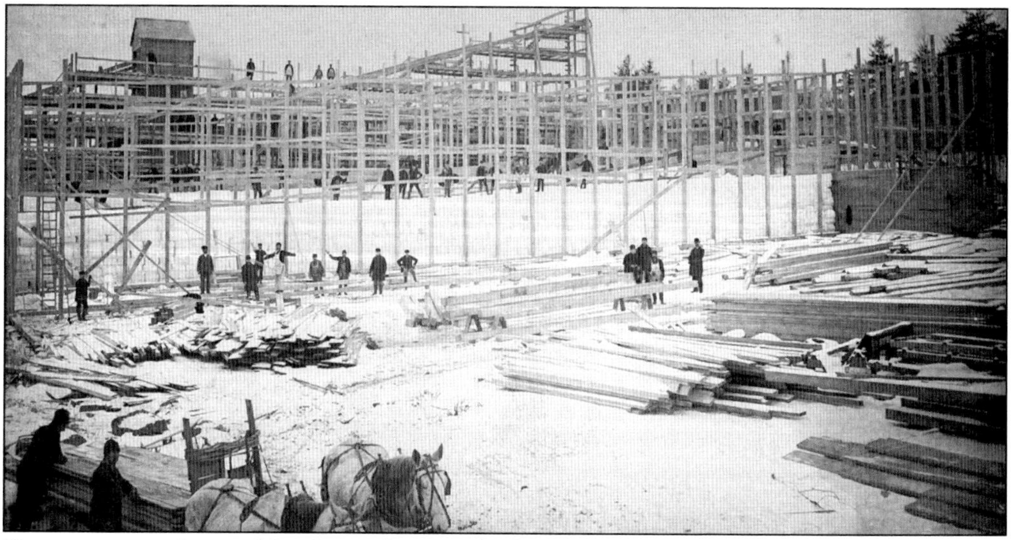

Huge ice storage houses like these, photographed in the winter of 1889–1890, were constructed on the south shore of Lovell Lake. They were filled with stacked blocks in the winter; the ice remained frozen and could be shipped to Boston year-round.

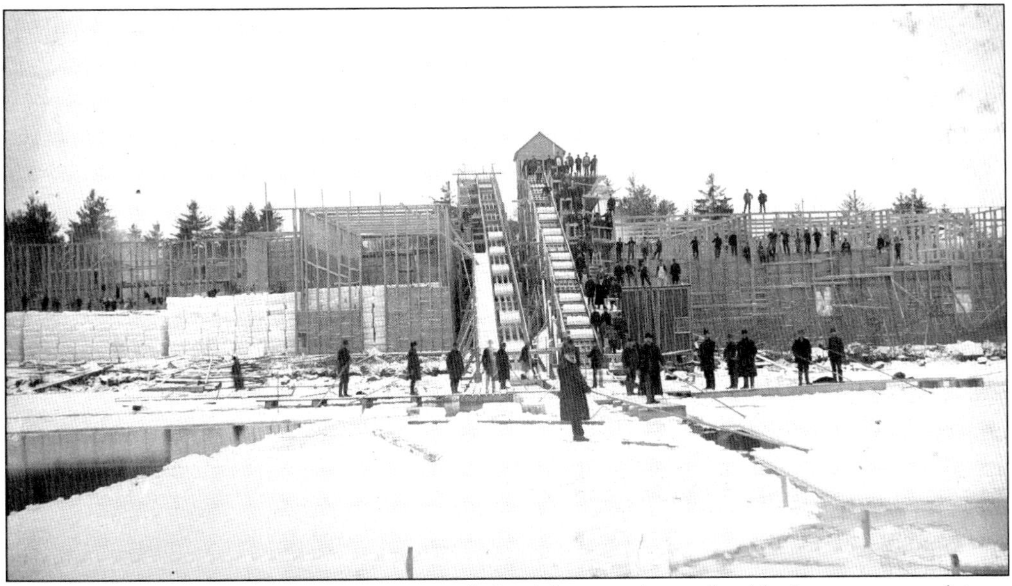

Elevators were used to lift the ice out of the lake to where the blocks were stored in a double-walled house under sawdust. The cakes visible here were 44 inches square and weighed over 600 pounds each. Before shipping, the ice cakes were cut in half twice, creating enough blocks for four ice boxes.

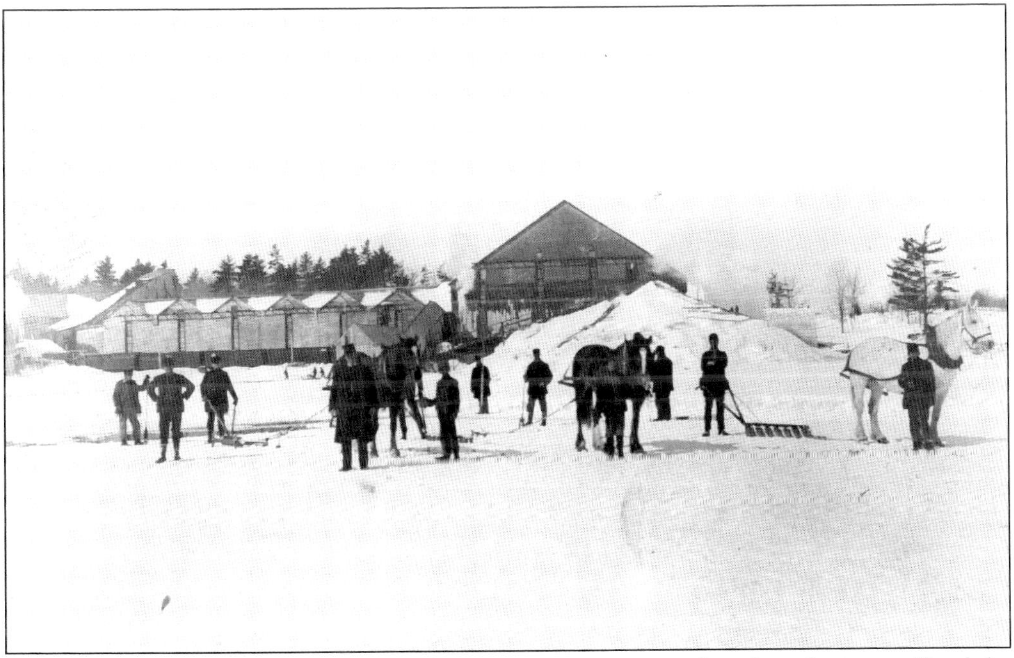

As the ice industry grew, horses were used to scrape away snow, mark and cut the ice, and haul the blocks to shore. Often, the animals would fall in the water. Each horse wore a choke-hold collar that the men could grab, cutting off the horse's breathing and causing it to bloat from the air in its body. The horse would then float to the surface and could be rescued before it strangled.

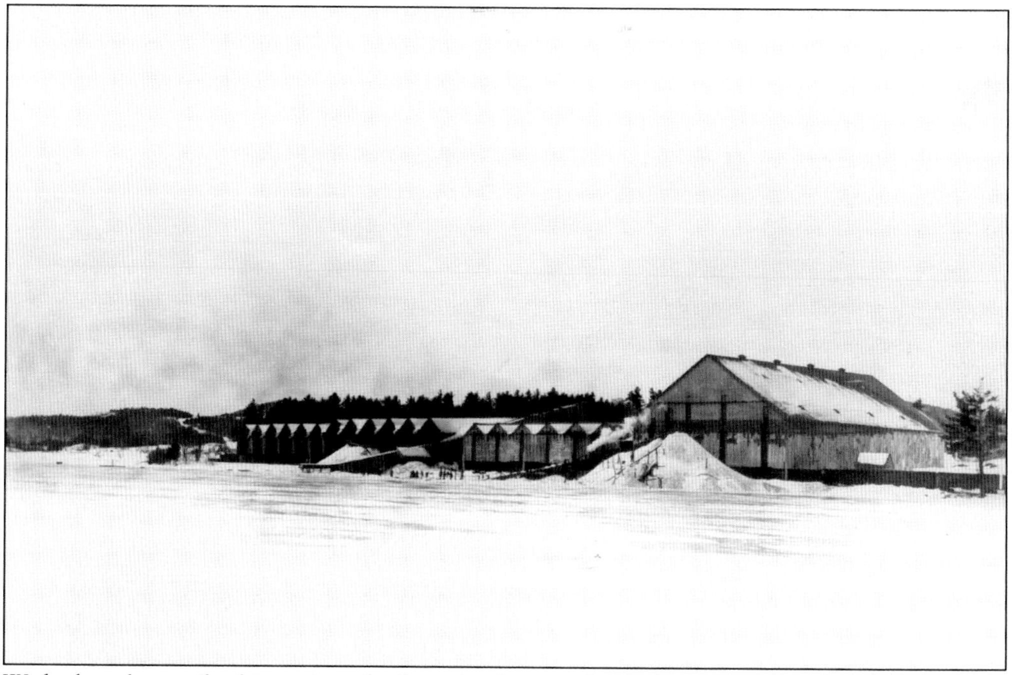

With the advent of refrigeration, the huge ice houses shown here were torn down in the early 1930s. All that remains today are some concrete footings, although a boardinghouse once used by the workers still stands on Lovell Lake Road.

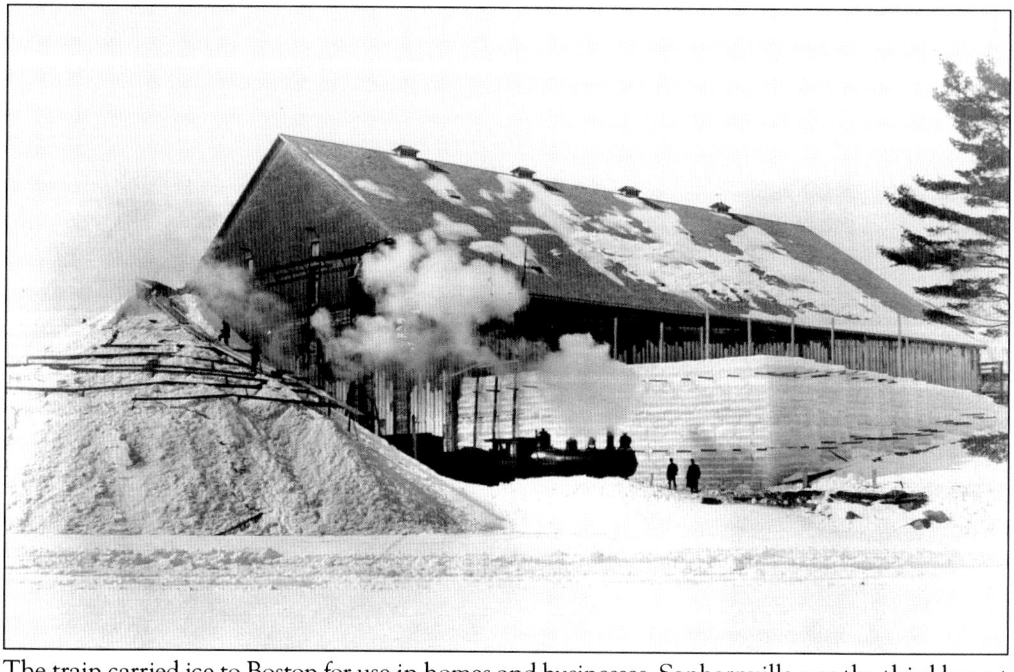

The train carried ice to Boston for use in homes and businesses. Sanbornville was the third largest producer on the Boston and Maine line after Milton, New Hampshire, and Wakefield, Massachusetts. Note the very large pile of ice shavings; the blocks were shaved to give uniformity.

Five

Other Villages

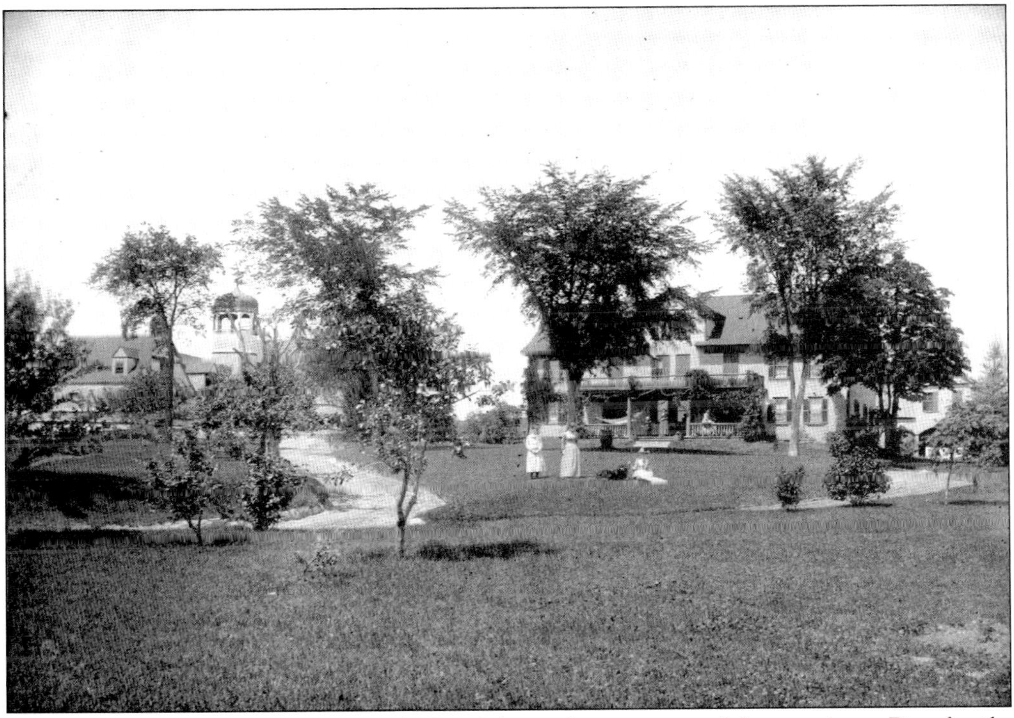

The Dow Homestead, on Province Lake Road, housed generations of the prominent Dow family. The imposing house had a view of Great East Lake at one time, and the spectacular barn was built in the European style. More recently, the estate has been in the Bancroft family for decades.

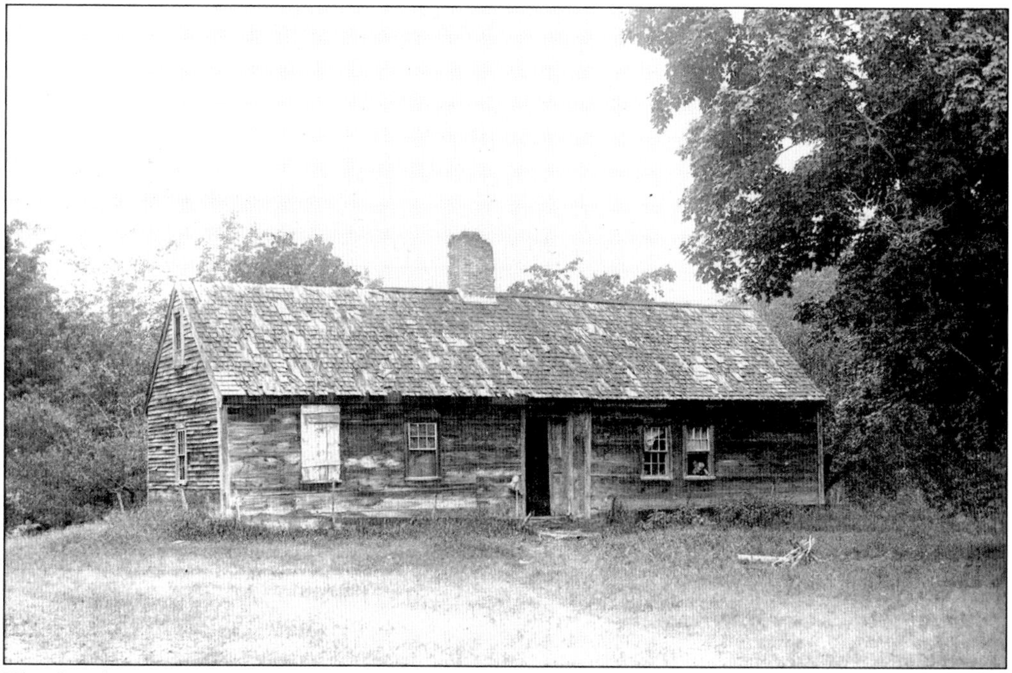

The Sarah Copp House was a traditional board house, a style common in the 18th and 19th centuries. It was located in East Wakefield, in the woods beyond the Dow Homestead.

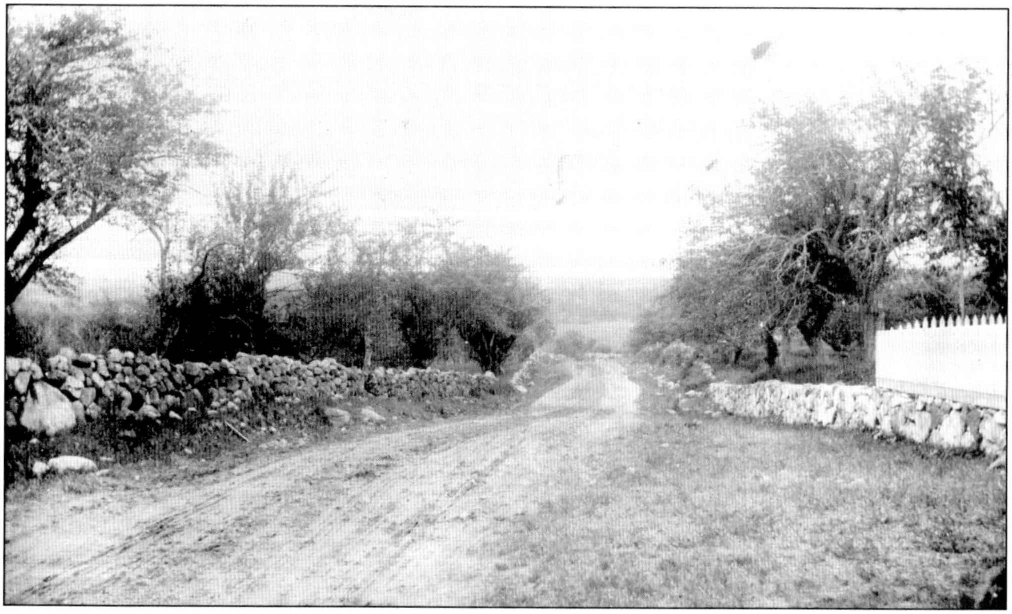

Province Lake Road is pictured in the late 19th century.

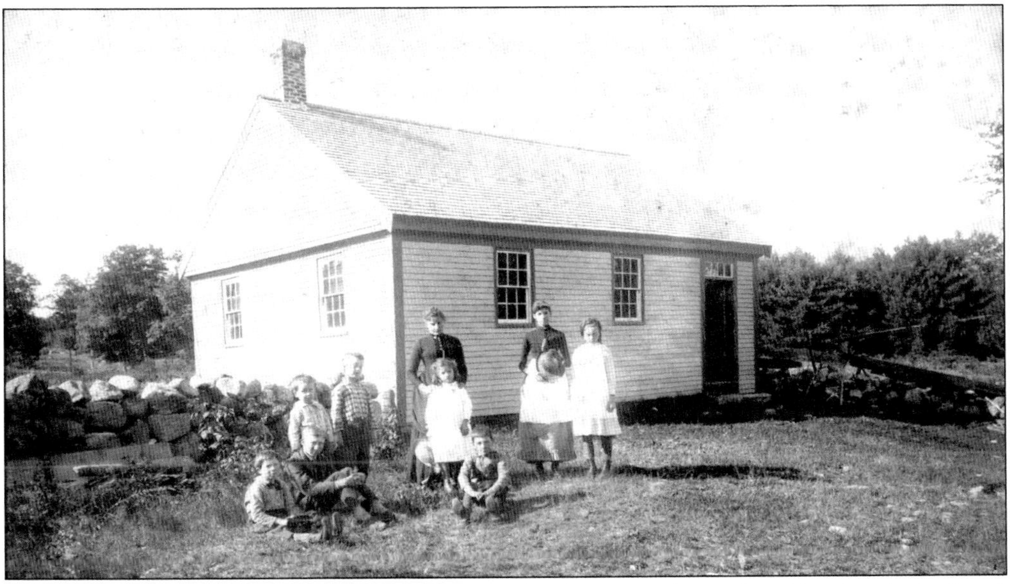

The Dow School, not to be confused with Dow Academy, was located on Province Lake Road. It closed in 1906 and was replaced in District 8 by the new East Wakefield School. The building later became a private home. Here, teacher Sarah Weeks and her students pose in front of the schoolhouse in 1888.

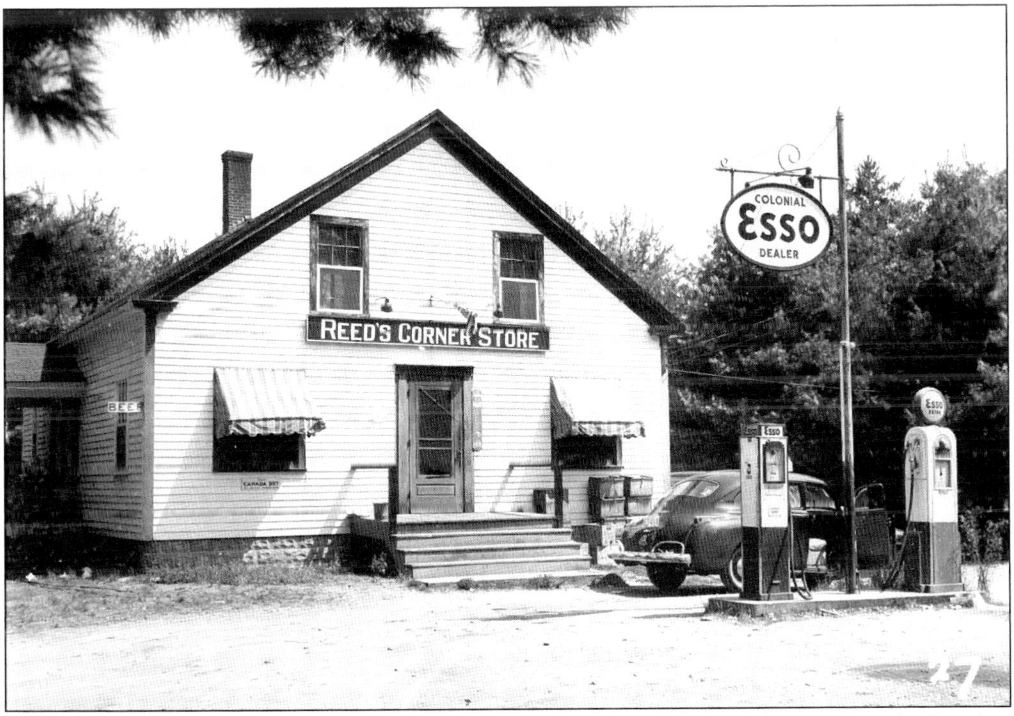

Reed's Corner Store was located at the corner of Acton Ridge Road and Province Lake Road in East Wakefield. Today, it is still a convenience store and gas station.

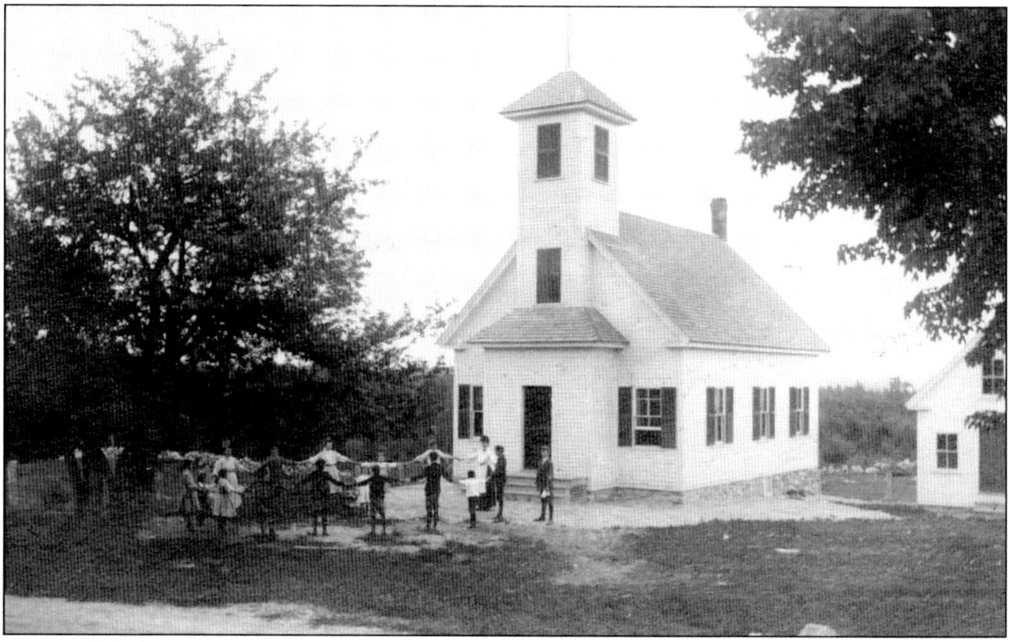

East Wakefield's new District 8 Schoolhouse was built on Province Lake Road near the railroad station in 1906. Previously, students from the village of East Wakefield had traveled to the Wakefield Corner School by train; the Dow School was thought to be inconveniently located. The structure still stands but now serves as a church.

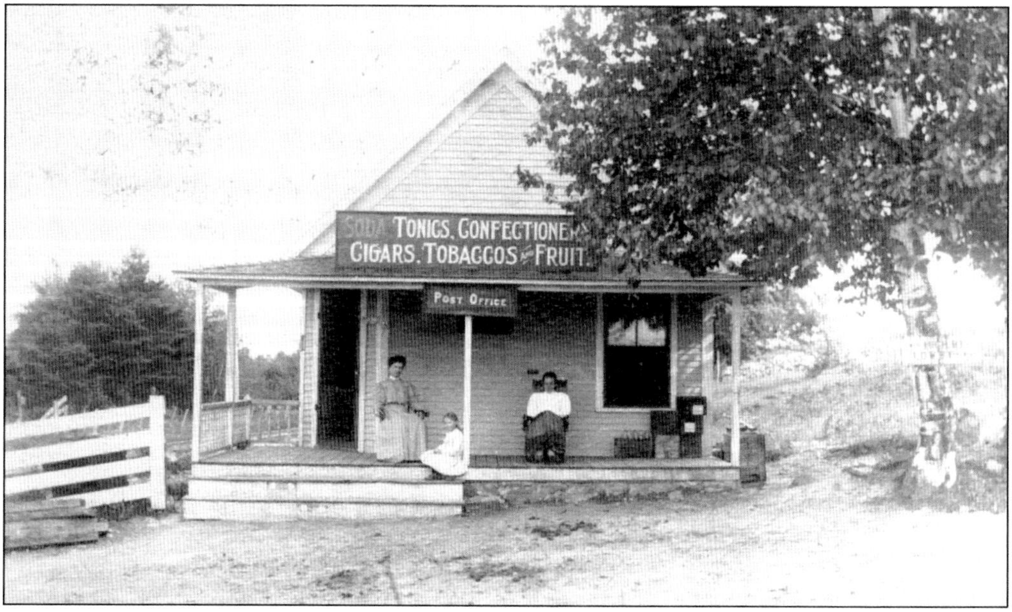

This building, one of several that housed the post office, still stands beside the railroad tracks in East Wakefield. Note the sign advertising tonic and confections.

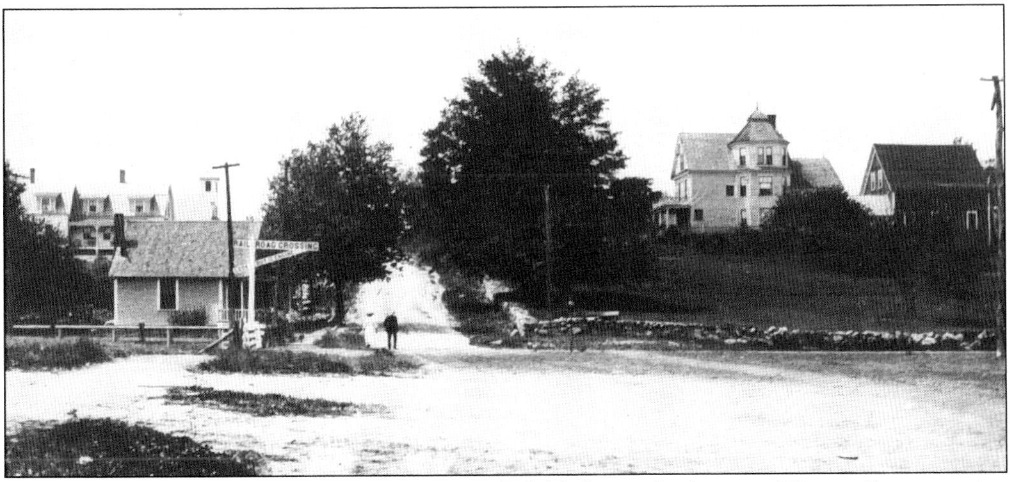

This view of Province Lake Road in East Wakefield shows the house of Ernest Scott, station agent and onetime postmaster, and the little post office building. The sign warns, "Railroad crossing. Look out for the engine."

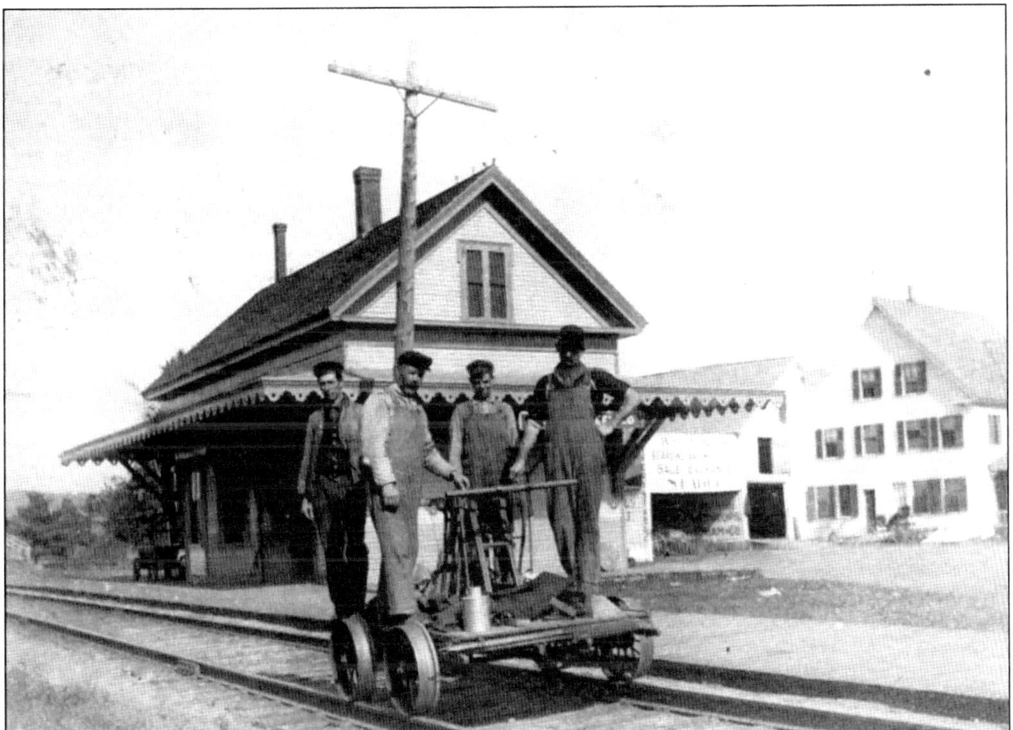

Four men on a handcar stop at the East Wakefield train station. These cars, propelled down the railroad tracks by manpower, were used mostly for track inspection and maintenance.

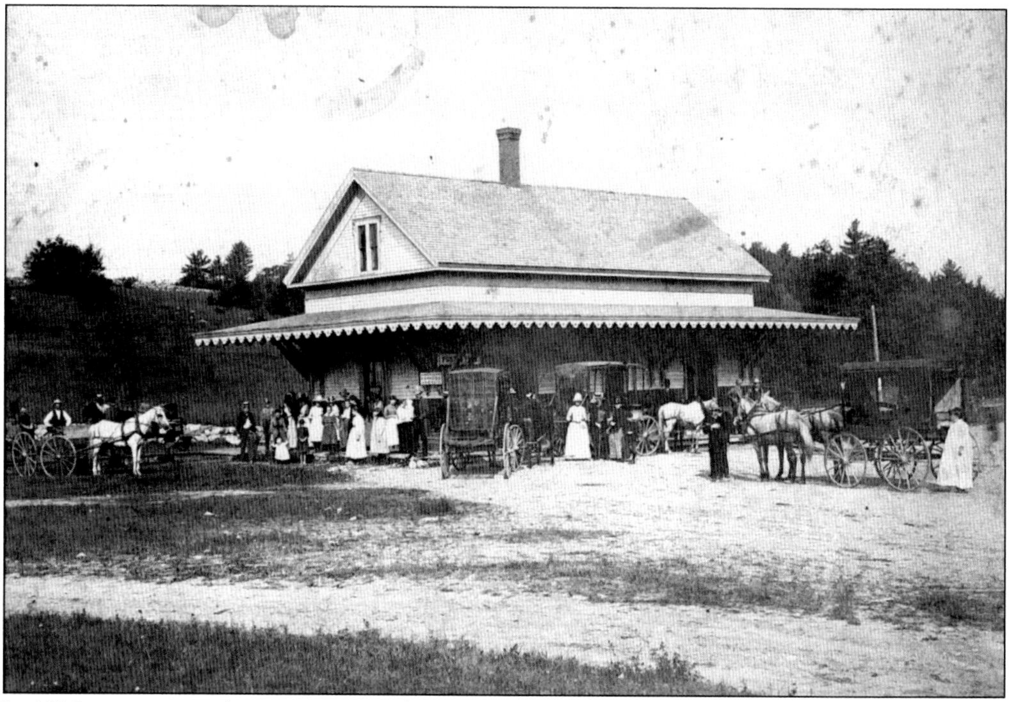

In 1900, carriages and wagons wait at the East Wakefield railroad station to take arriving visitors to the local guest houses. The East Wakefield post office was also housed in the building at this time. The name of the station was later changed from East Wakefield to Burleyville, to reduce confusion between the three Wakefield stations.

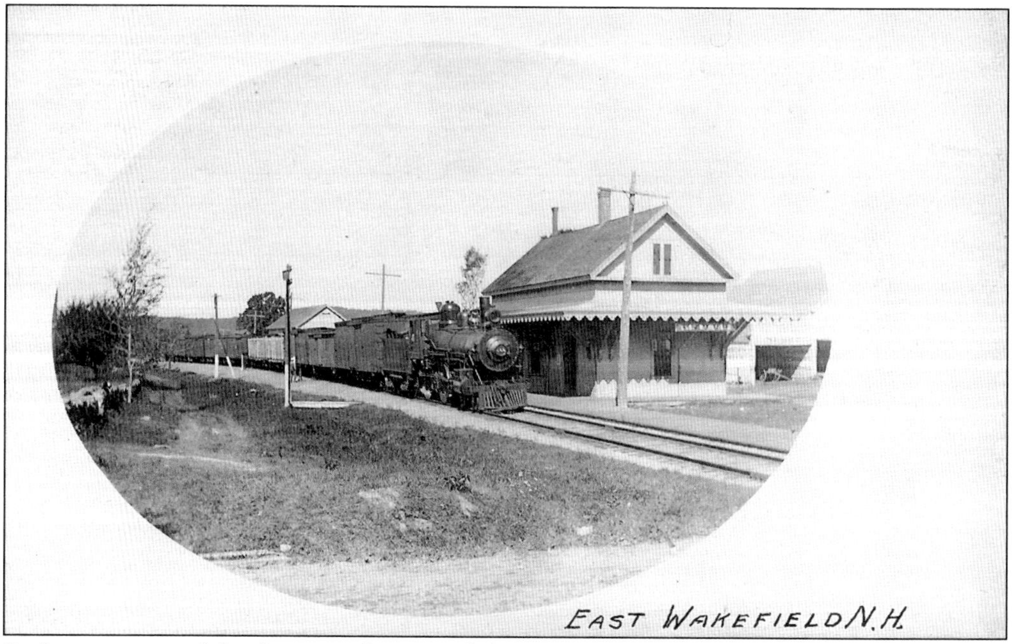

Both passenger and freight trains frequented the East Wakefield station. Summer visitors came to stay in the inns in East Wakefield and over the border in Maine, and lumber and other goods were sent out on the trains.

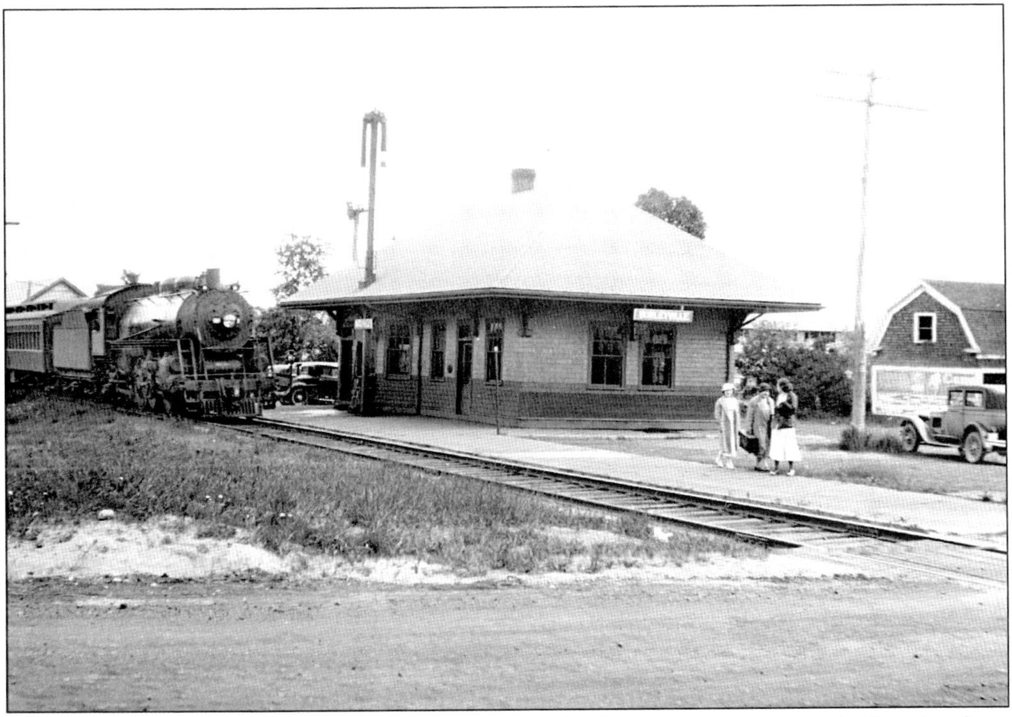

After a fire destroyed the Burleyville station in 1910, this less ornate station was built in its place. Train service to East Wakefield/Burleyville finally ended in 1956.

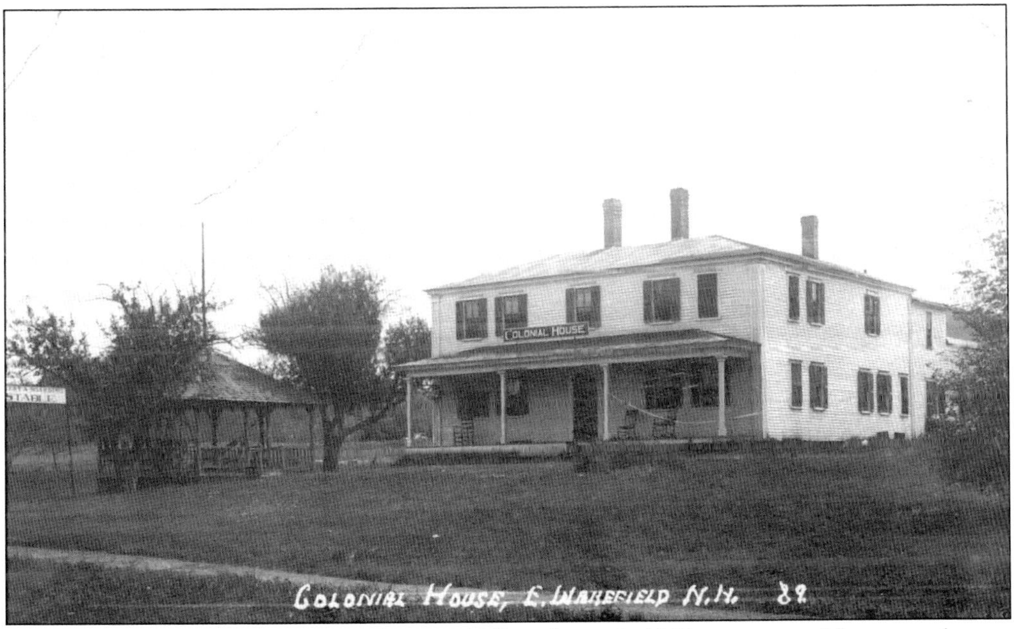

Colonial House, run by Almon and Hattie Hill in the early 1900s, was one of four guest houses in East Wakefield and could accommodate about 20 visitors. Many people came from the city for extended summer vacations to eat homemade, farm-fresh food and enjoy the country air.

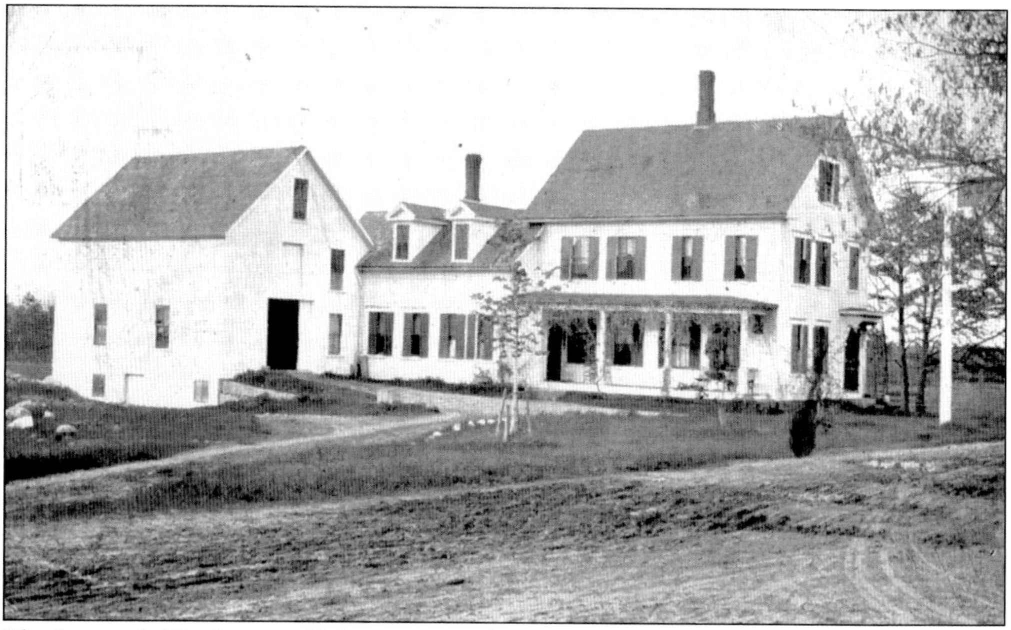

The Sunnyside Hotel, originally known as Kershaw House, could lodge approximately 25 people. The hotel was built by the first agent of the East Wakefield station.

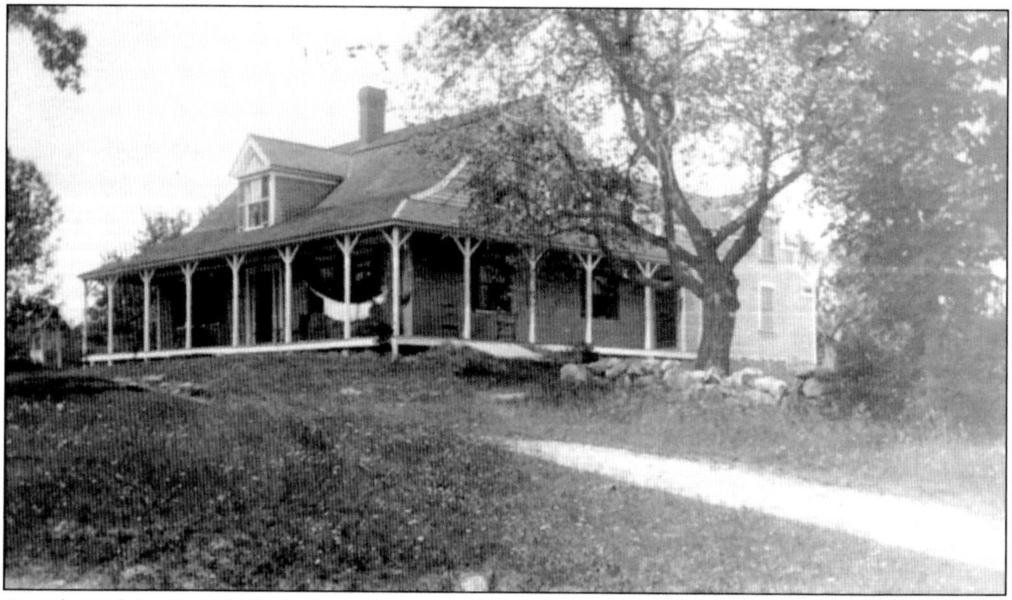

Another of the East Wakefield guest houses, Pevey House has since been destroyed by fire.

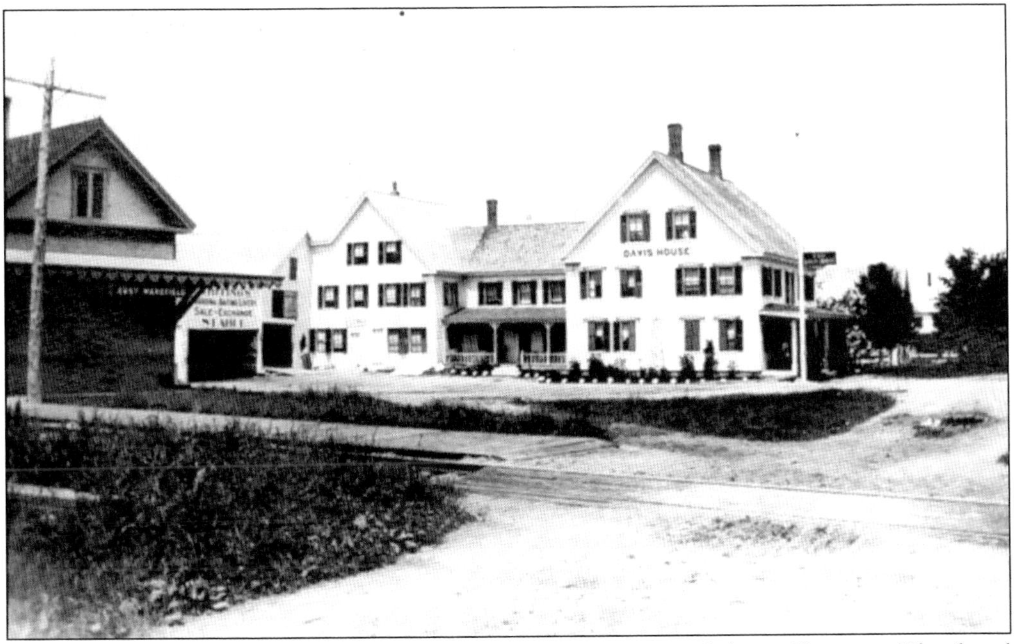

Davis House was the largest of the four inns, with a capacity of about 40 guests. This hotel and its livery stable stood adjacent to the railroad station. In 1910, a fire swept through East Wakefield, and Davis House was burned down along with the station. The Newfield Farmers' Union was later built on the site.

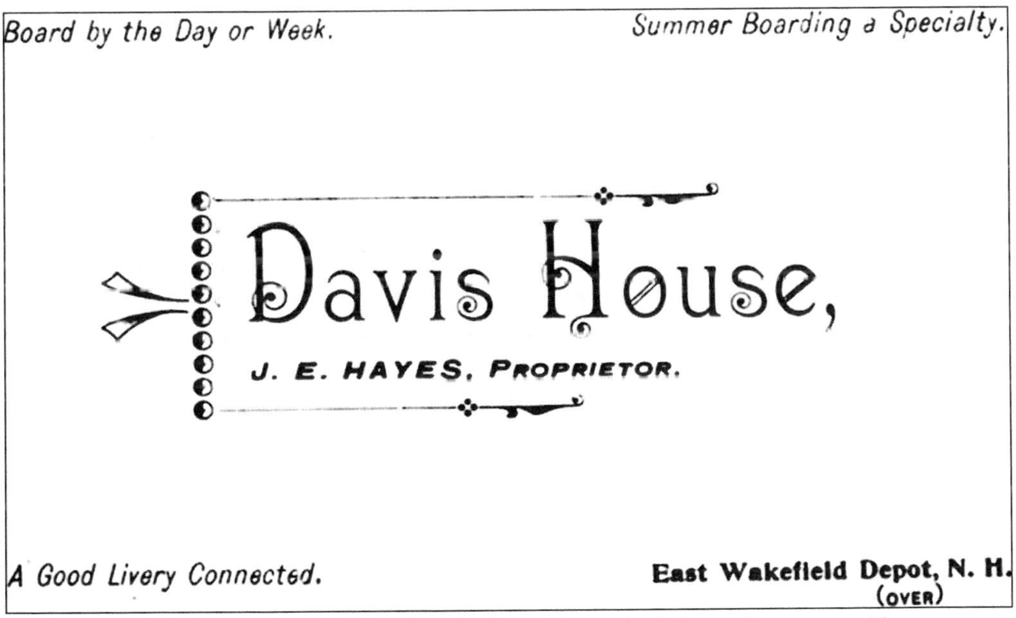

Board by the Day or Week. *Summer Boarding a Specialty.*

Davis House,

J. E. HAYES, PROPRIETOR.

A Good Livery Connected. **East Wakefield Depot, N. H.**

(OVER)

This Davis House business card included the local train schedule on the reverse side.

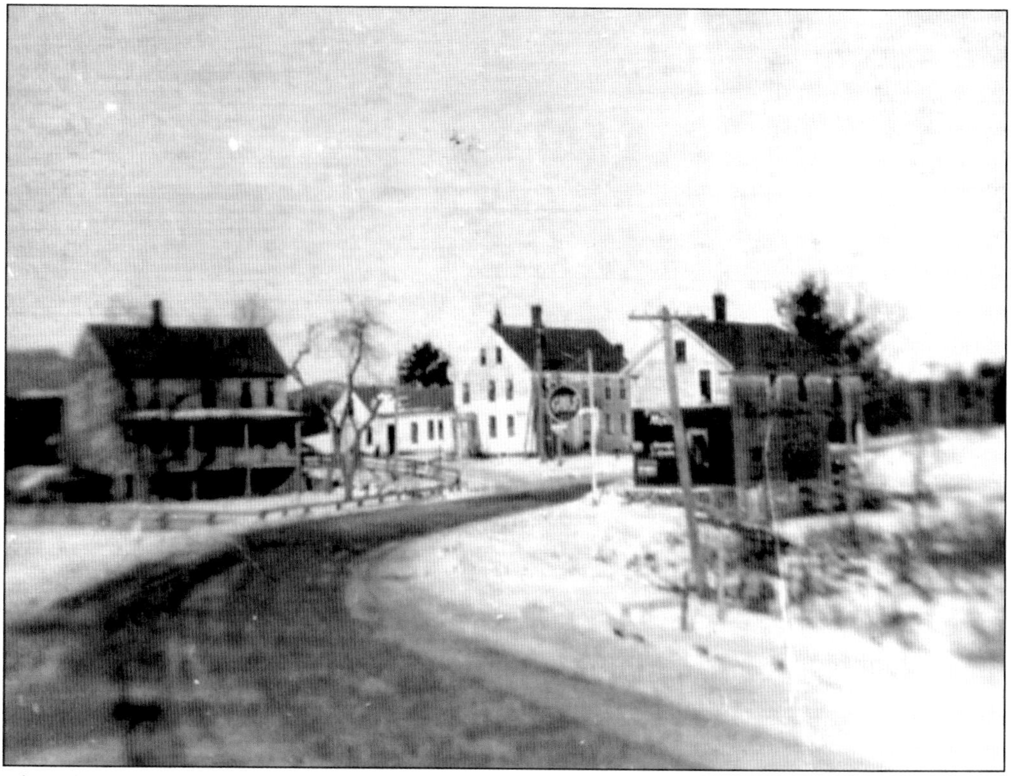

The village of Woodman was named after a local family. This 1930 photograph shows Province Lake Road, as well as Ballards Ridge Road going off to the left.

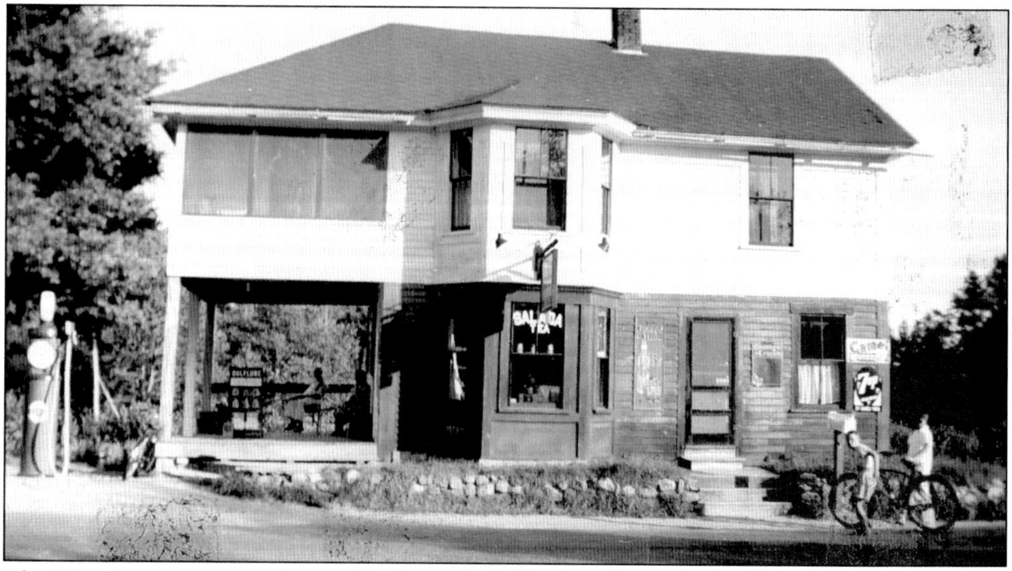

The Woodman store, once located on Province Lake Road, is no longer standing. Note the signs for Orange Crush and Salada tea.

Photographed in the early 1900s, the Chick House is located in Woodman at the corner of Province Lake Road and Ballards Ridge Road. The Woodman post office was once situated here.

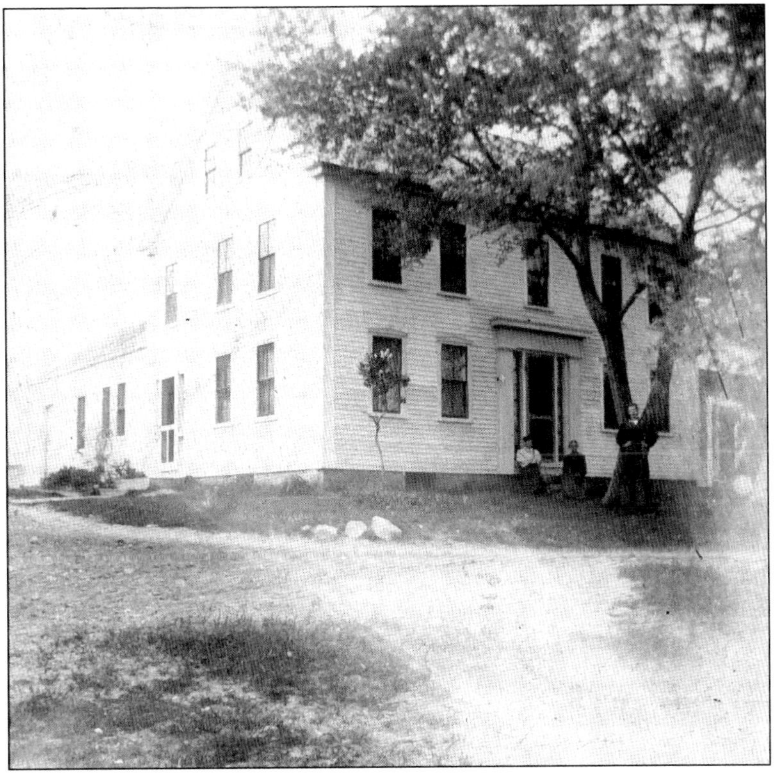

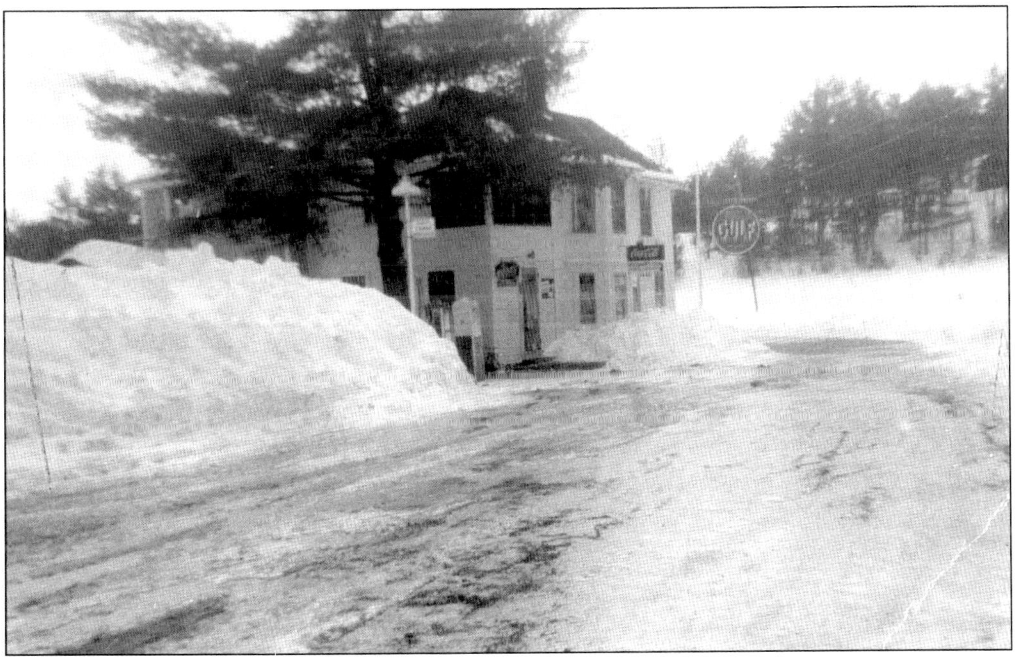

The Woodman store experiences a snowy day in 1953.

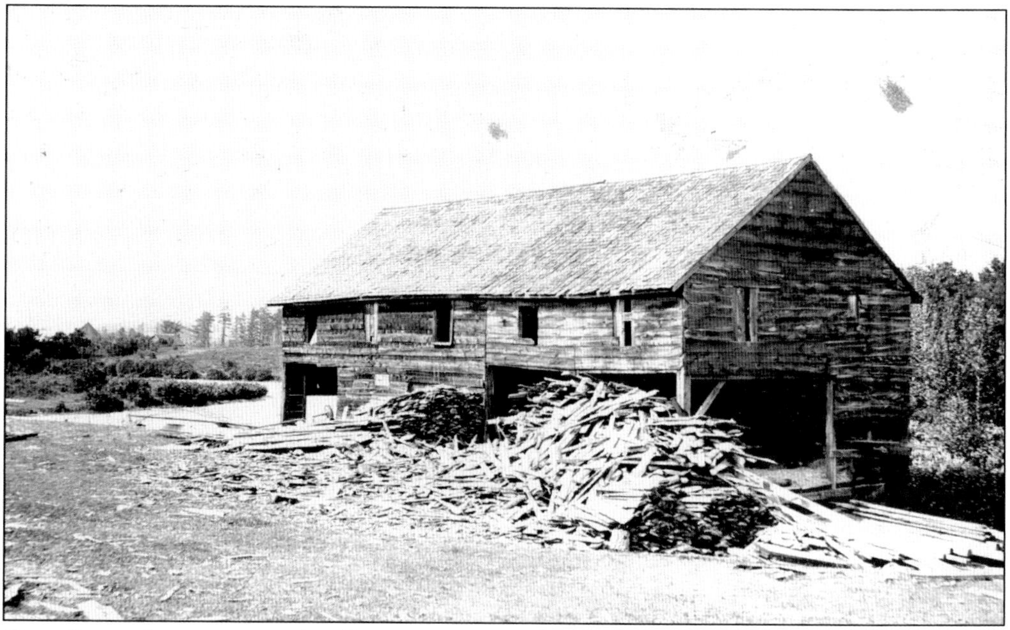

One of several water-powered mills processing wood in Wakefield, George Chick's mill operated in Woodman in the late 1800s and early 1900s.

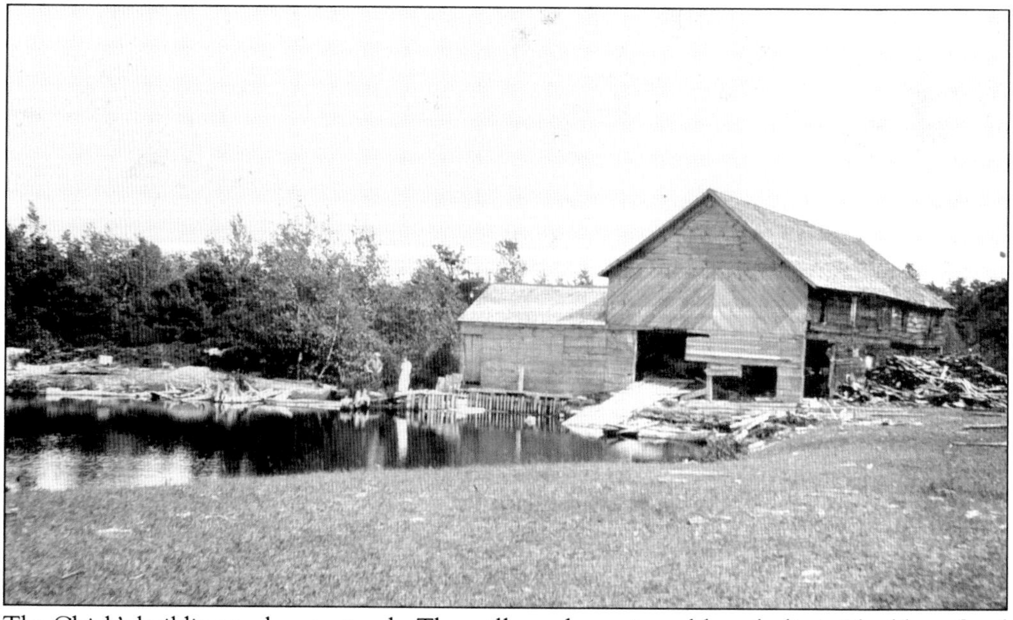

The Chick's building no longer stands. The mill pond remains, although diminished by a flood that took out the dam.

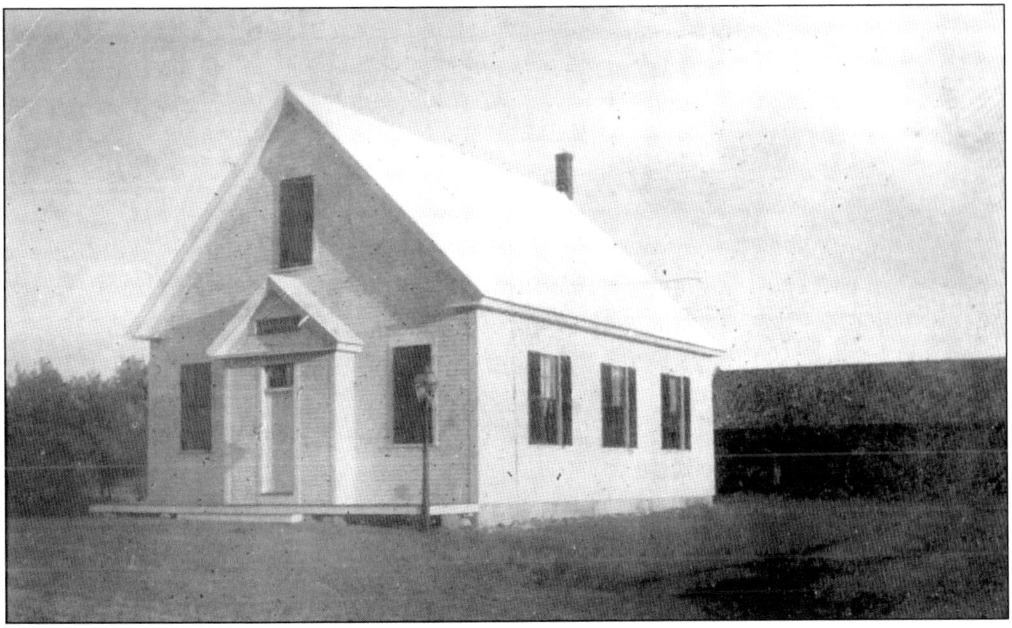

The Advent Chapel was built in Woodman in the 1890s. Located next to the cemetery on Province Lake Road, the building was used by the Advent Christian Society, and occasionally other denominations, until the 1960s. Though still standing, it no longer hosts regular services.

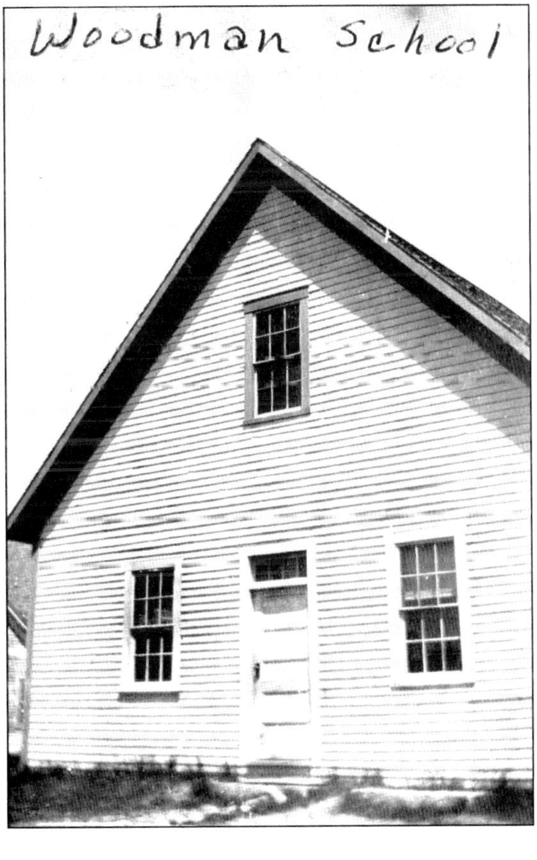

The District 11 School in Woodman opened next to the chapel on Province Lake Road in 1923.

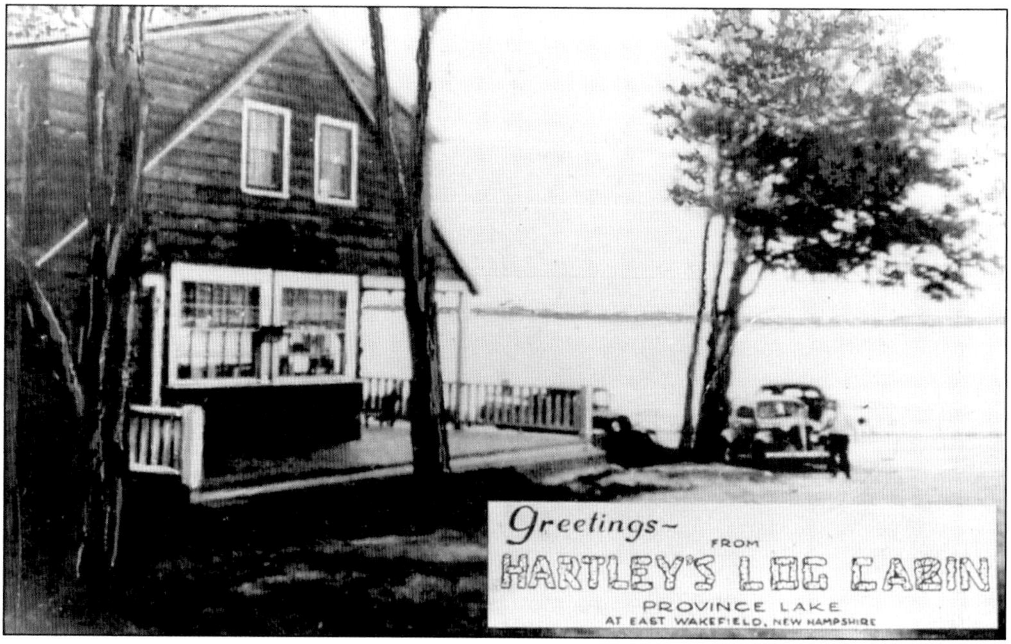

"Greetings from Hartley's Log Cabin," once located on Province Lake at the corner of Province Lake Road and Bonnyman Road.

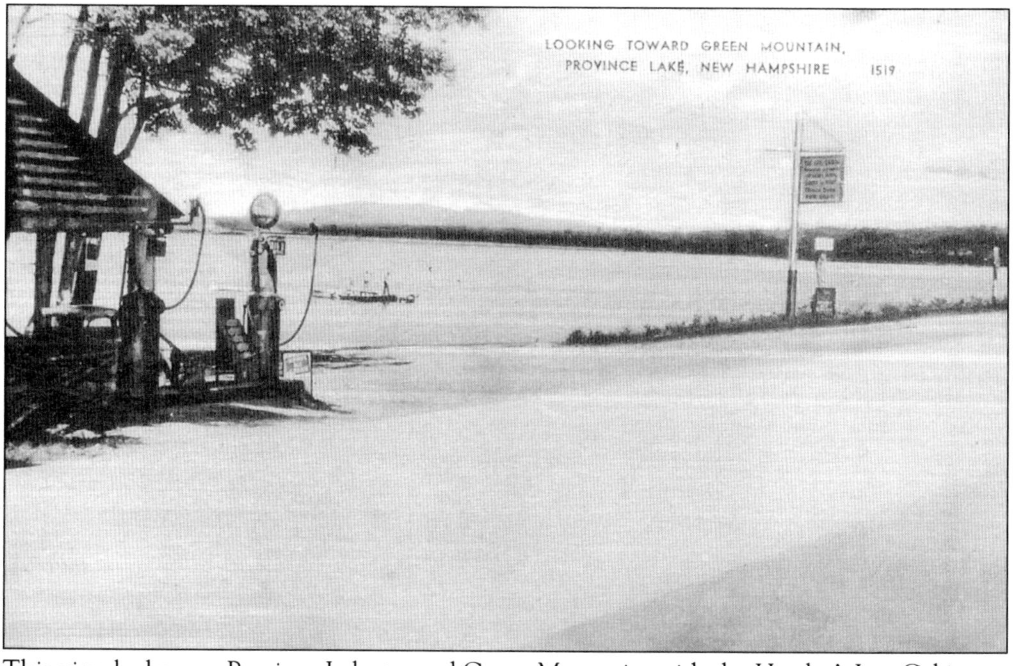

This view looks over Province Lake toward Green Mountain, with the Hartley's Log Cabin gas pumps in the foreground.

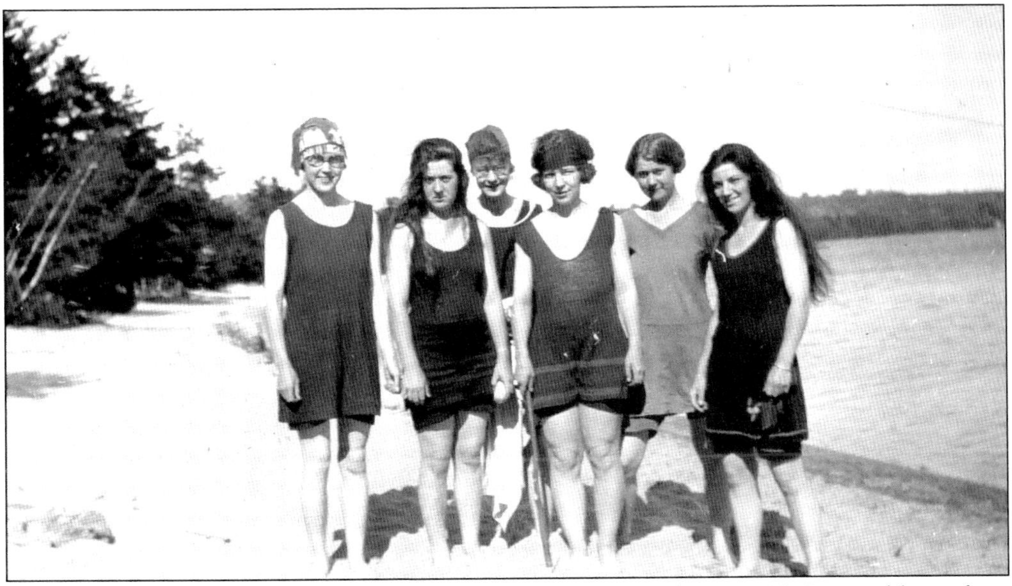

Local girls enjoy a day of sun and swimming at Great East Lake in 1923. Pictured here, from left to right, are Julia Bishop, Margaret Paul, Louise Paul, Caroline Paul, Katherine Paul, and Doris Brackett.

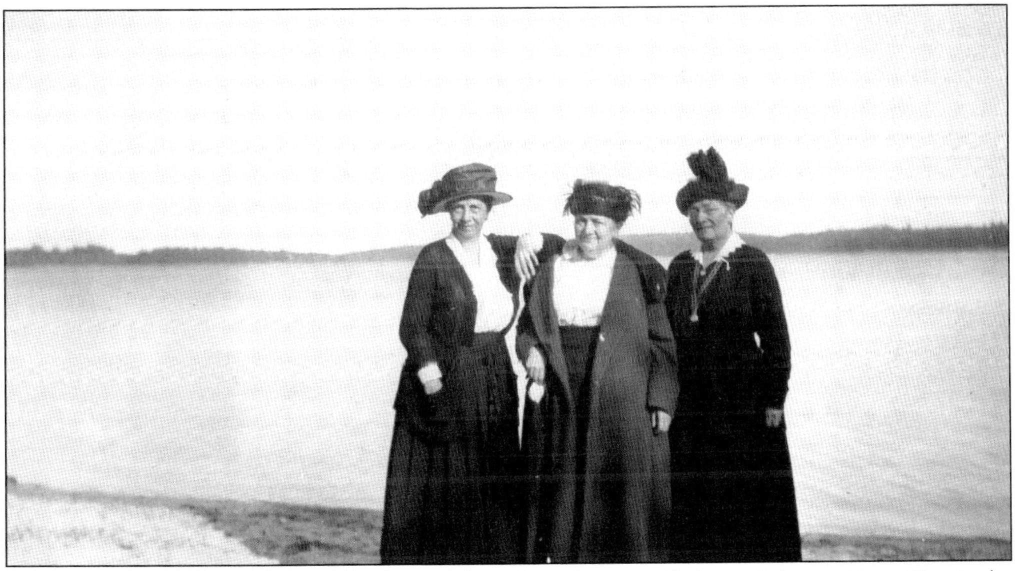

No bathing suits or beach hats for these ladies. Spending a well-dressed day at Great East Lake are, from left to right, Josephine Stowell, Annie Paul, and Carrie Hall.

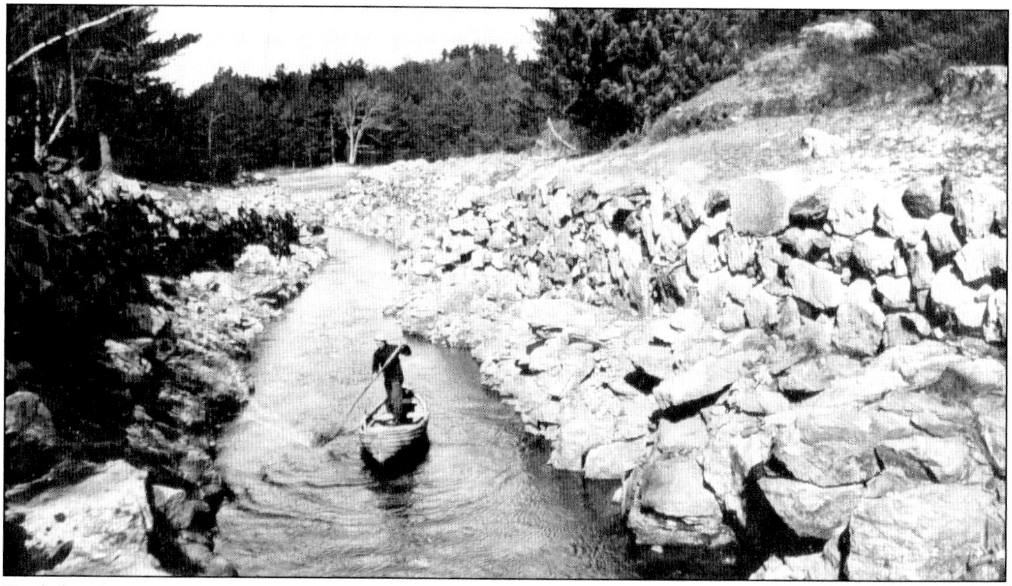

Built by the Great Falls Manufacturing Company of Somersworth, the Newichawannock Canal between Great East Lake and Horn Pond was begun in the 1850s, but the Civil War slowed its completion. The walls of the canal were built of local stone and laid dry (with no mortar).

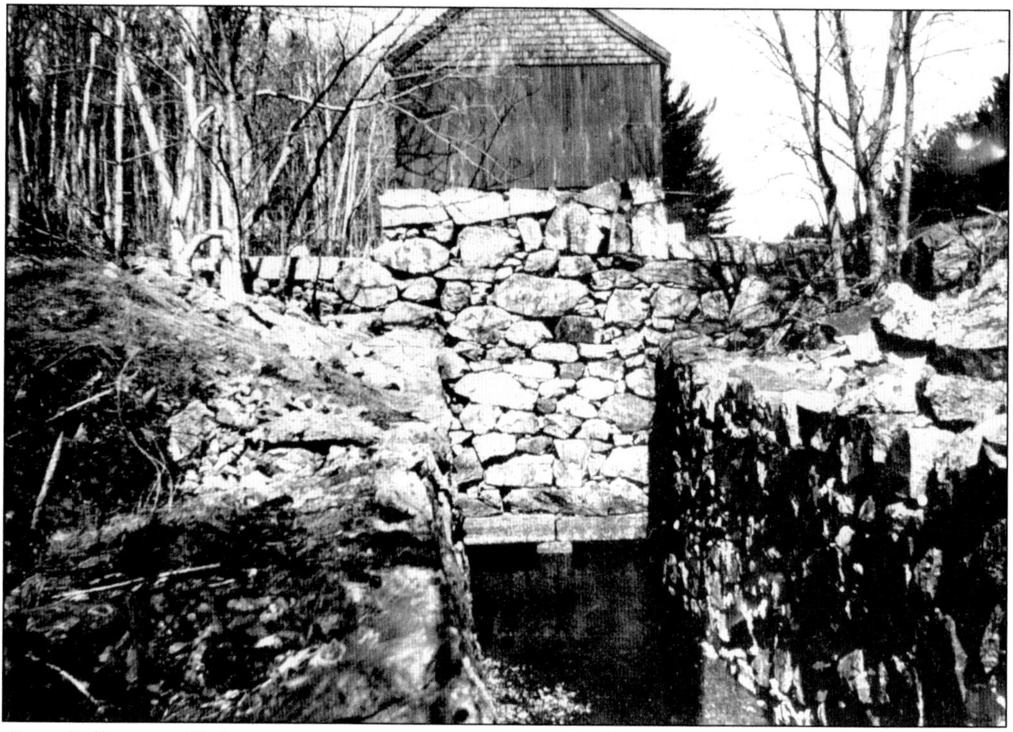

Great Falls controlled many water sources to ensure a steady supply for the mills in Somersworth. The canal allowed the mills to draw on the water of Great East Lake. Sometimes heavy usage lowered the water level until the lake became a stump swamp, to the dismay of residents and visitors alike. The company was eventually forced to modify the gates to maintain a minimum water level of 10 feet in the lake.

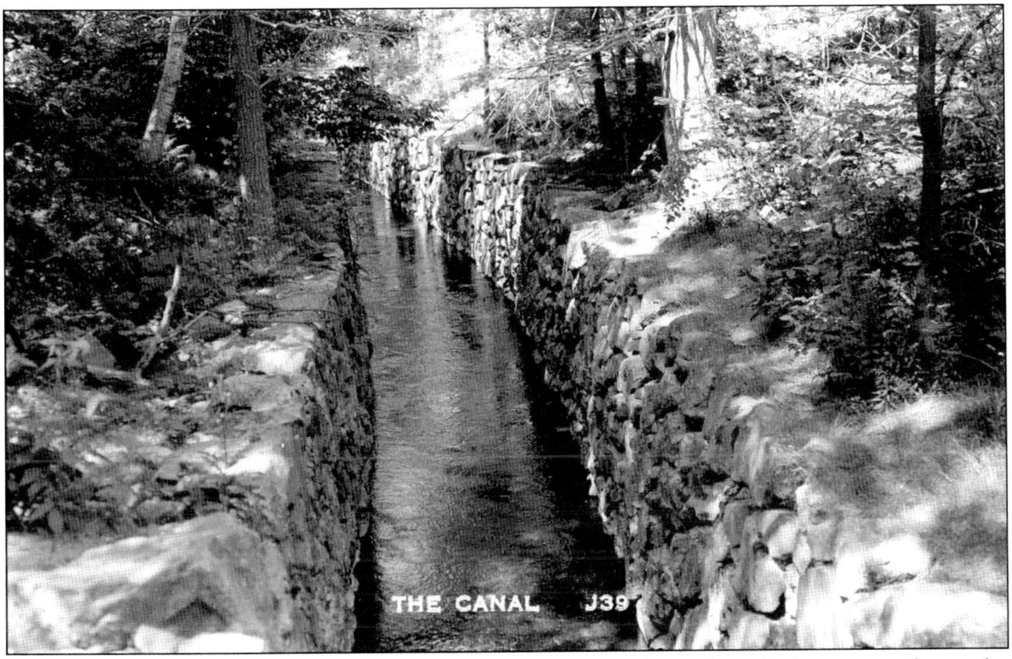

The Newichawannock Canal, with the stonework still standing after all these years, forms the dividing line between New Hampshire and Maine.

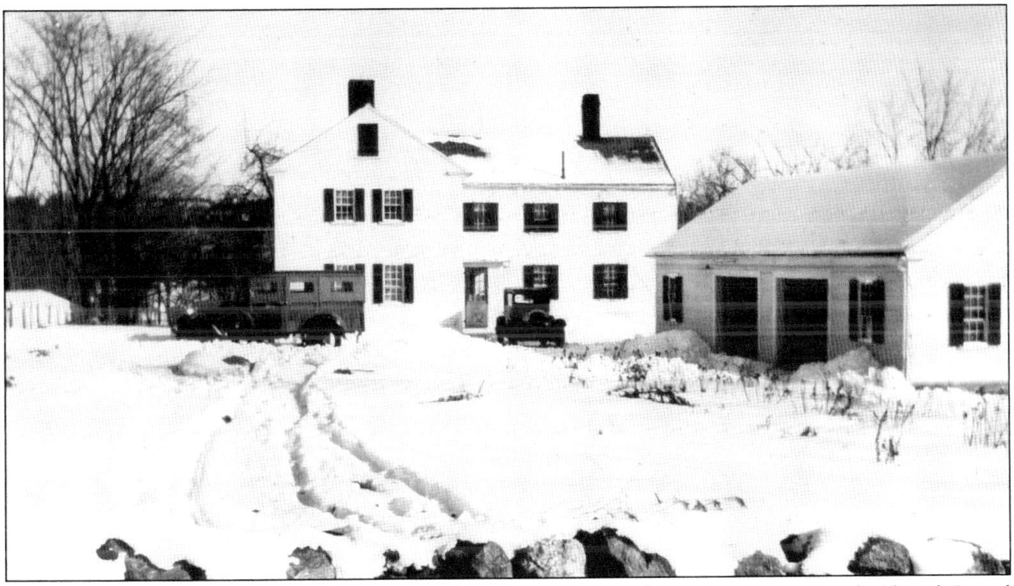
Canal Farm is located next to the Newichawannock Canal on the Horn Pond side of Canal Road. The house was built in 1817 by John Paul Jr., a Sanford, Maine, resident who had settled on the site because of the three nearby mills. He hoped that the area would become the town's next thriving village.

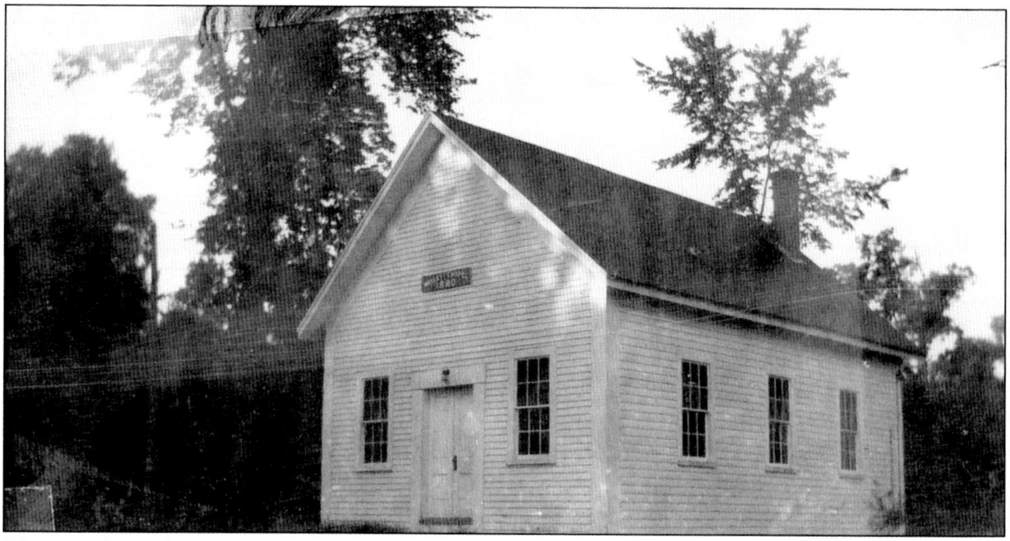

The Wesley Chapel, which still stands on North Wakefield Road in North Wakefield, is shown in 1880 shortly after its construction. Although a Methodist chapel, it was also used for Baptist services.

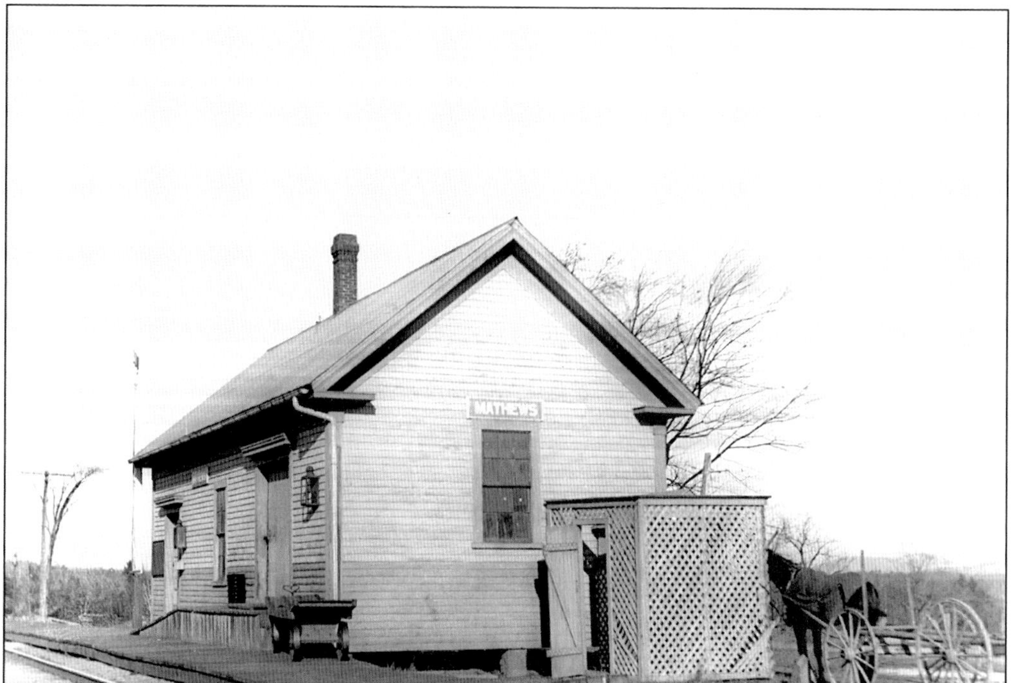

The North Wakefield railroad station, photographed in 1914, was called Mathews Station after longtime station agent John Mathews. The last train stopped here in 1948.

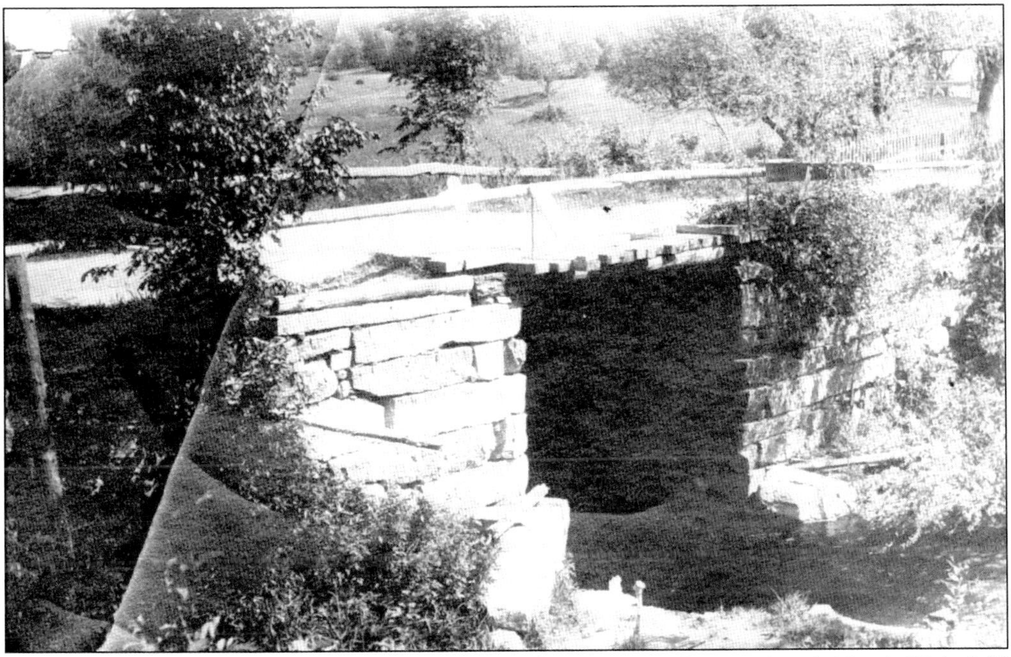

Pictured in 1900, Mathews Bridge spans Pine Brook to connect Route 16 with North Wakefield village. The road formerly served as the highway from North Wakefield to Pine River.

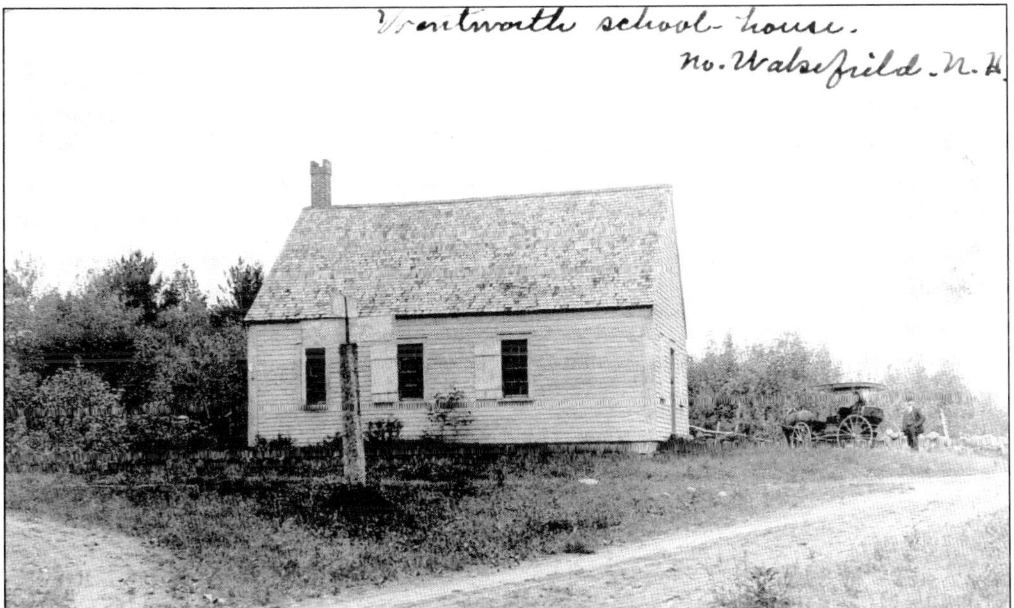

The Wentworth Schoolhouse, seen prior to 1915, served North Wakefield (District 6). The building was located at the junction of Leighton Corner Road, Pine River Pond Road, and Ballards Ridge Road, but is no longer standing.

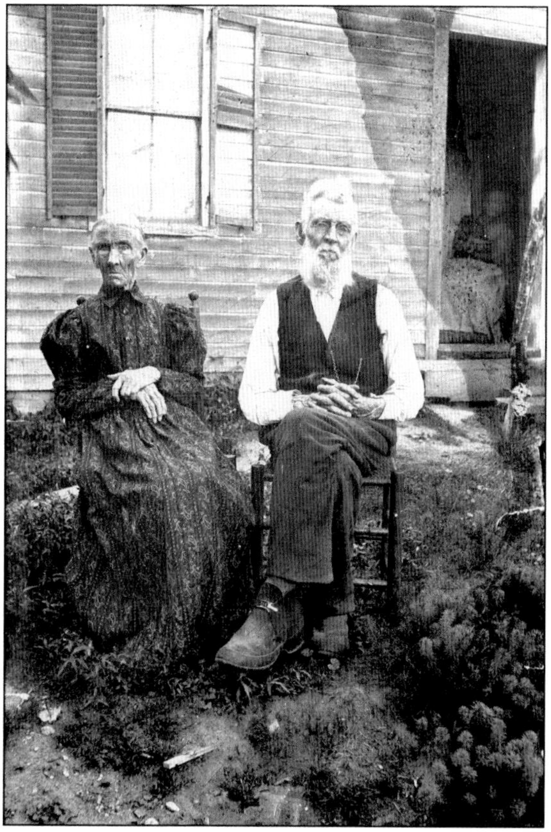

Elder Joseph Spinney sits with his wife, Elizabeth Spinney, in front of their home in South Wakefield. Elder Spinney was a Freewill Baptist and Adventist preacher in the South Wakefield (Spinney) Meeting House for more than 50 years.

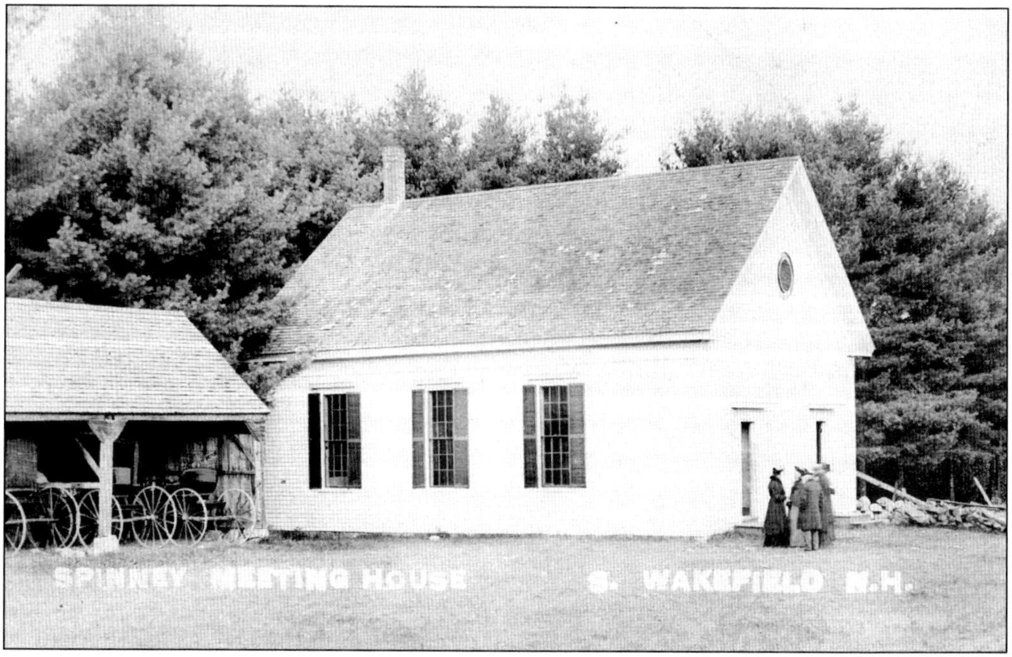

The Freewill Baptist meetinghouse was built in South Wakefield in the late 1700s and later named after Elder Joseph Spinney. The structure is located on what is now Route 109.

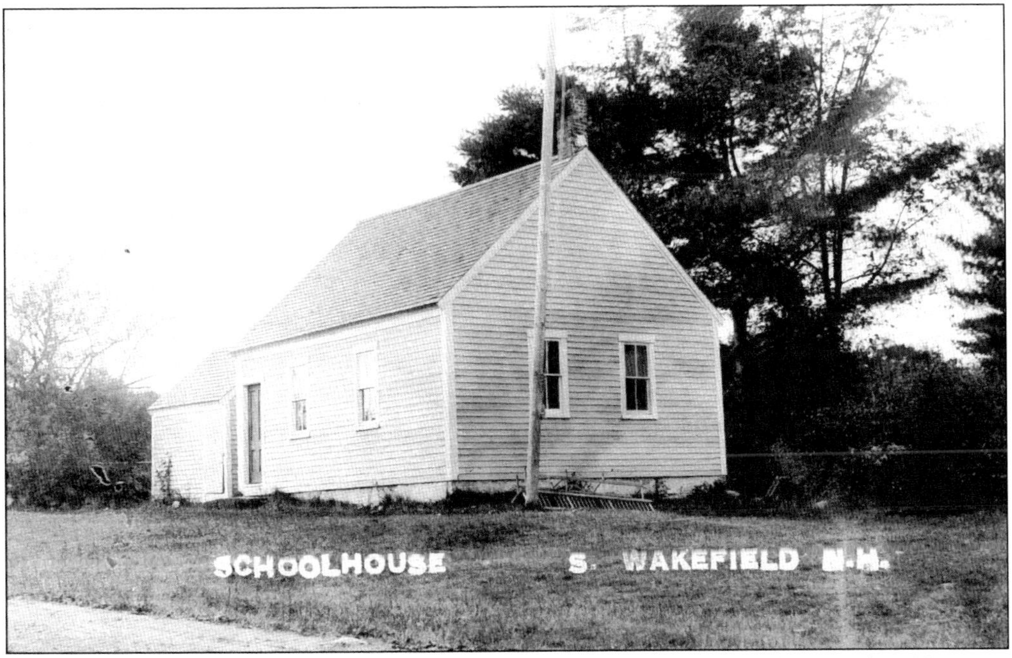

The South Wakefield Schoolhouse, photographed in 1907, was reportedly moved to Union to become a private home.

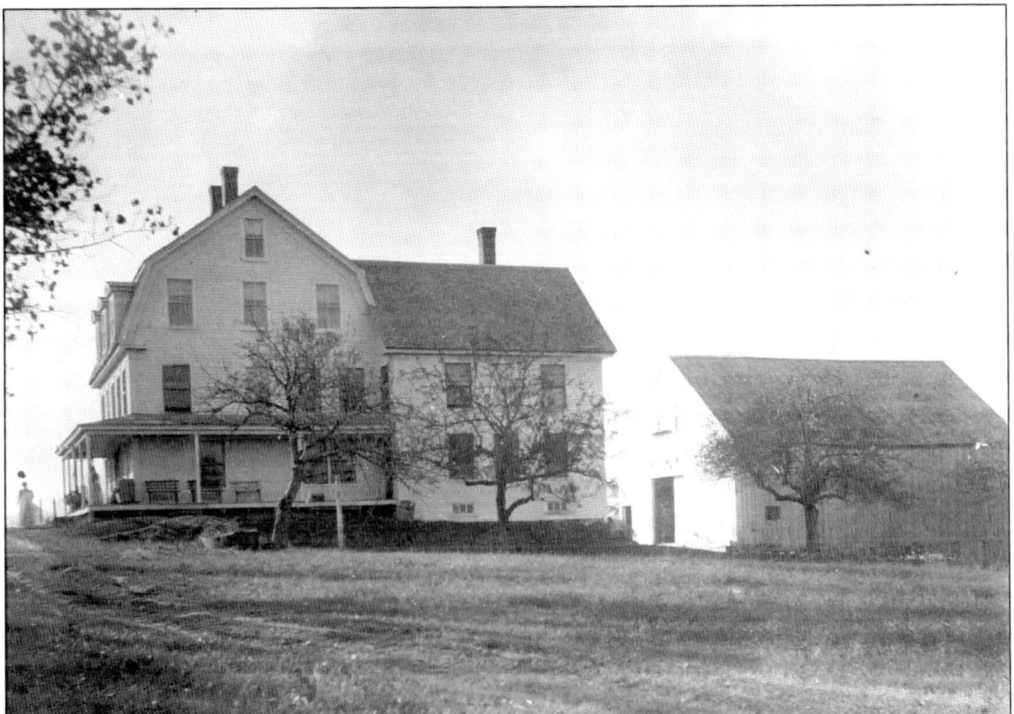

Garland House, an inn located in South Wakefield near Lovell Lake, had a capacity of 30 guests. The room rate was $1 for the day or $5 for the week.

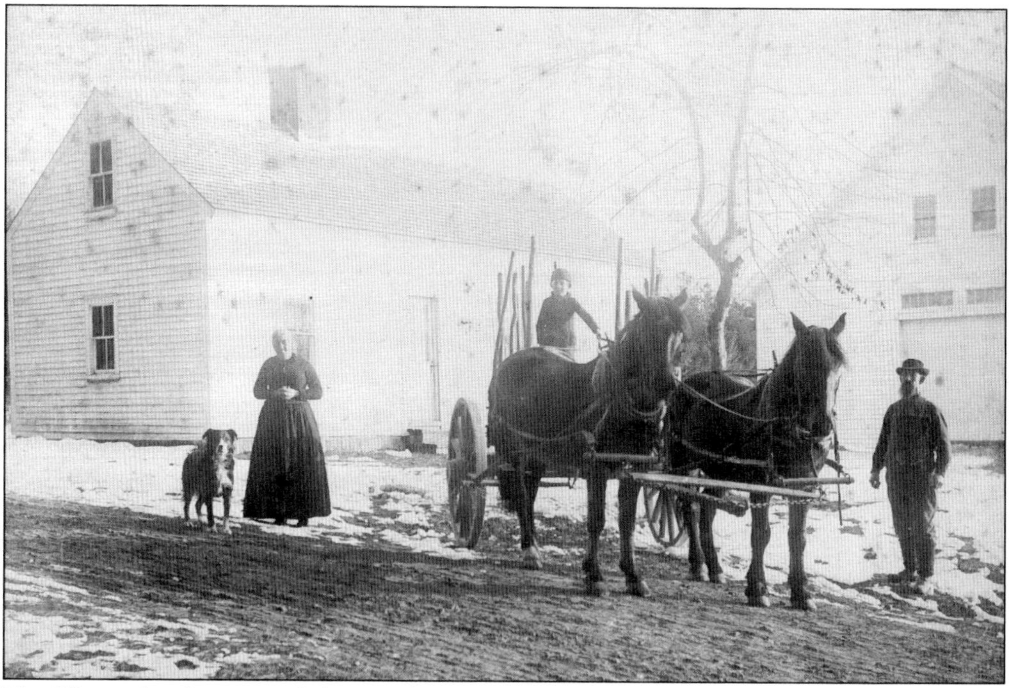

The Wiggin family occupied this South Wakefield farm for 102 years. Frank J. and Mildred E. Wiggin, with their son Harvey Wiggin, are pictured here in the late 1800s or early 1900s. The family supplied the Boston and Maine trains with milk, vegetables, ice, and water until 1911. The Wiggin family remained dairy farmers until World War II, when Harvey and his wife Myra sold their entire herd of cattle to the government.

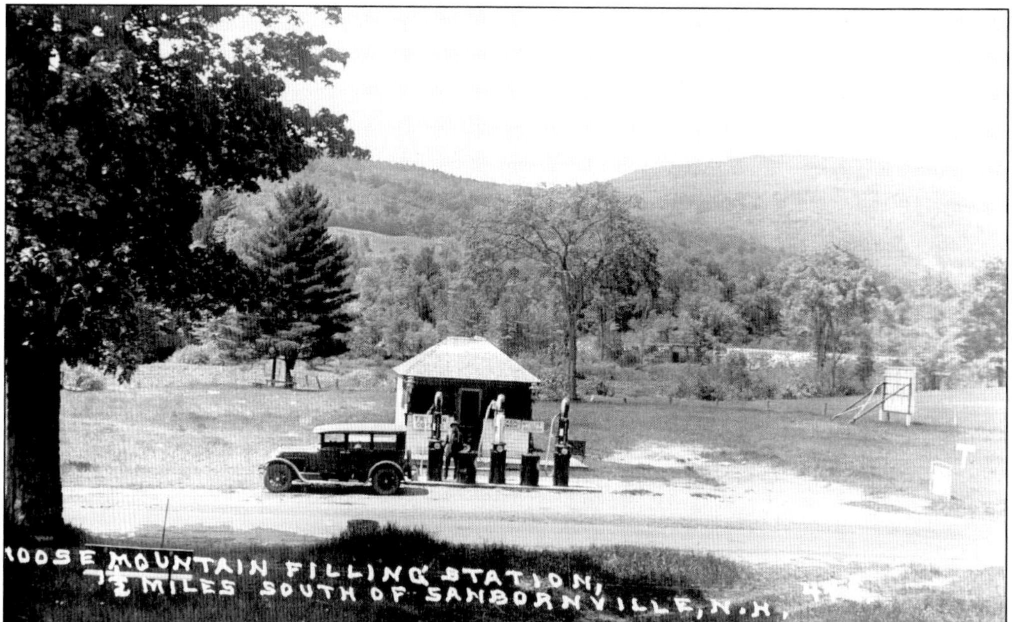

The Moose Mountain Filling Station, photographed in 1920, stood one and a half miles south of Sanbornville on what is now Route 153.

Six

BROOKFIELD

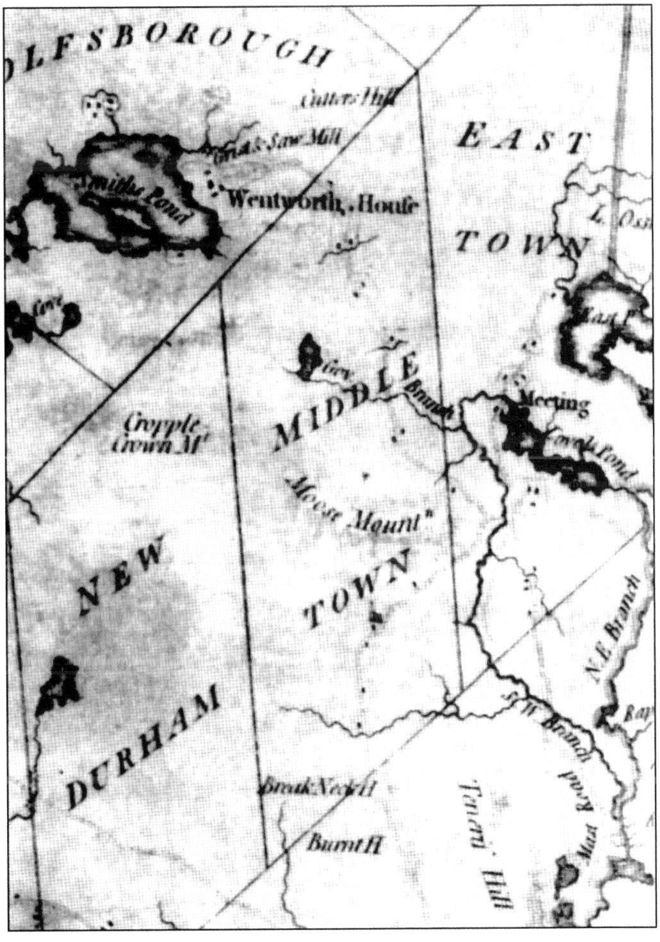

Capt. Samuel Holland was commissioned by Gov. John Wentworth to map all of New Hampshire; he completed the task in 1774. This map showed Middle Towne with Moose Mount, Governor's Branch (river), and that portion of Governor's Road that wound through the Northern or Second Division to Wentworth House in Wolfeboro. In December 1794, the Second Division was incorporated as Brookfield.

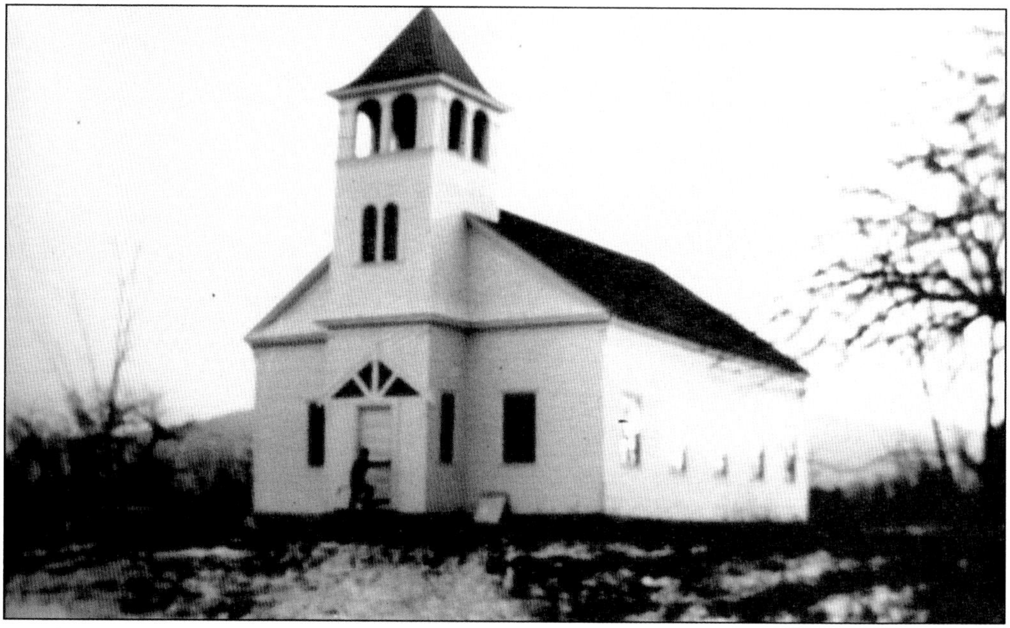

Brookfield residents voted to build a meetinghouse in 1804 and to bring in two quarts of rum and a "mug of cyder" to "vendue," or bid off the construction. Not until 1823 was the building constructed, with a "decent pulpit," singing seats, pews without doors, and plastered walls. The long-anticipated cast bell, given to the town by Frank Hutchins, was dedicated at a memorable ceremony in 1907 and still calls citizens to the annual town meeting in March. The town house served purposes other than just meetings, however. Worship services by the Methodists and the Second Adventists were held here for many years. From 1890 to 1941, the town library occupied a small room at the front of the building. This room was converted to a kitchen in the 1950s. Through the 20th century, the building provided a community space for entertainments ranging from minstrel shows and dances to potluck suppers.

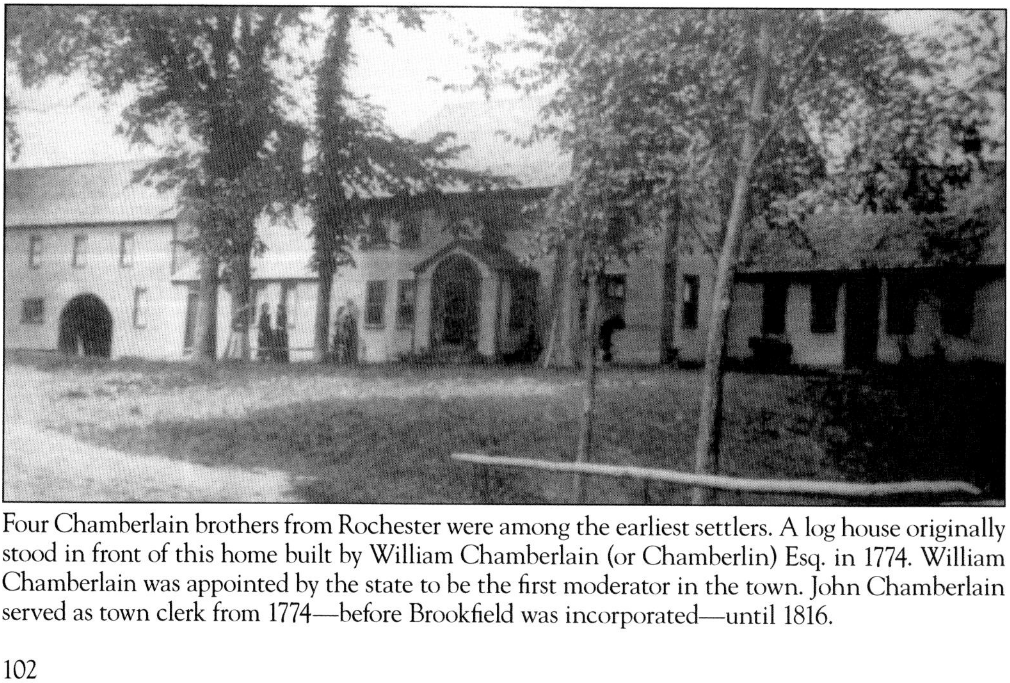

Four Chamberlain brothers from Rochester were among the earliest settlers. A log house originally stood in front of this home built by William Chamberlain (or Chamberlin) Esq. in 1774. William Chamberlain was appointed by the state to be the first moderator in the town. John Chamberlain served as town clerk from 1774—before Brookfield was incorporated—until 1816.

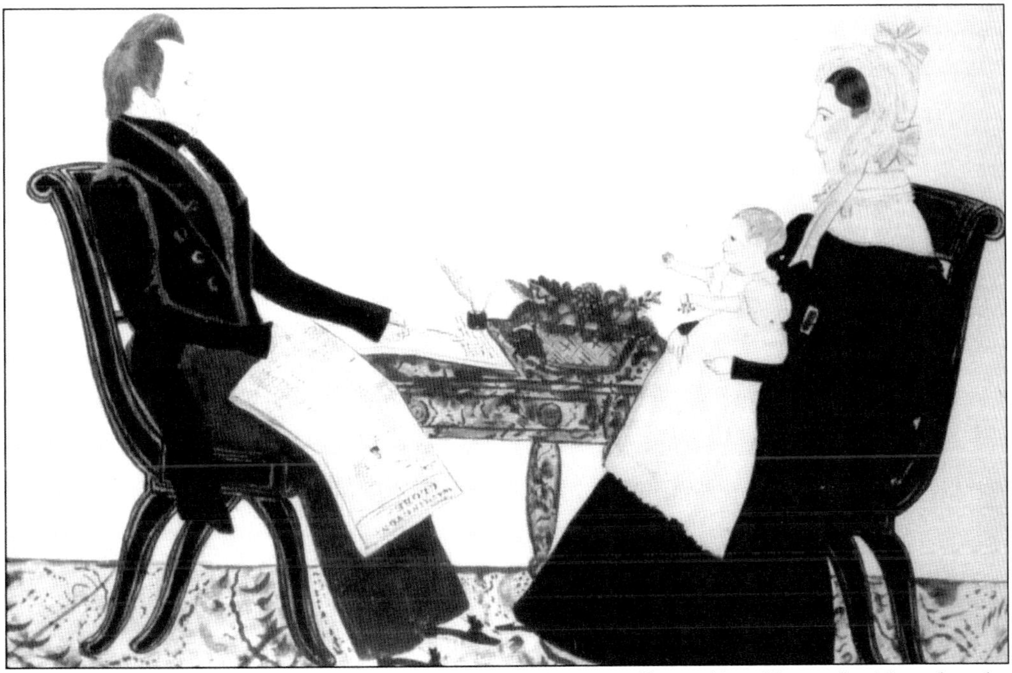

Squire Trueworthy Chamberlain commissioned a likeness of himself and his wife, Abigail, to be painted by the itinerant limner Joseph H. Davis around 1835. Everyone in Brookfield admired the artist's accurate final touch of Chamberlain reading the *National Intelligencer*, a newspaper expressing the squire's favorite political prejudice. (Private collection.)

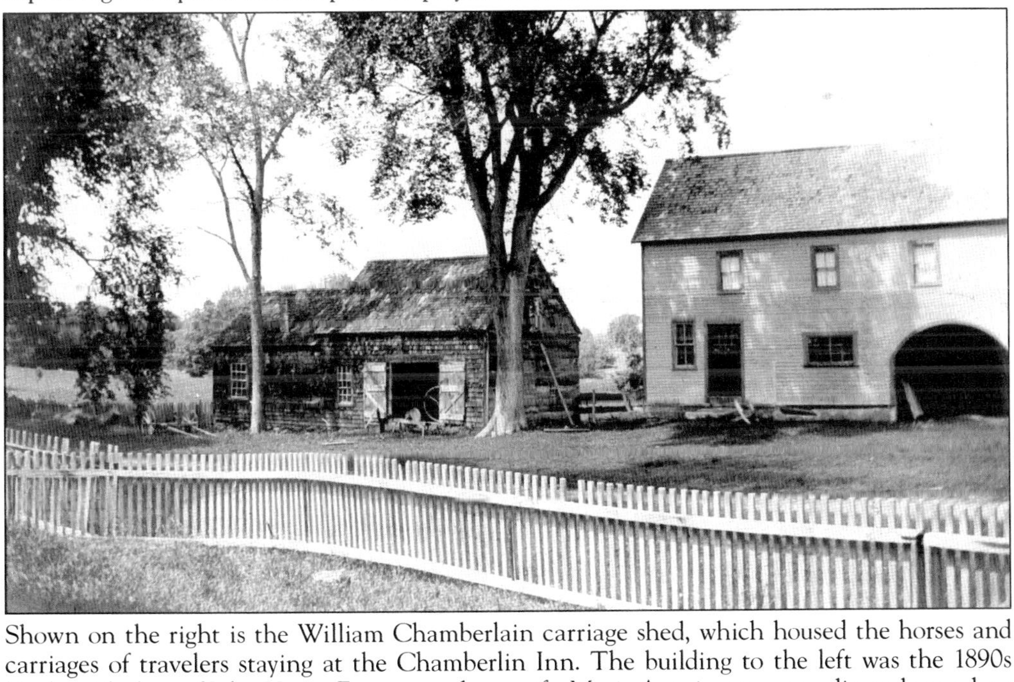

Shown on the right is the William Chamberlain carriage shed, which housed the horses and carriages of travelers staying at the Chamberlin Inn. The building to the left was the 1890s blacksmith shop of John Henry Ferguson, whose wife, Marie Antoinette, was a direct descendant of William Chamberlain and the great-grandmother of the present owner. The buildings were taken down in 1905.

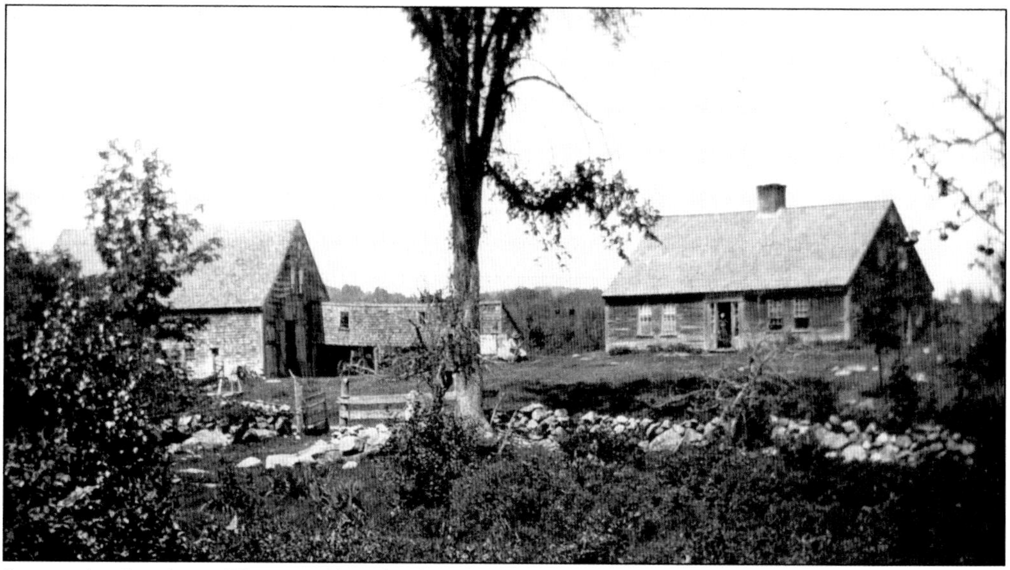

Joining his brothers, Thomas Chamberlain built his home on Mountain Road. Thomas was a Minuteman, serving from 1777 to 1780. He operated both a gristmill and sawmill on Hanson Brook. A wool-processing mill with "one machine for carding wool and dressing cloth" was also located here. Thomas's son Thomas Jr. owned a tannery, Willey and Chamberlain, across the road, and a fourth Chamberlain brother, James, had a cider mill and a maple-sapping operation nearby.

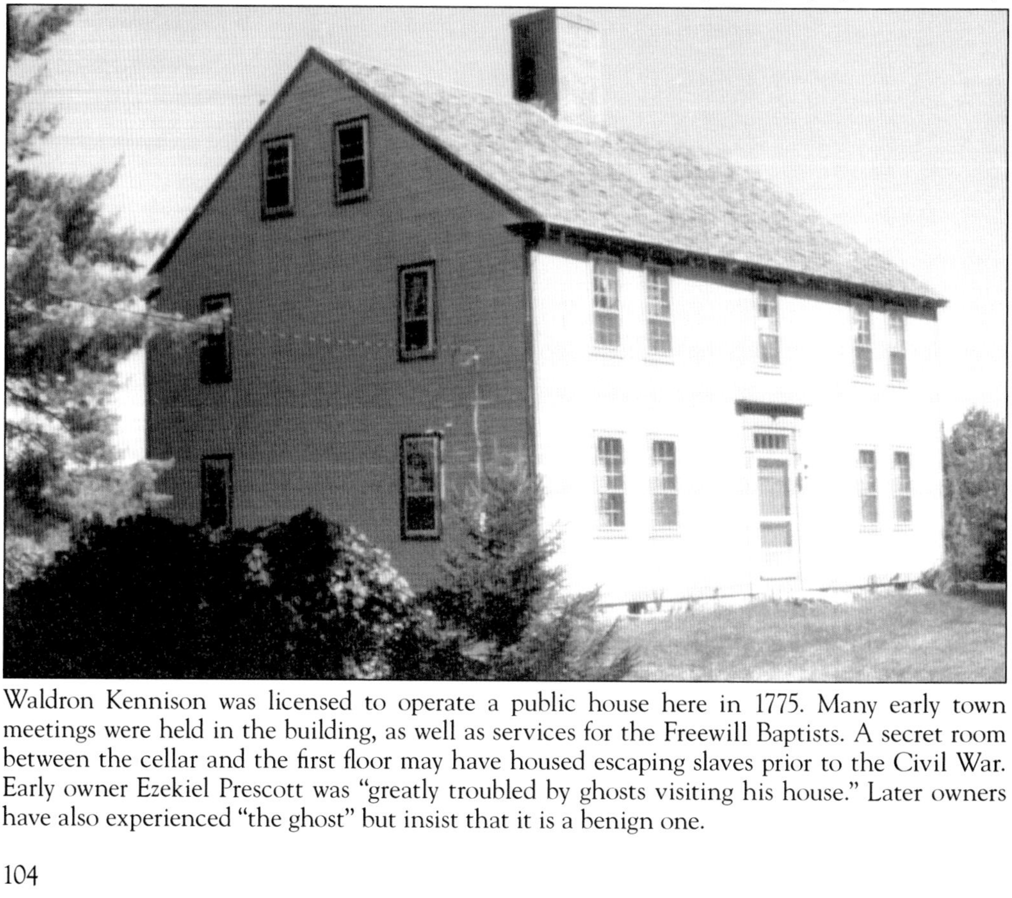

Waldron Kennison was licensed to operate a public house here in 1775. Many early town meetings were held in the building, as well as services for the Freewill Baptists. A secret room between the cellar and the first floor may have housed escaping slaves prior to the Civil War. Early owner Ezekiel Prescott was "greatly troubled by ghosts visiting his house." Later owners have also experienced "the ghost" but insist that it is a benign one.

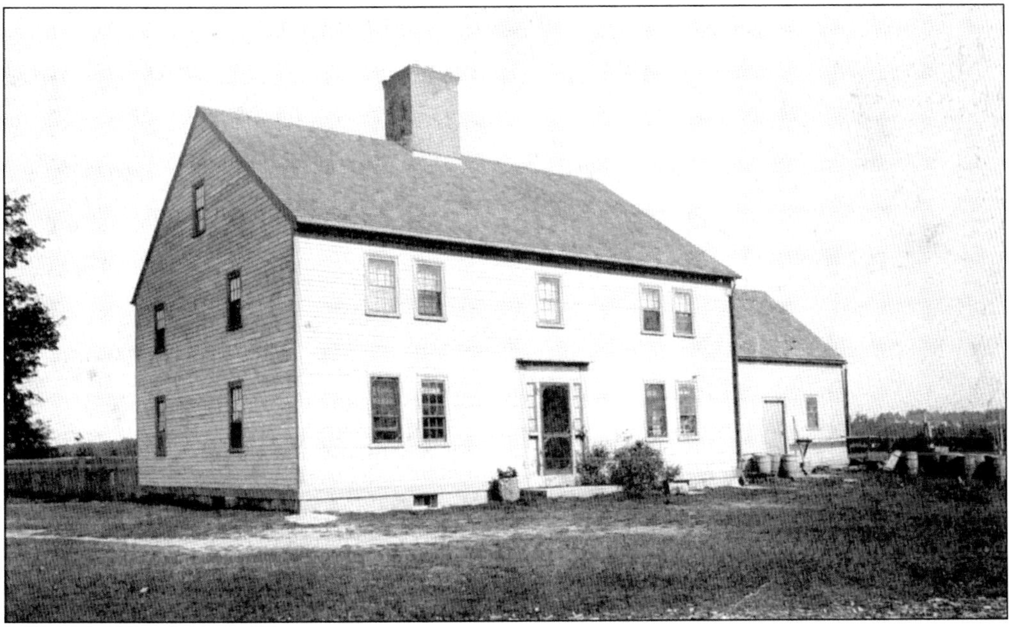

Built in the 1770s by Ezekiel Sanborn Sr., this farm was a prosperous one. When Sanborn's estate was probated in 1830, the first horse and wagon to appear in any Brookfield inventory was listed among his possessions. Ezekiel Jr. married Abigail, daughter of William Chamberlain, and became a prosperous farmer and joiner, or carpenter. Father and son and their families lived in the house, with each side having a cooking fireplace. In the 1870s, it was a successful dairy farm.

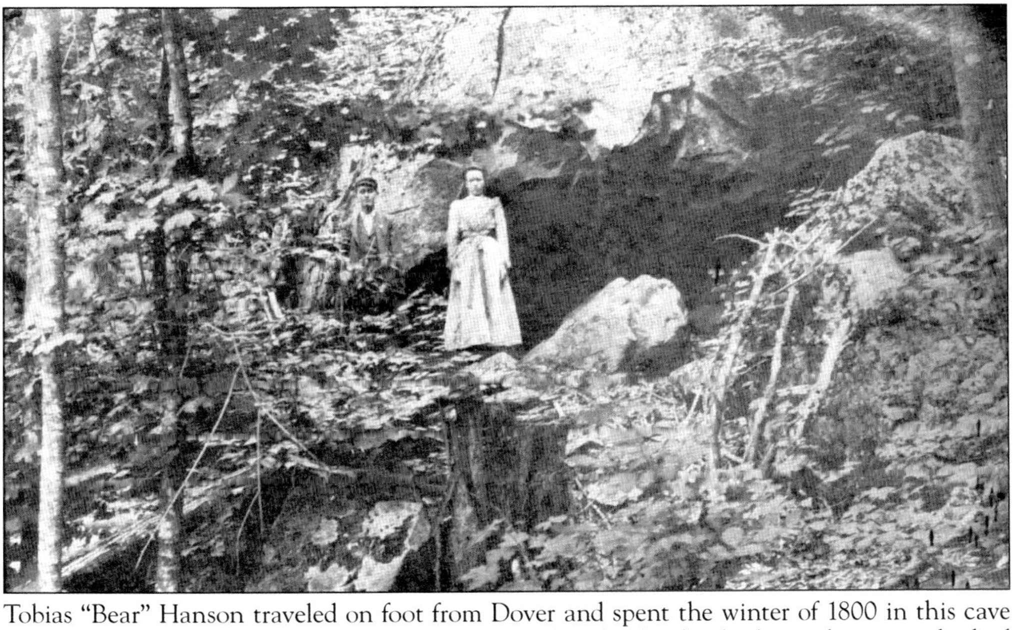

Tobias "Bear" Hanson traveled on foot from Dover and spent the winter of 1800 in this cave on Moose Mountain. He acquired his nickname when he fought the bear whose cave he had appropriated, and won. Another encounter occurred when he was surprised by a bruin; he jumped on and rode "bearback" until he managed to grab a pine knot and deal the bear a murderous blow. Pictured at the cave around 1900 are an unidentified companion and Lillian West.

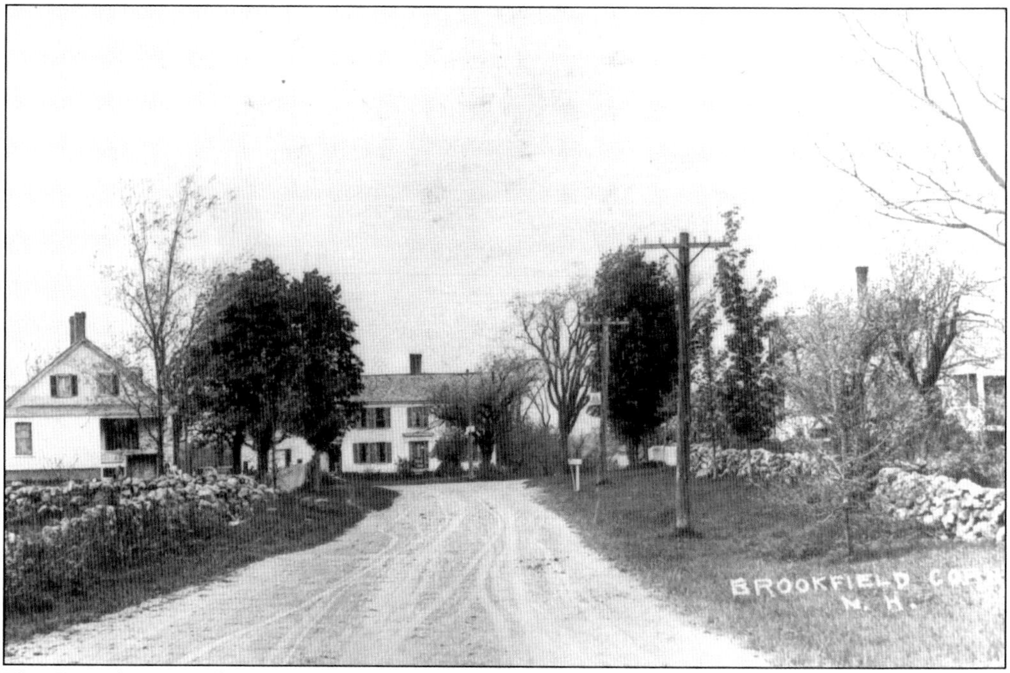

The Daniel Wiggin house at Brookfield Corner was the site of many town meetings. The 1815 meeting was memorable, for "where the meeting was holden [the floor] broke down and the voters fell with it. No lives were lost nor no one badly hurt." The voters continued the meeting in the road outside the house. Wiggin billed the town 15£ for damages. The house served as the post office for many years in the 19th century.

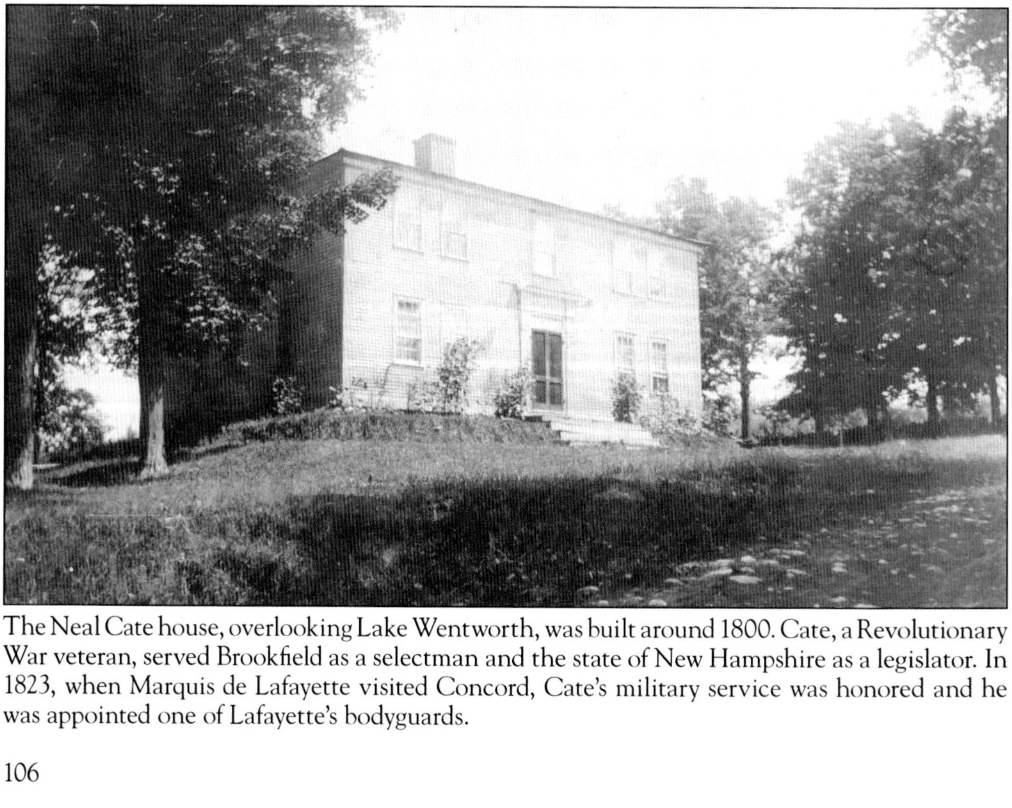

The Neal Cate house, overlooking Lake Wentworth, was built around 1800. Cate, a Revolutionary War veteran, served Brookfield as a selectman and the state of New Hampshire as a legislator. In 1823, when Marquis de Lafayette visited Concord, Cate's military service was honored and he was appointed one of Lafayette's bodyguards.

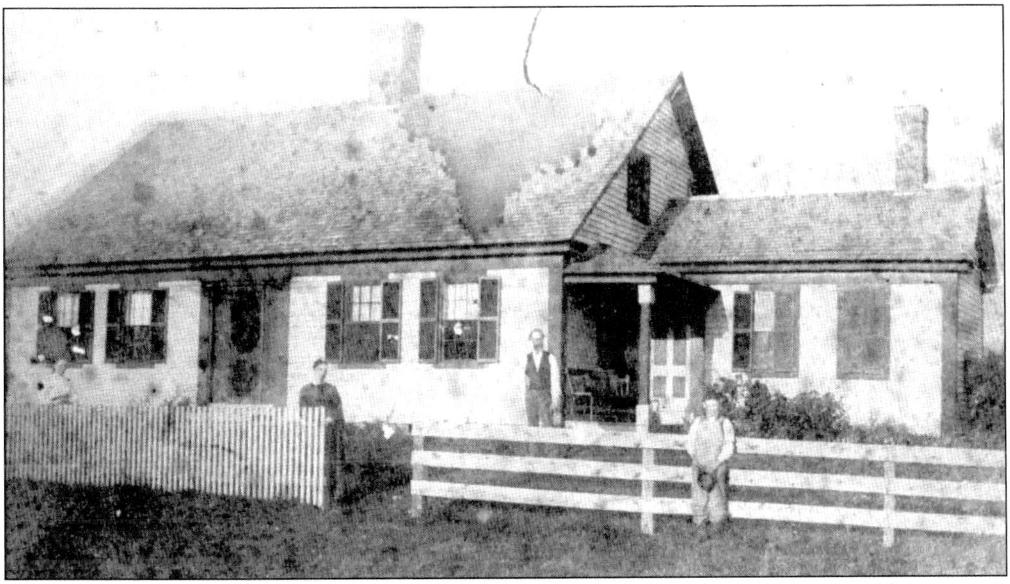

This was the first of six tenant farms owned by Albert and Nathaniel Haven of Portsmouth from 1811 to 1849. The Havens owned all the stock on the farms but the produce was by the "halves." In later years, Charles Colman, a descendant of early settler Dudley Colman, and his wife, Salome, owned this home. A preacher, Charles held Adventist meetings in surrounding towns and in the Churchill schoolhouse.

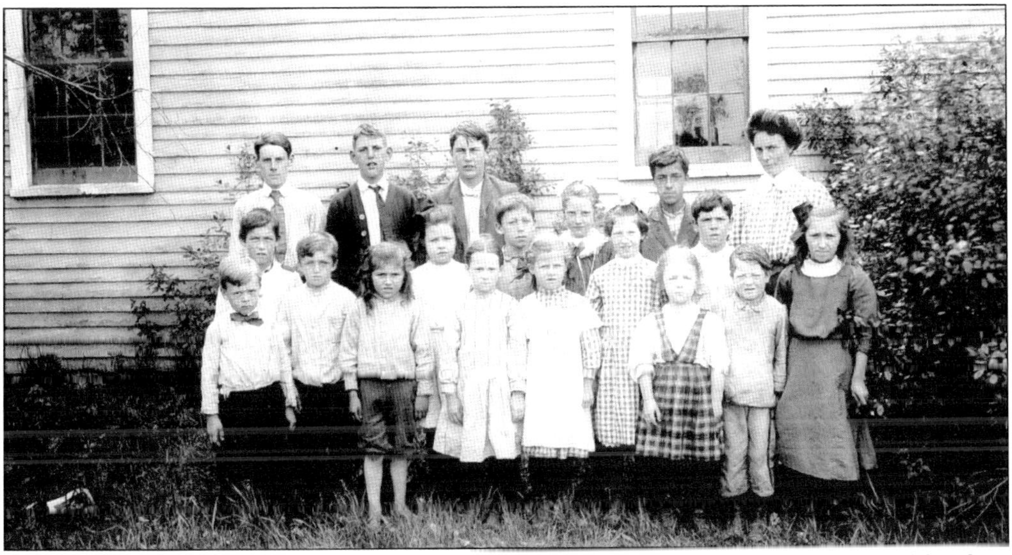

Nathaniel and Joseph Churchill settled on Tumbledown Dick Road on land owned by their wives, Patience and Sally, who were daughters of wealthy Newmarket merchant John Tash. Two of Joseph's sons, John T. and Joseph T., became prominent merchants, innkeepers, stage operators, and state legislators. Churchill School, built opposite John T.'s home on Governor's Road, is shown here in 1910. Pictured from left to right are the following: (first row) Fred Churchill, Bruno Lampron, Neal Cate, Clorinda Lampron, Alberta Mills, Jewel Watson, Mary Brown, Roy Burroughs, and Evelyn Cate; (second row) Warren Burroughs, Dorothy Jackson, Almon Lampron, Bessie Rines, and Dana Burroughs; (third row) John L. Hutchins, John Lang, Leon Willey, Wilfred Lamford, and teacher Alice Churchill.

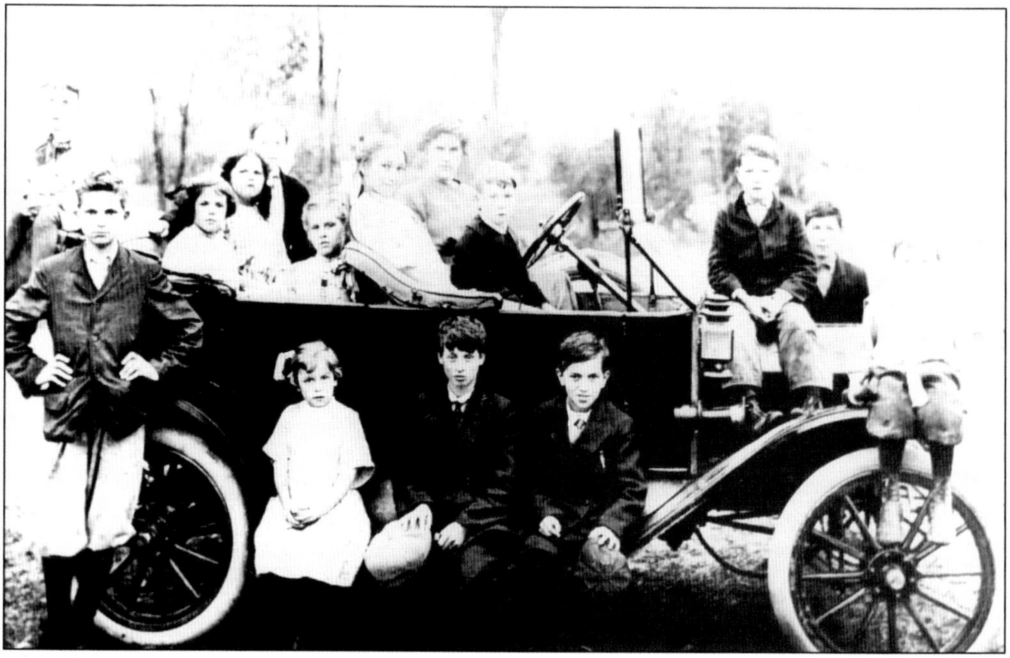

Churchill School students pose in 1911. Most are unidentified, but Myron, Neal and Evelyn Cate are among the students. In the back seat is Lillian West (née Brown), who lived on Mountain Road for over 90 years. She recalled driving the cows to pasture before school and, in later years, driving the snow roller over impassable roads.

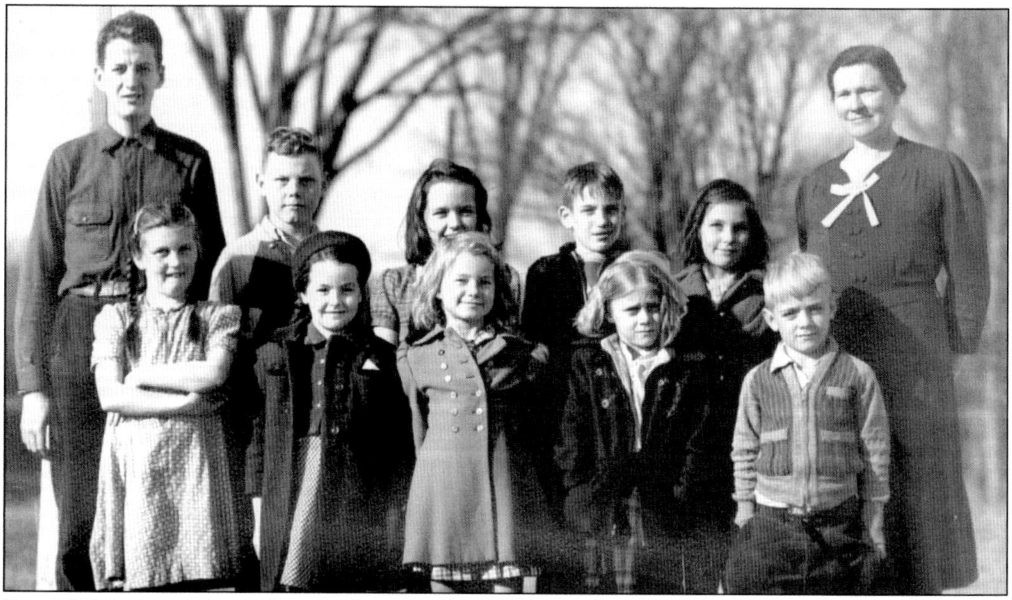

Eva Willey was enshrined in the hearts of her Churchill School pupils as a superb and caring educator. She brought a number of important school programs to Brookfield, including many rural health programs. Shown at the one-room schoolhouse in 1941 are the following, from left to right: (first row) Barbara Hooper, two unidentified students, Roberta Nason, and Teddy Nason; (second row) Chester Chellman, Ralph Dodier, Marilyn Nason, Richard Shortridge, unidentified, and teacher Eva Willey.

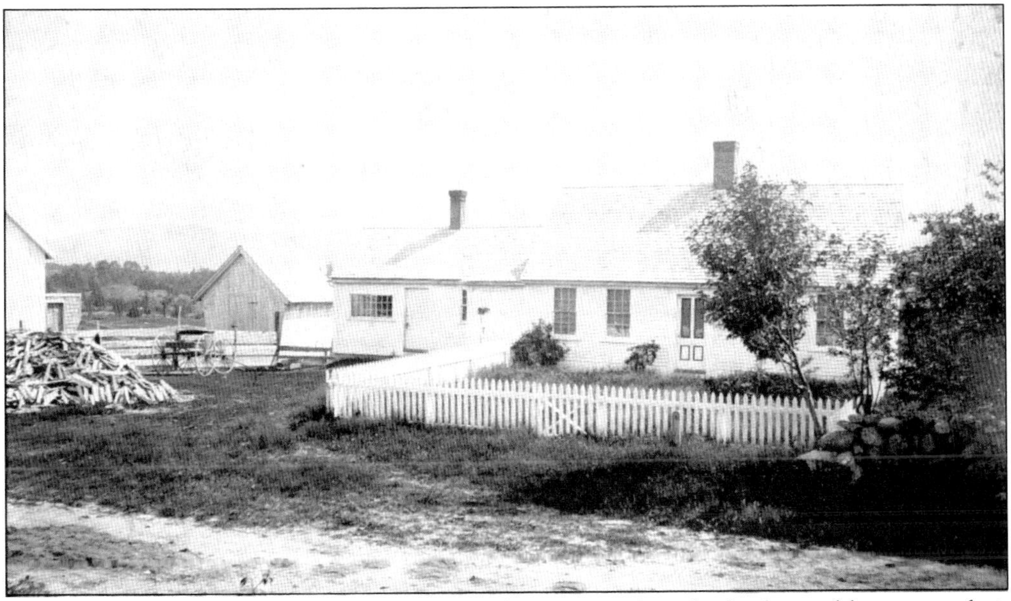

Hannah and Pamela Hackett, daughters of Col. James Hackett, built identical homes on their father's property. James Sr. was the builder of the *Ranger*, John Paul Jones's famed ship. Retiring to Brookfield, James Sr. opened a shop that was run by his son James Jr. after his death. The Hackett house and barn comprised one of the Wallace Wright dairy farms, which in the 1920s marketed Greathome Milk.

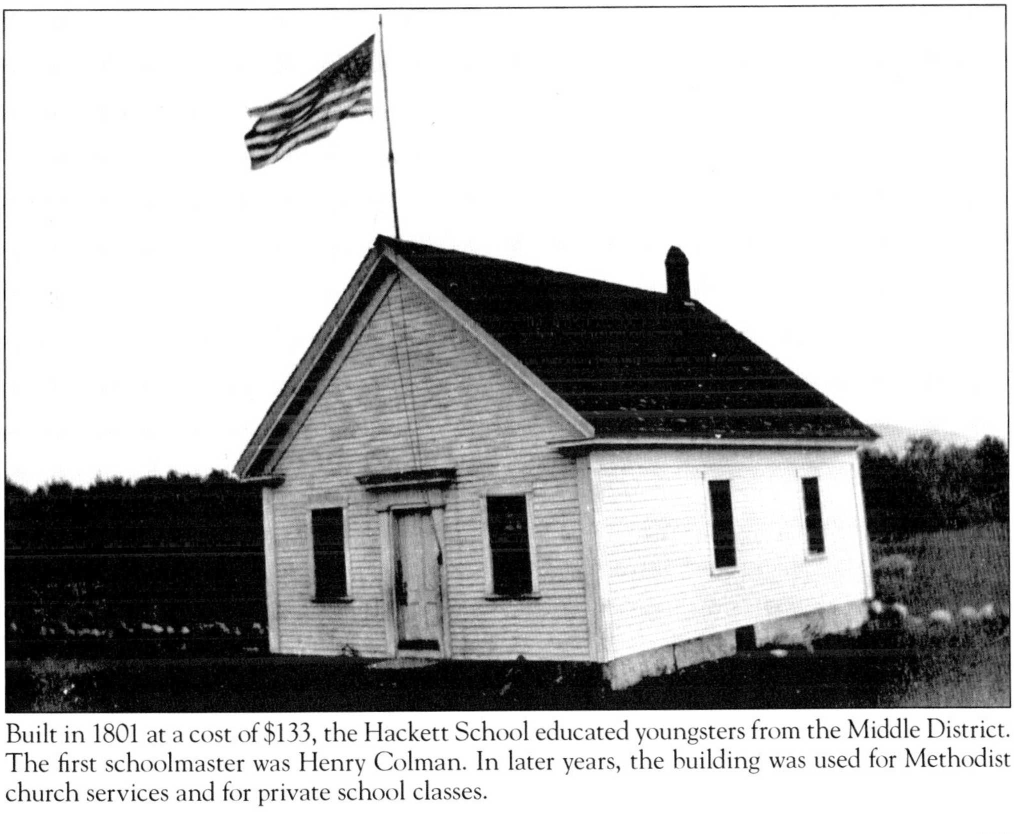

Built in 1801 at a cost of $133, the Hackett School educated youngsters from the Middle District. The first schoolmaster was Henry Colman. In later years, the building was used for Methodist church services and for private school classes.

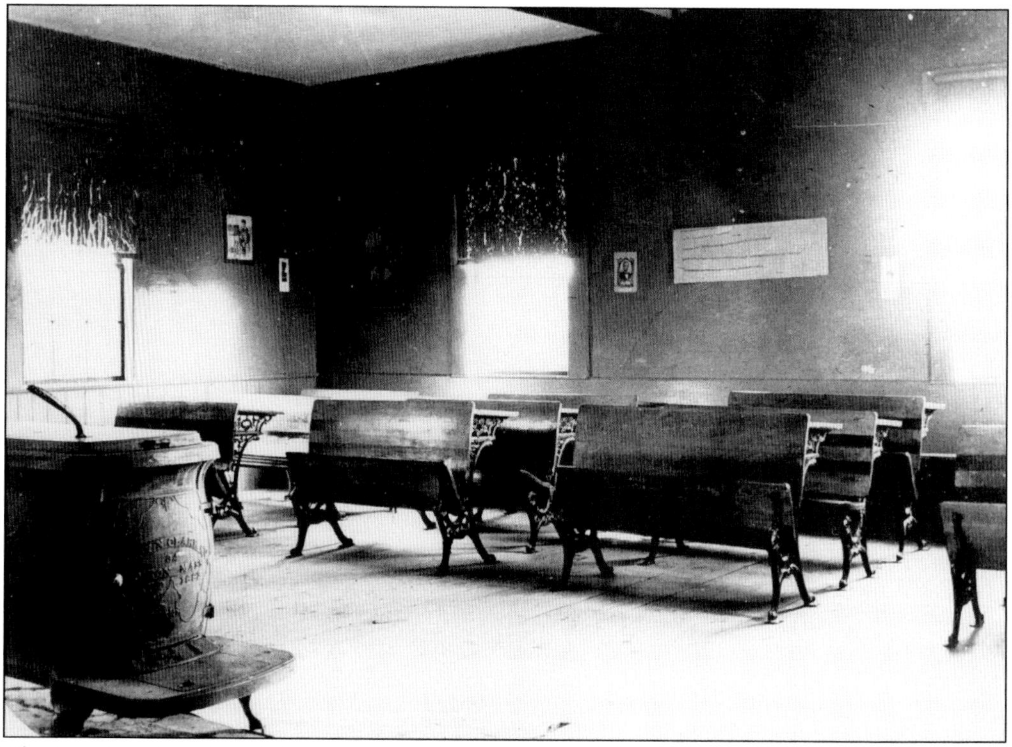

The interior of Hackett School is pictured prior to 1920. The schoolhouse stands on its original location, but has long been converted to a private home.

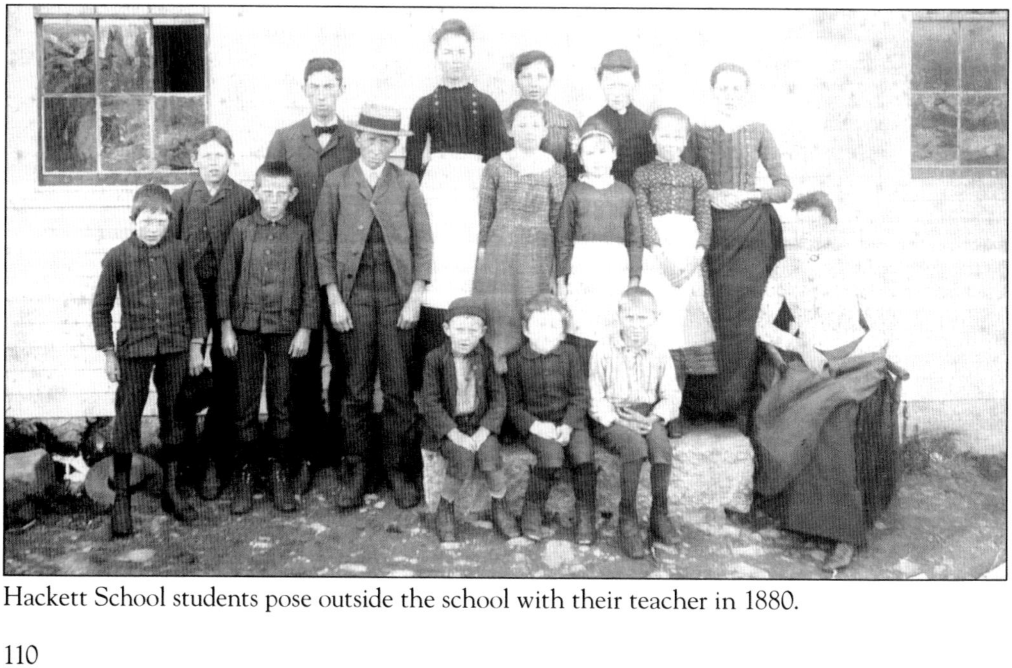

Hackett School students pose outside the school with their teacher in 1880.

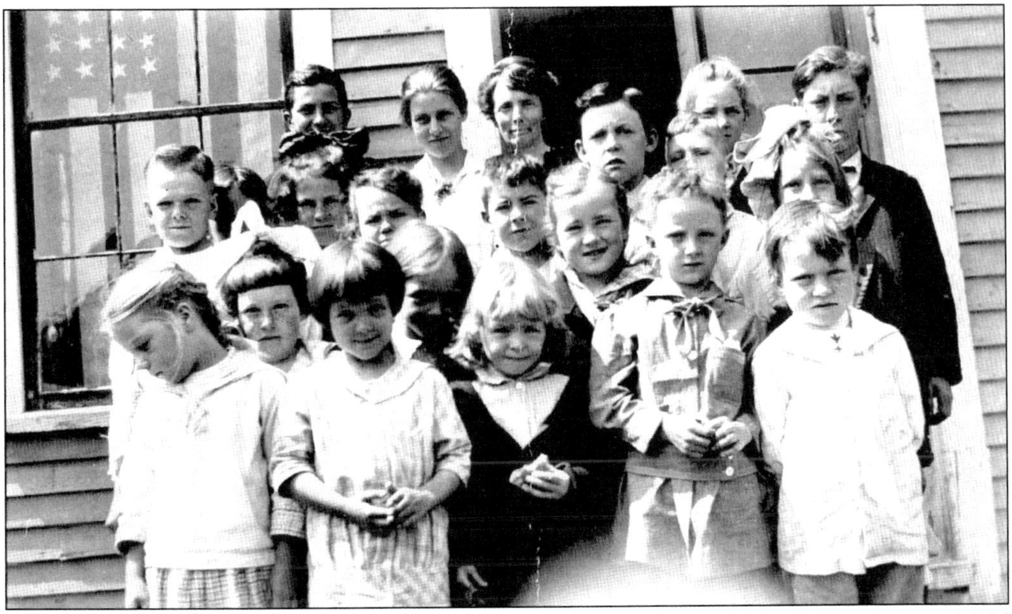

For one year, 1919, the Churchill and Hackett Schools were combined at the store at Brookfield Corner. In its early years, the store sold merchandise ranging from spirituous liquors to silk gloves. The second floor served many uses—as a courtroom for legal hearings, a meeting place for the Know Nothing Party in the 1850s, and the businesses of Beniah Whitehouse and Frank Shortridge, who made hoops for mackerel kits and finished sale shoes from a factory in Farmington. The building was torn down in the 1920s.

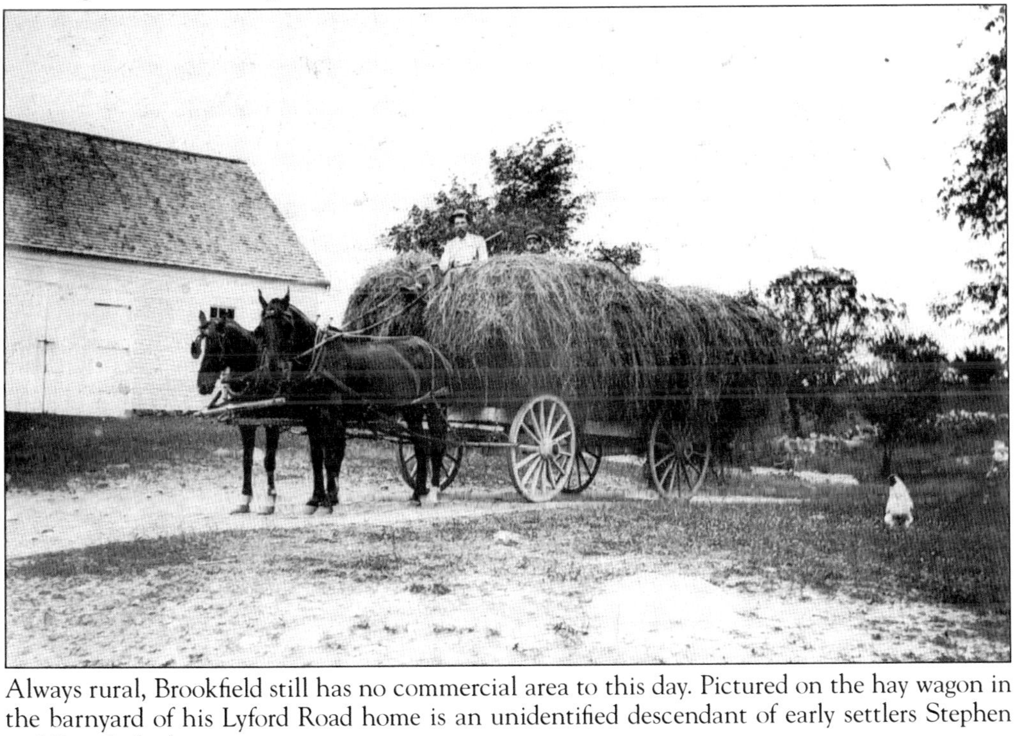

Always rural, Brookfield still has no commercial area to this day. Pictured on the hay wagon in the barnyard of his Lyford Road home is an unidentified descendant of early settlers Stephen and Sara Lyford.

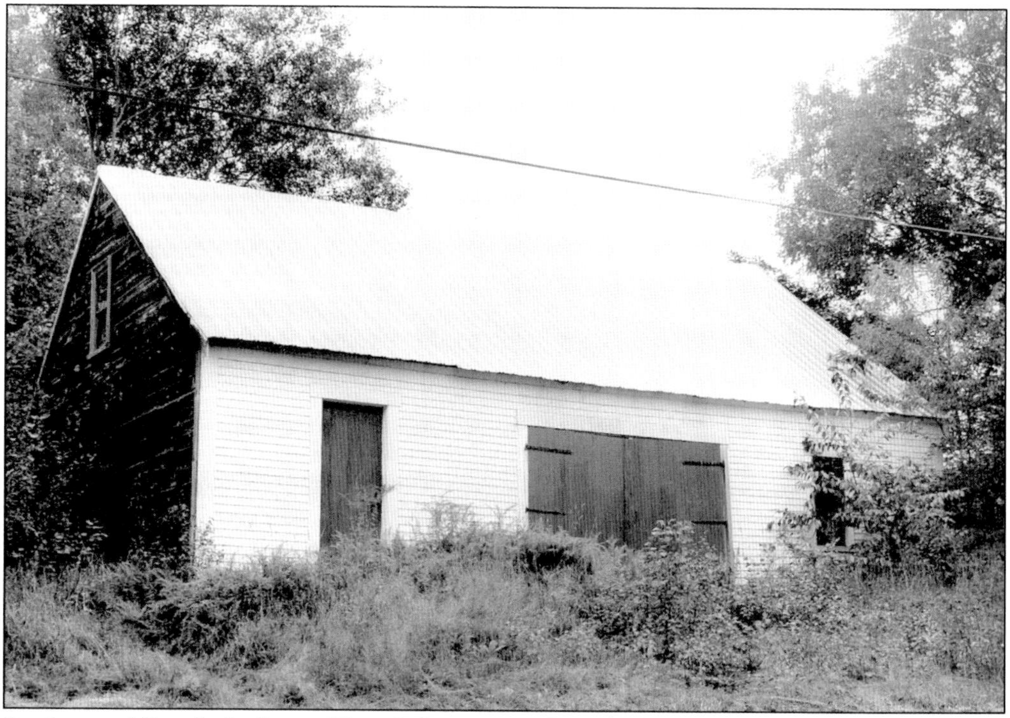

Stephen and Sara Lyford's son Theophilus remained on the homestead and served in the state legislature in 1852 and 1853. Betsy, daughter of Theophilus and Mary Lyford (née Goodhue), married John S. Hutchins, also a state legislator. Hutchins built this cider mill opposite the family home around 1834.

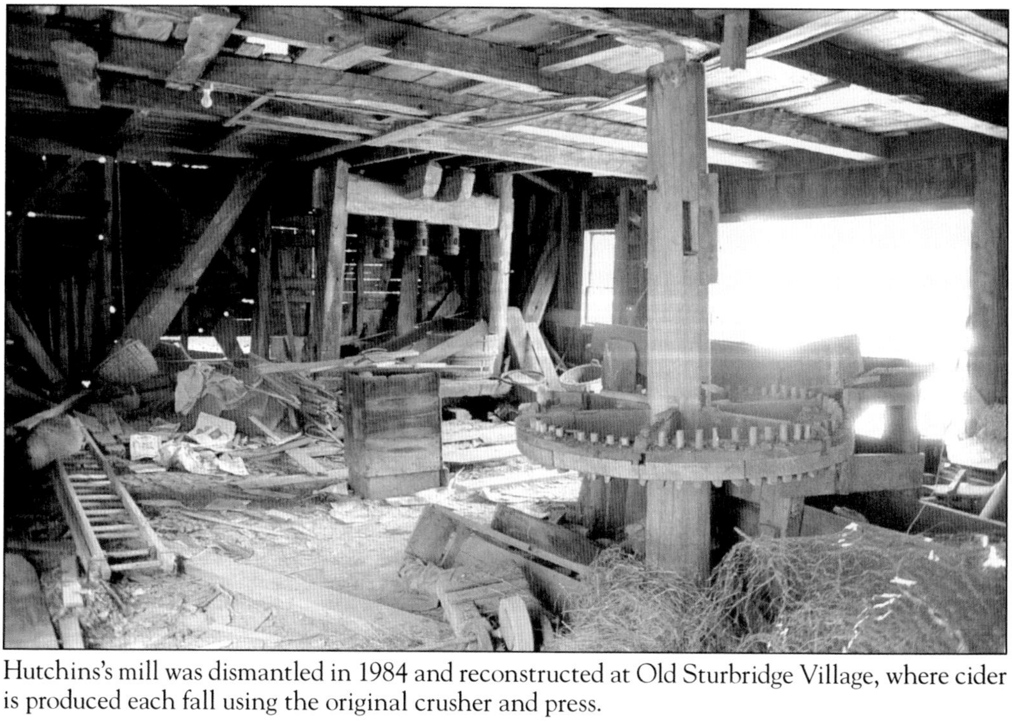

Hutchins's mill was dismantled in 1984 and reconstructed at Old Sturbridge Village, where cider is produced each fall using the original crusher and press.

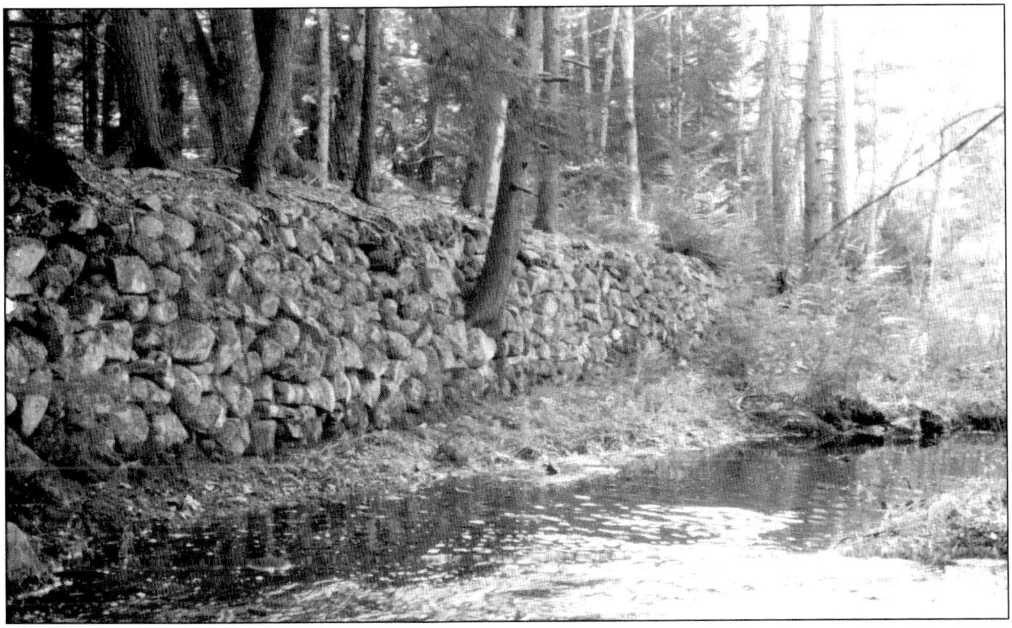

Robert Pike settled in Brookfield in 1785 and, according to an early deed, was a "clothier." His fulling mill, which processed cloth with steam and pressure, appeared on the town tax record in 1796. Pike also ran a sawmill, the only evidence of which is this dam built in 1828. The dam is an impressive 200 feet long, 8 feet high, and 8 feet thick. The mill was burned to the ground in 1855 by a suspected arsonist.

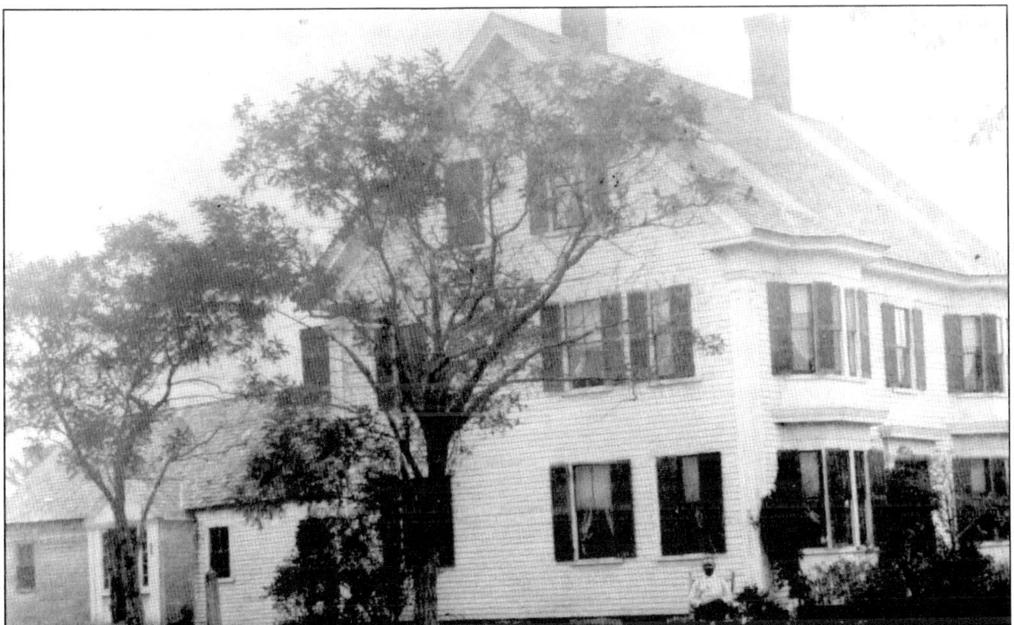

Josiah Robinson, a tanner whose business was located on nearby Pike Brook, settled here in 1778. His son Walter built the original four-room home around 1800, and in 1876 Walter's son Noah added an eight-room section to the original. The large house accommodated boarders for a number of years.

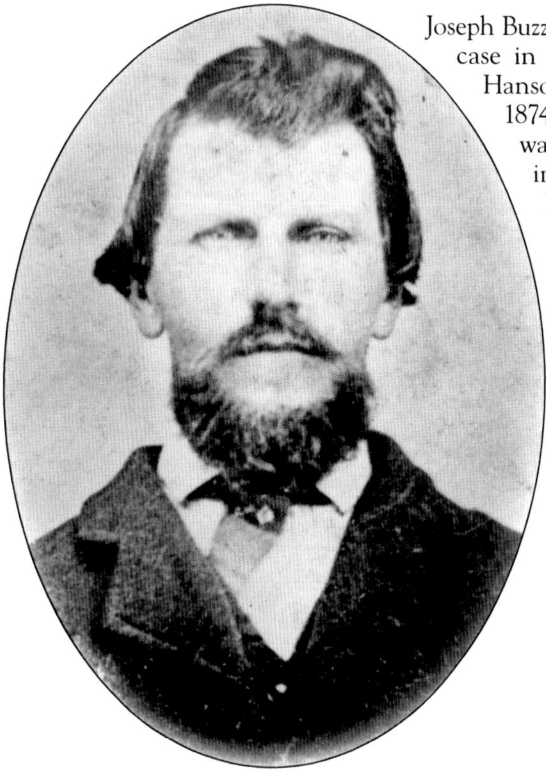

Joseph Buzzell was at the center of a celebrated murder case in Brookfield. Buzzell's rejected bride, Susan Hanson, was shot in her home on November 3, 1874. Charles Cook confessed to the crime and was tried and sentenced to prison. Although implicated by Cook as the person who hired him to commit the act, Buzzell was tried and found not guilty. Later evidence proved Buzzell's guilt, but since trying him again involved double jeopardy, he was charged only with being an accessory. At the second trial, he was found guilty and died by hanging on July 10, 1878. (Thom Hindle collection.)

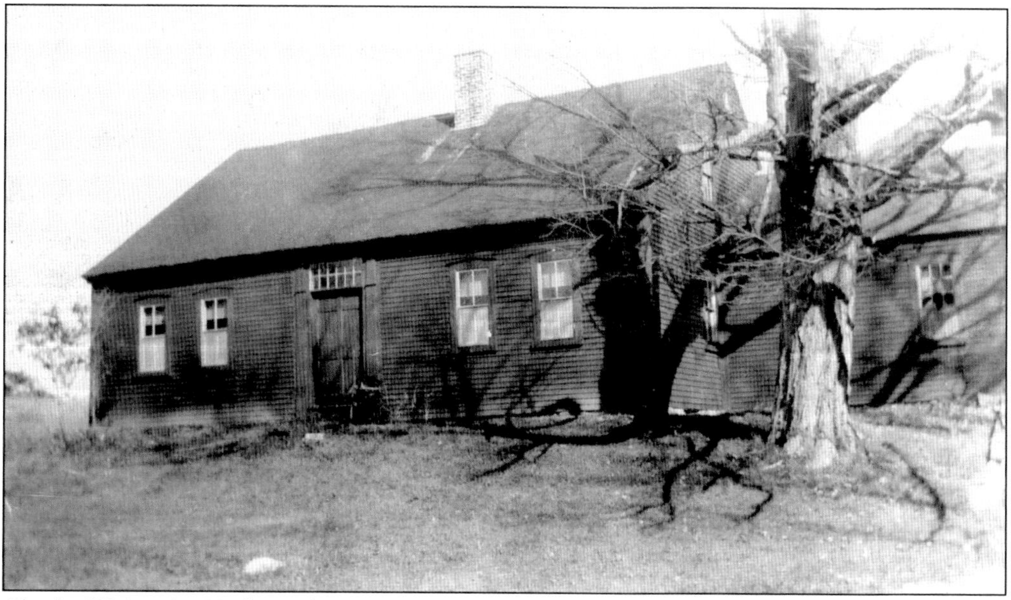

Charles Witham's 1800 home began a journey on a blistering hot day in 1850. A team of oxen was moving the house from Union to Cottle Hill Road in Brookfield. Whether it was the result of the heat or the barrel of cider the drivers stopped to consume along the way, the house never reached its destination, remaining right where the men stopped to rest at the foot of a long hill.

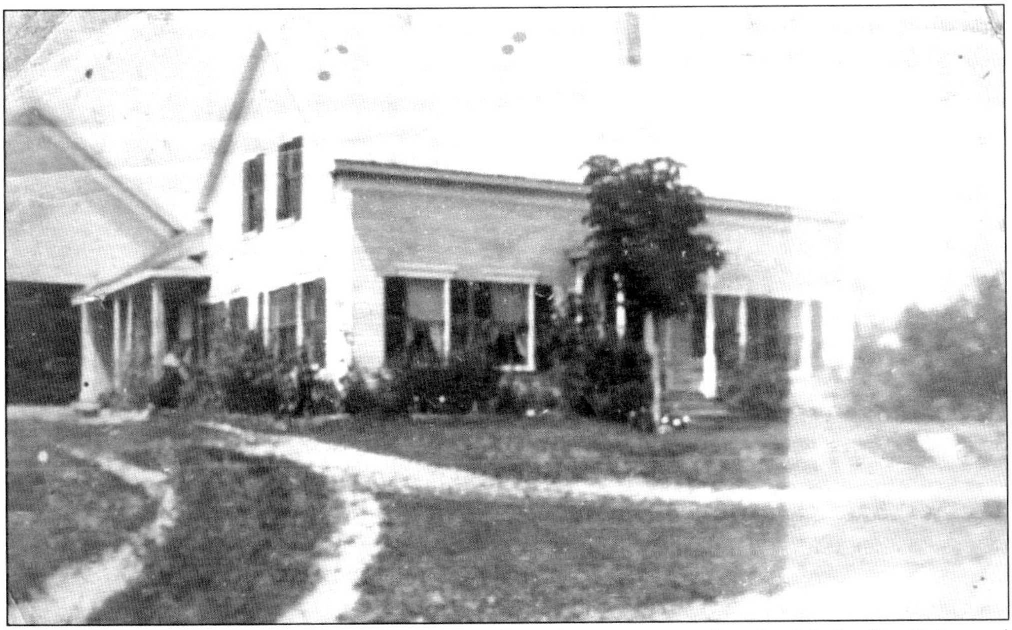

Built around 1840, the structure above served as the parsonage for the Methodist Episcopal Society. The first pastor was Rev. Henry Nutter, who was followed by five other ministers. The parsonage was sold to Robert L. Chamberlain in 1880, and the proceeds went to the Methodist Society of Cottonboro. Chamberlain served Brookfield as town clerk for 12 years and selectman for 2. He is pictured below with his wife, Gertrude (née Hanson), in their home in 1895.

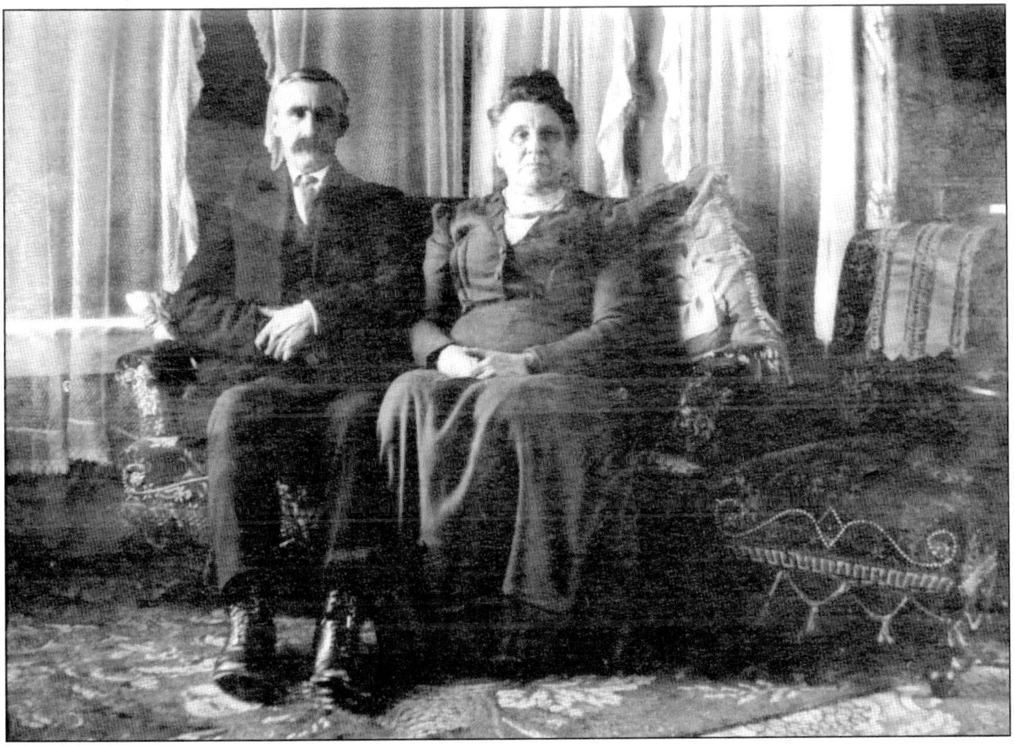

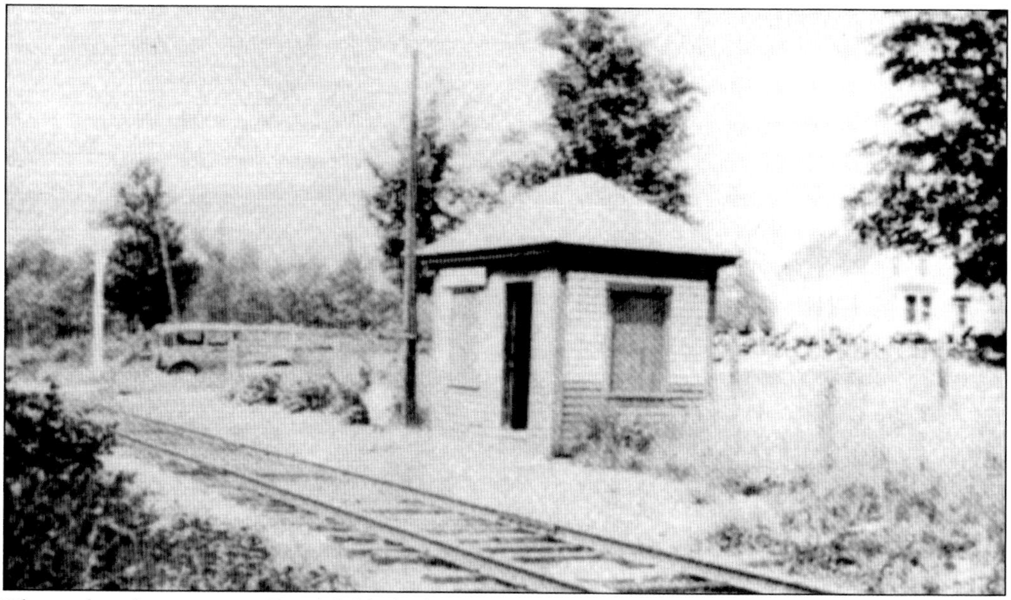

The railroad station in Brookfield, little more than a flag stop, was called Pike's Crossing. Brookfield students could hop on the train at the crossing and be transported to Wolfeboro and Brewster Academy, where they attended high school.

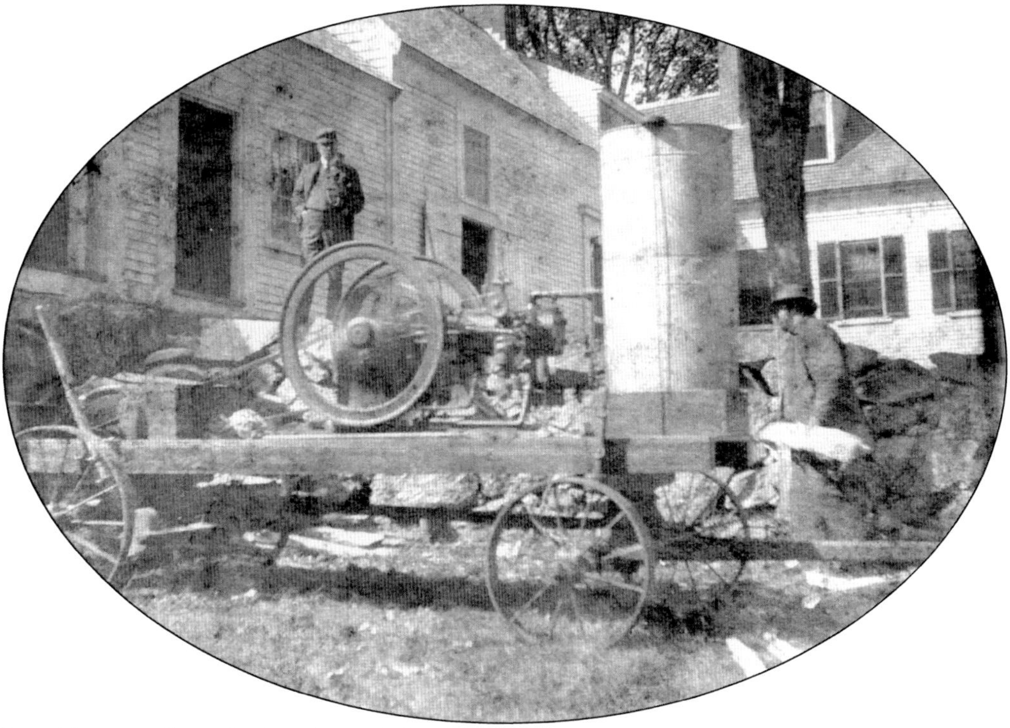

Portable sawmills took the place of the larger operations. This one runs in the yard of the Ferguson house in 1904. Observing is Thomas Bowden, whose wife, Adaline, was a descendant of William Chamberlain.

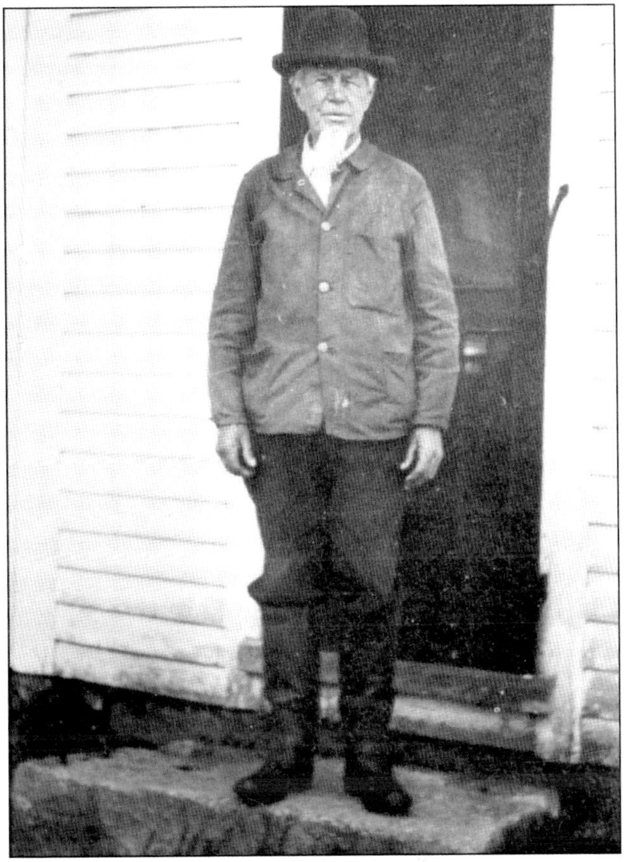

Joseph Smith Wentworth, seen at right around 1910, made hundreds of shoes in his shop on Stoneham Road. Dozens of shops, like the one seen below, were scattered throughout town well into the 20th century.

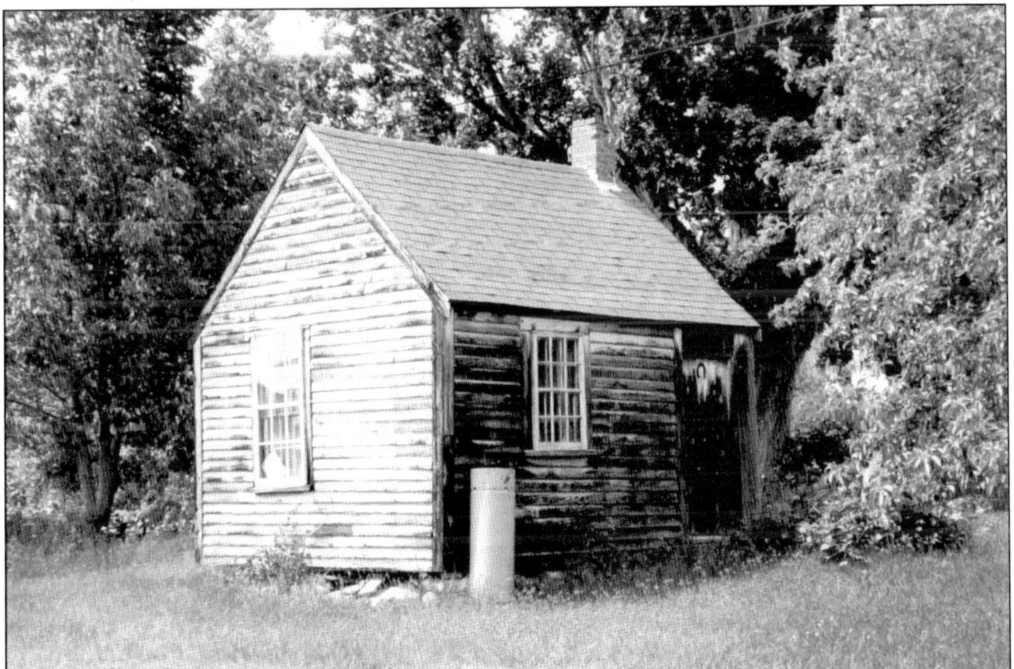

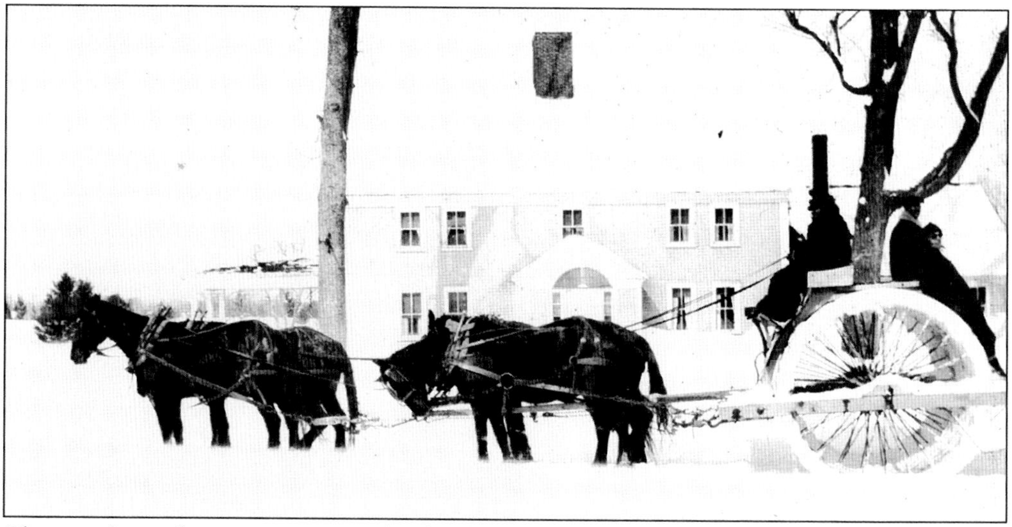

Clearing the roads was a monumental task. This snow roller is shown in front of the Chamberlain House around 1900.

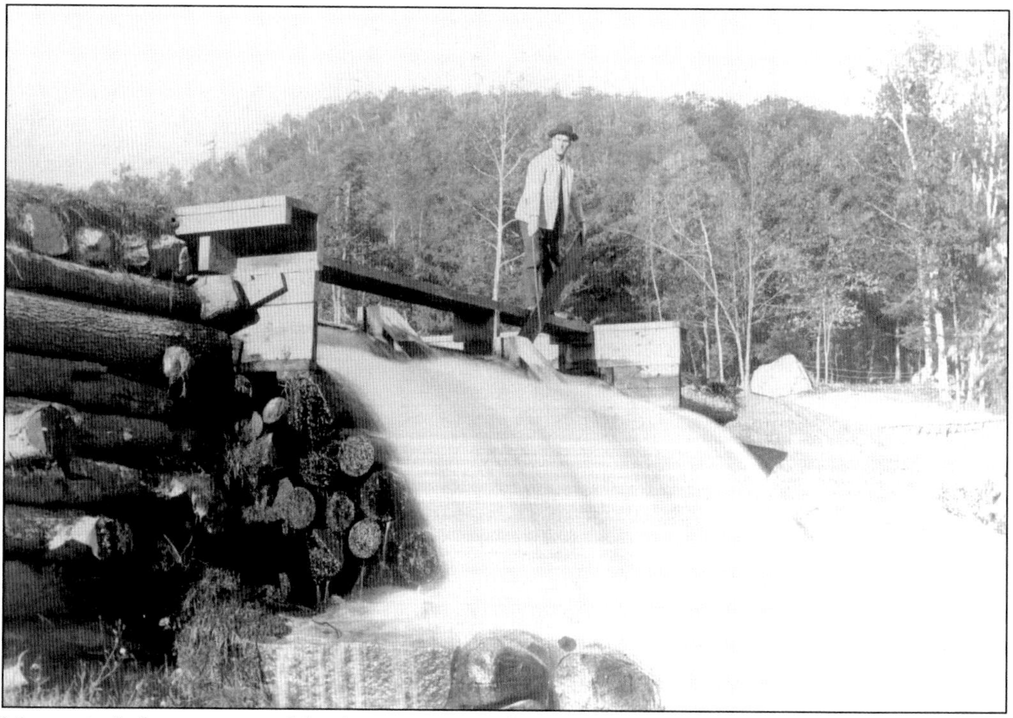

Mountain Lake was created by damming up Tobias Hanson's old cranberry bog. At one time, a lumber mill stood on the shore and a huge sawdust pile was created. One day, the sawdust pile, full of methane and decomposing matter, exploded with a roar. Gladys Churchill and her parents were fishing on the lake and had the terrifying experience of seeing the lake covered with smoldering sawdust.

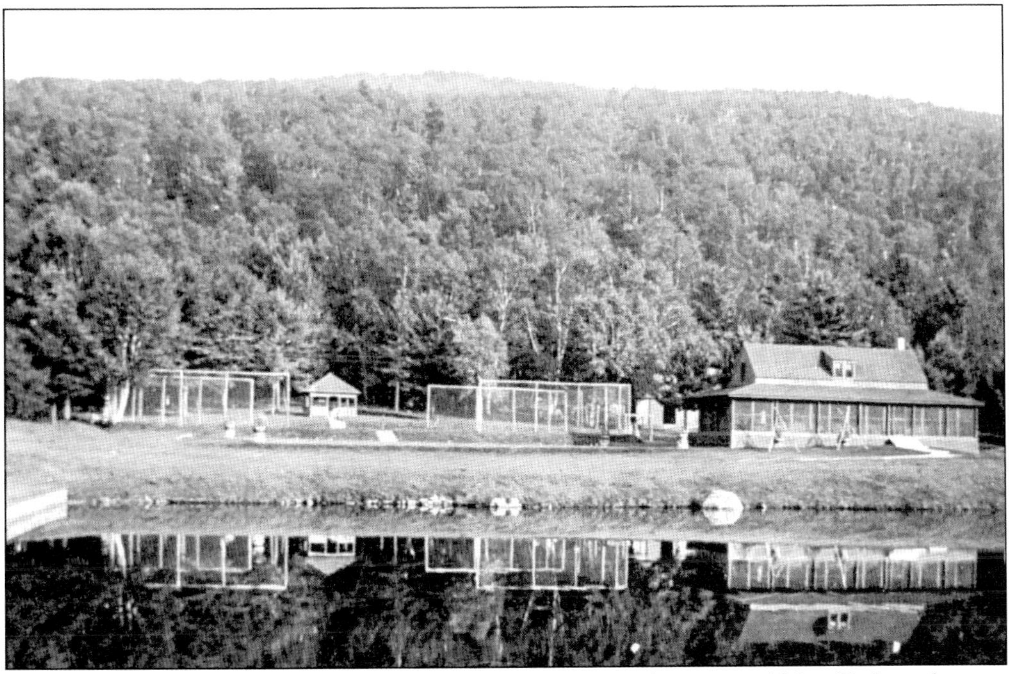

At the beginning of the 20th century, families from Massachusetts and New York, seeking to escape the noise and impure air of the city, bought land and built summer retreats. The Harrises, owners of Hudson and Harris Theaters in New York, built Mountain Lake Camp with a rustic lodge and bright, blue-stained outbuildings that included a stable, ice house, "auto house," boathouse, and summer house near the lake.

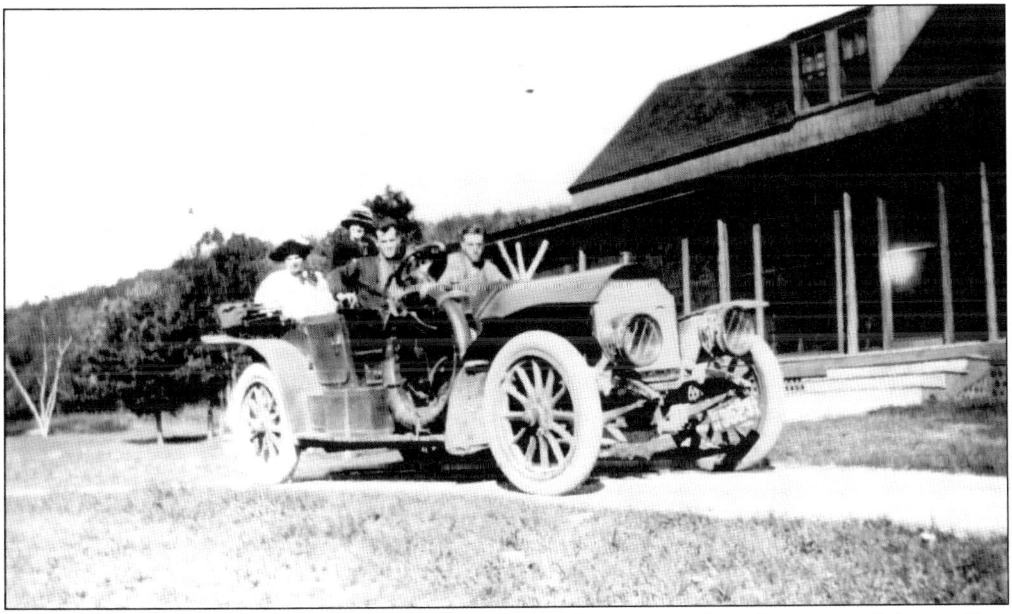

Theater folk were transported to Mountain Lake Camp in a Simplex, one of the earliest automobiles. Chauffeur George Mitchell picked up guests at the Sanbornville station and gave them a wild "initiation" ride up and down the steep hills and through Churchill Brook. It was widely reported that the shrieks of the city women could be heard all the way to Sanbornville.

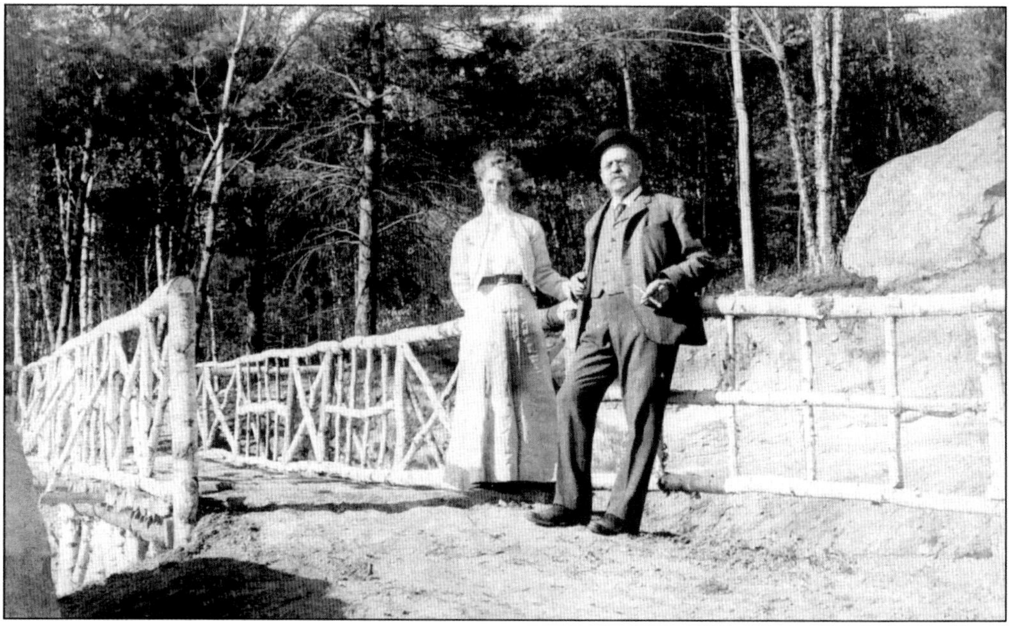

Henry B. Harris and his wife, Renee, spent several summers at Mountain Lake Camp, entertaining friends from New York and enjoying the rustic atmosphere. Local caretaker Langdon Brown tended the property when the Harrises were not in residence. The Harrises booked first-class passage on the *Titanic* in April 1912. On the journey, Harris stepped into the crowd of doomed passengers, so that his wife, boarding a lifeboat, would be spared his final moments. Renee Harris became Broadway's first female producer, introducing Charles Coburn, Barbara Stanwyck, Judith Anderson, and the playwright Moss Hart.

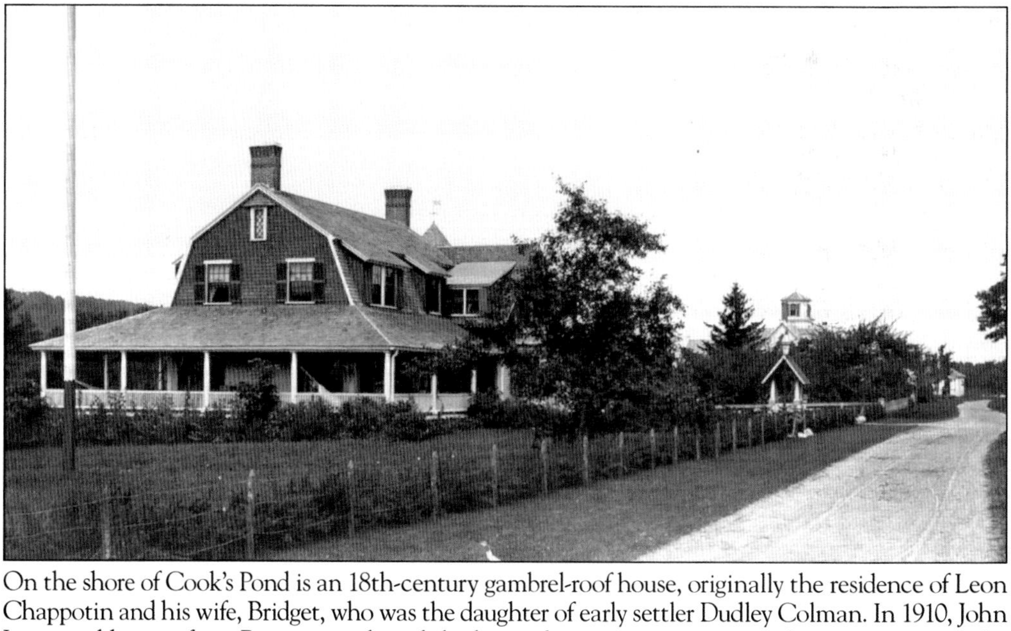

On the shore of Cook's Pond is an 18th-century gambrel-roof house, originally the residence of Leon Chappotin and his wife, Bridget, who was the daughter of early settler Dudley Colman. In 1910, John Lee, an alderman from Boston, purchased the house for use as a summer residence. Lee turned the structure, added wings on each side, and built the barn, complete with a bowling alley.

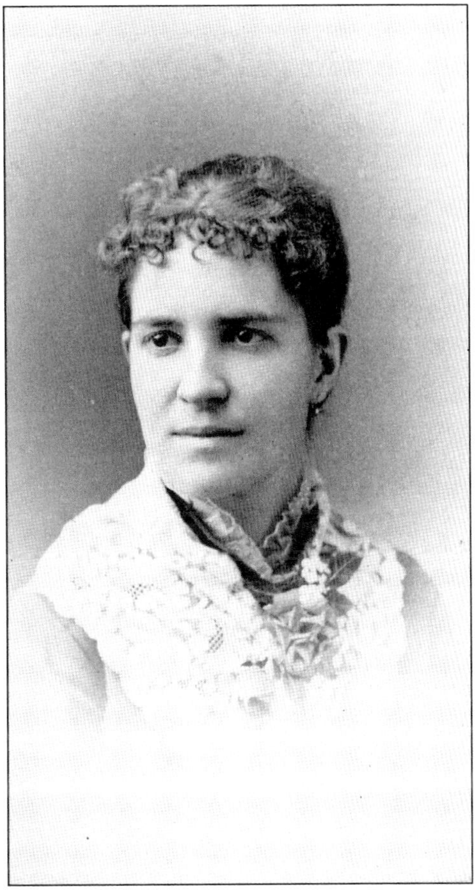

In 1912, Jennie Barker Jones Pinkham (right) bought 50 acres and a stone house on Cook's Pond. She was the widow of Charles Hacker Pinkham, who was the son of Lydia E. Pinkham and president of the Lydia E. Pinkham Medicine Company of Lynn, Massachusetts. Jennie had five houses built for her children, one of which became known as Winter House, as it was used for the entire family to occupy while enjoying winter holidays and sports. Local workmen built the houses, which were staffed by Irish maids from Boston. The children enjoyed three ponies, horses, a cow, the lake, and three chauffeur-driven automobiles that transported the families to picnics on Tumbledown Dick Mountain. The postcard below of the mountain from Cook's Pond was sent by Jennie Pinkham to a friend in 1912 and extols the lovely view from her country home.

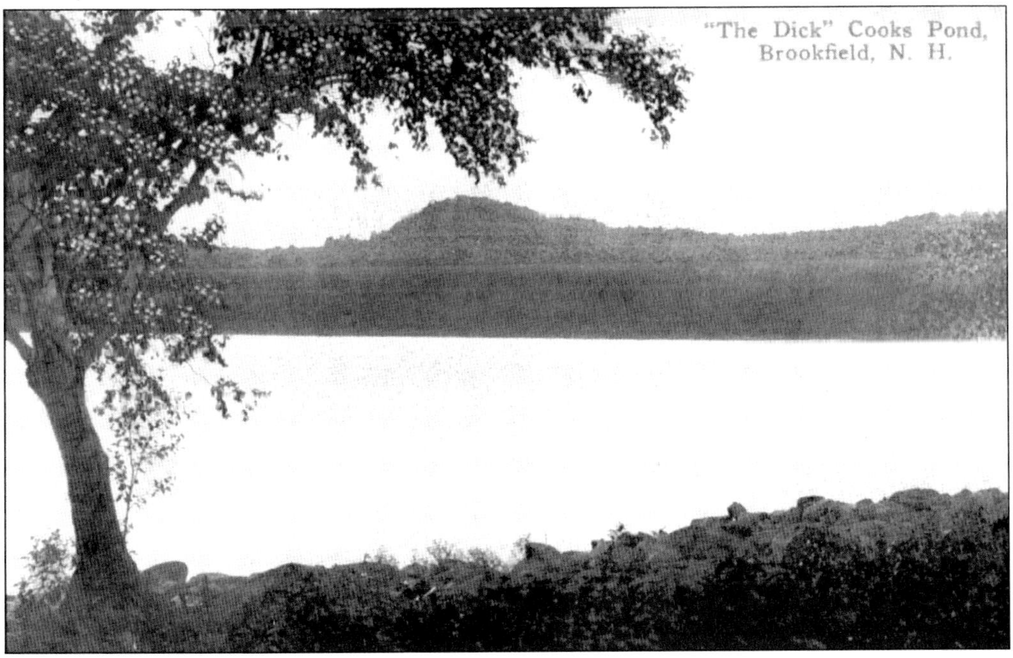

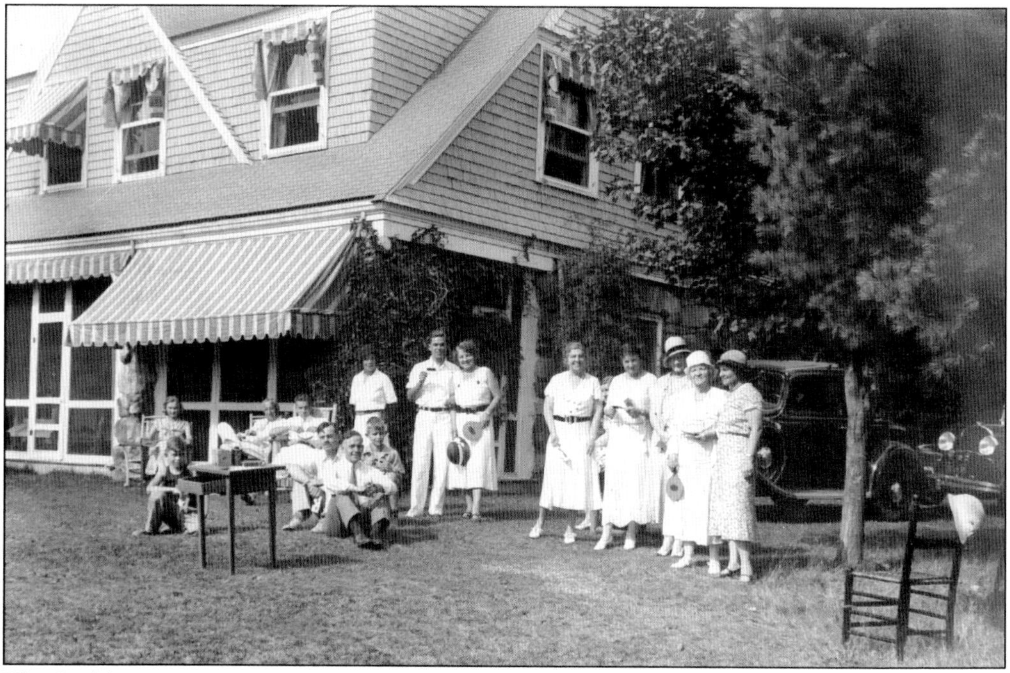

The Pinkhams enjoy a party with friends on the lawn of the family estate, Lynnmere, while looking at an eclipse through exposed film. Identified here are David W. Burnham, Ann Burnham, Hermon E. Smith Jr., Daniel R. Pinkham, Charles Burnham, Daniel R. Pinkham Jr., Olive W. Pinkham, Lyndon Burnham, Marion P. Smith, Lucy P. Burnham, Jennie Pinkham, and Elsie P. Haines.

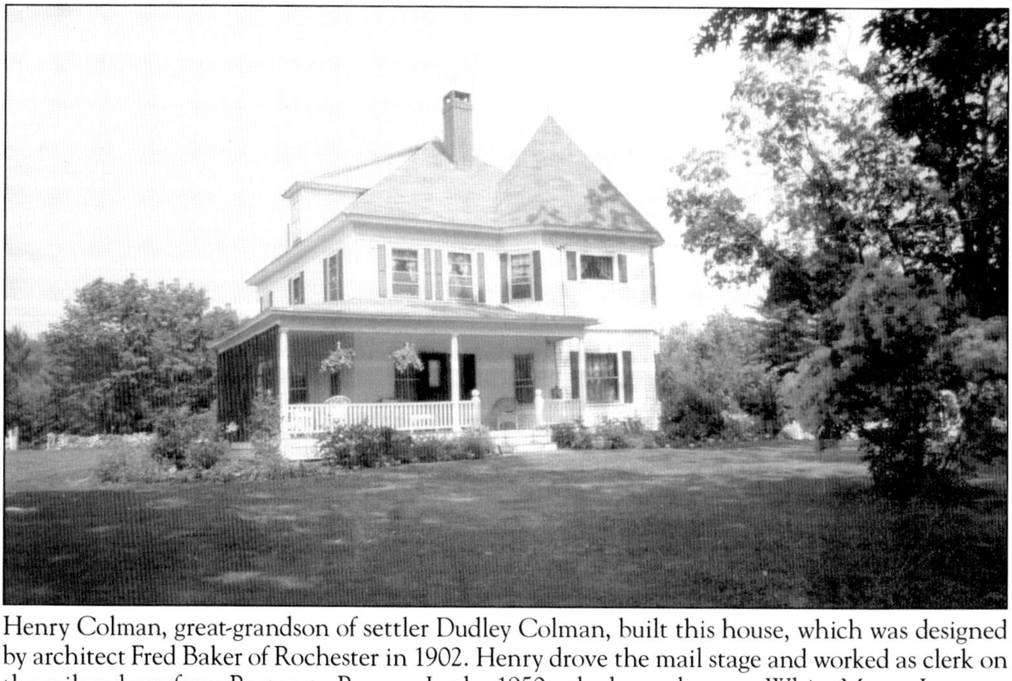

Henry Colman, great-grandson of settler Dudley Colman, built this house, which was designed by architect Fred Baker of Rochester in 1902. Henry drove the mail stage and worked as clerk on the railroad run from Boston to Bangor. In the 1950s, the house became White Manor Inn, run by Iola and Edward White, who grew all the produce featured in their famous Sunday dinners.

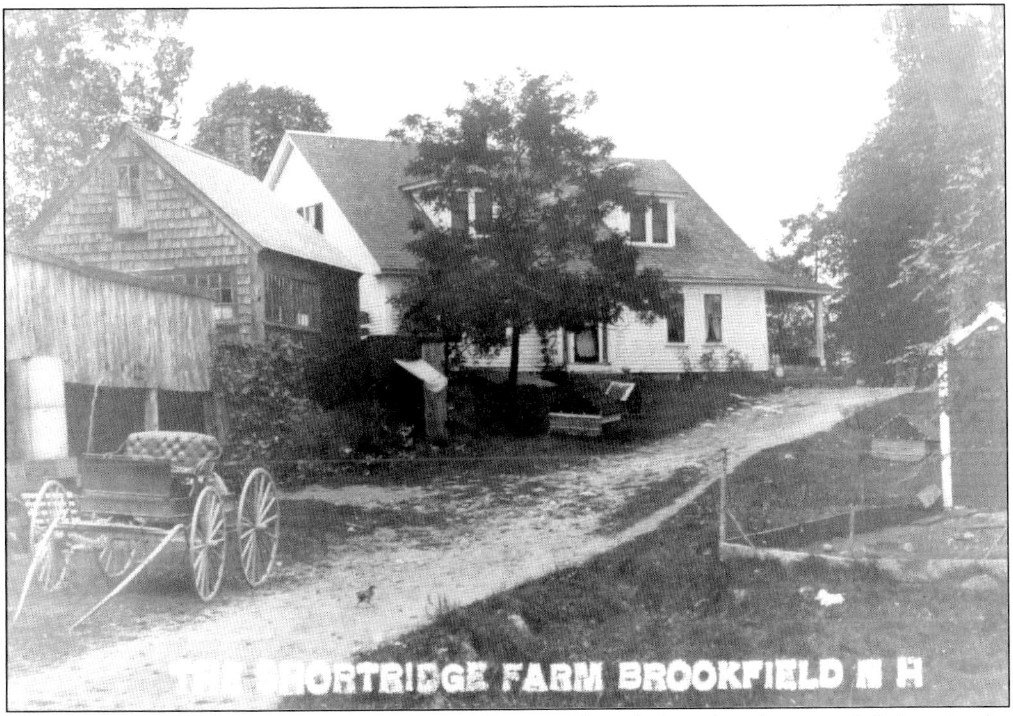

The Shortridge farm (above) was built around 1840. Identified in the photograph below, in the yard of the Shortridge home in 1910, are Marjorie Shortridge, Clotilda Morley, Josiah Morley, Harold Morley, Emma Shortridge, Ralph Shortridge, Grace Shortridge, Frank Clark, Lizzie Clark, Florence Morley, and Albert Shortridge.

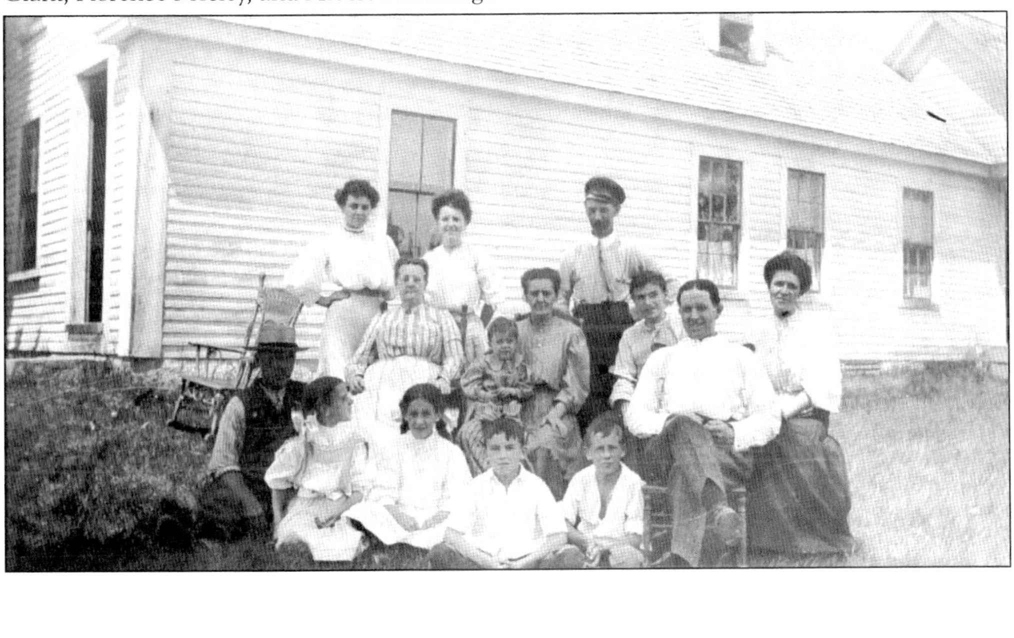

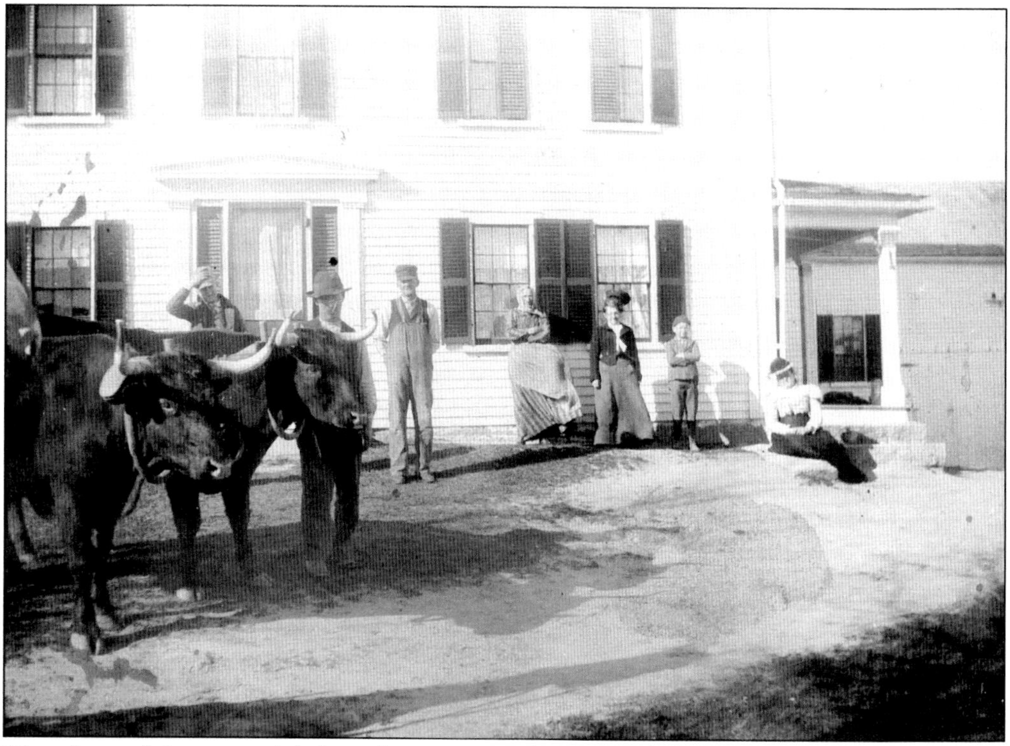

The advent of the automobile brought tourists to the area and, therefore, tourist homes became common. Wallace Lang and wife Abbie Lang (née Cotton) advertised "Tourist Accomodation [*sic*]—$.50 a night." Members of the Lang family are pictured in the front yard of the farm on Stoneham Road in 1901. Charles Thurston holds the oxen.

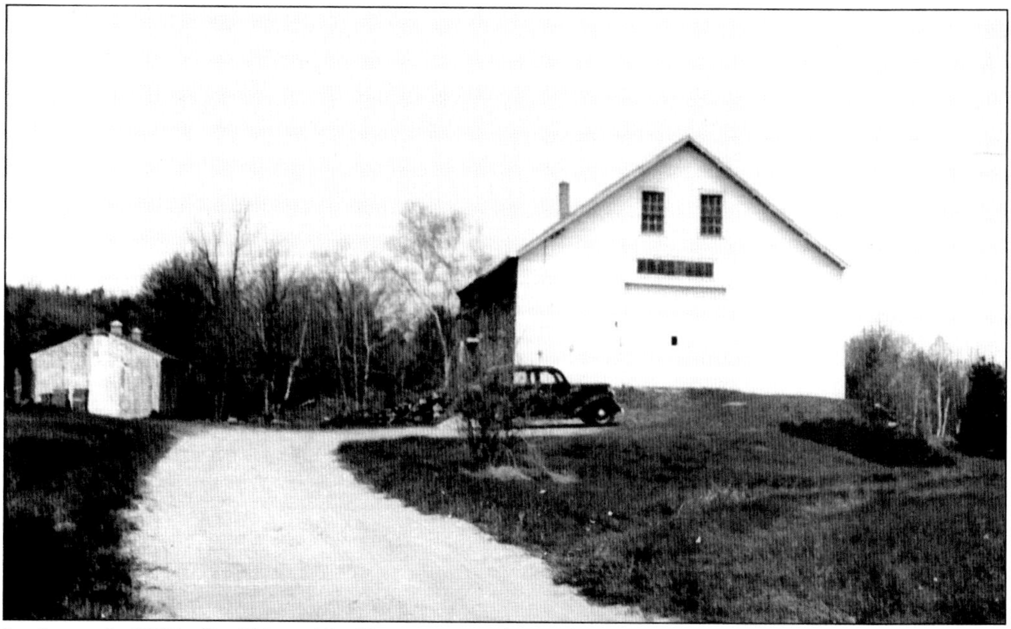

In the early 1950s, Dr. Edward L. Howes opened Northeast Biological Laboratories in the barn that was one of the outbuildings of the old Dudley Colman place.

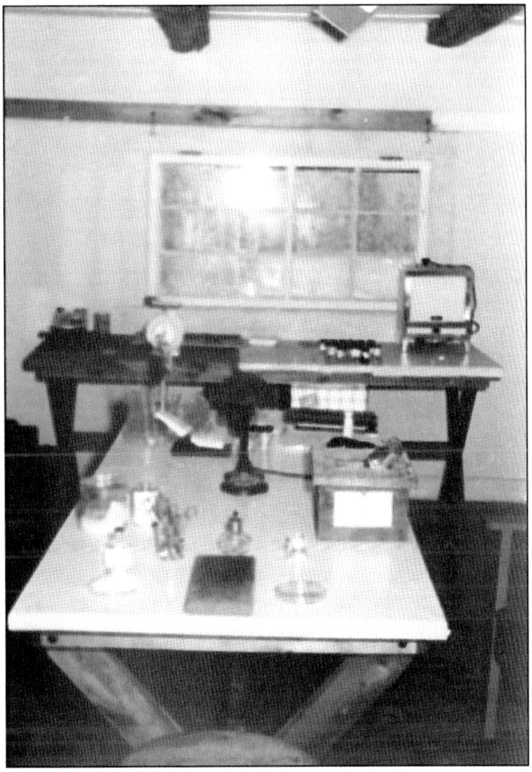

Cancer and wound-healing research was conducted at Northeast Biological Laboratories. Dr. Howes invented a suture, which the lab then manufactured.

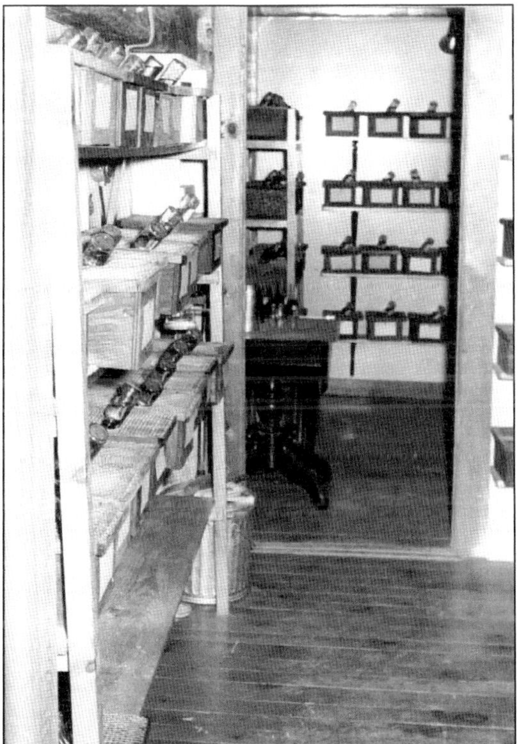

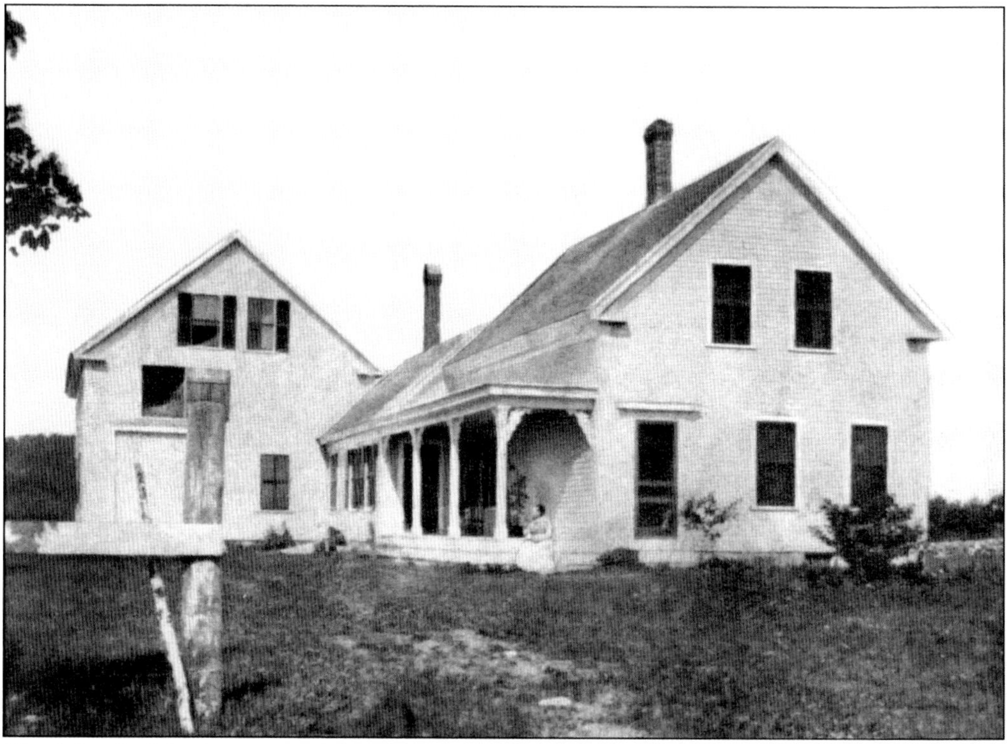

The John C. Pike home was located next to the Dudley Colman farm, which burned to the ground in 1942. Dr. Howes and his family then purchased the Pike house and used it as their summer home. Pike, who conducted a lumbering operation, built a simple, Greek Revival–style home that he later embellished with Victorian detail. The early house is quite hidden beneath its later finery.

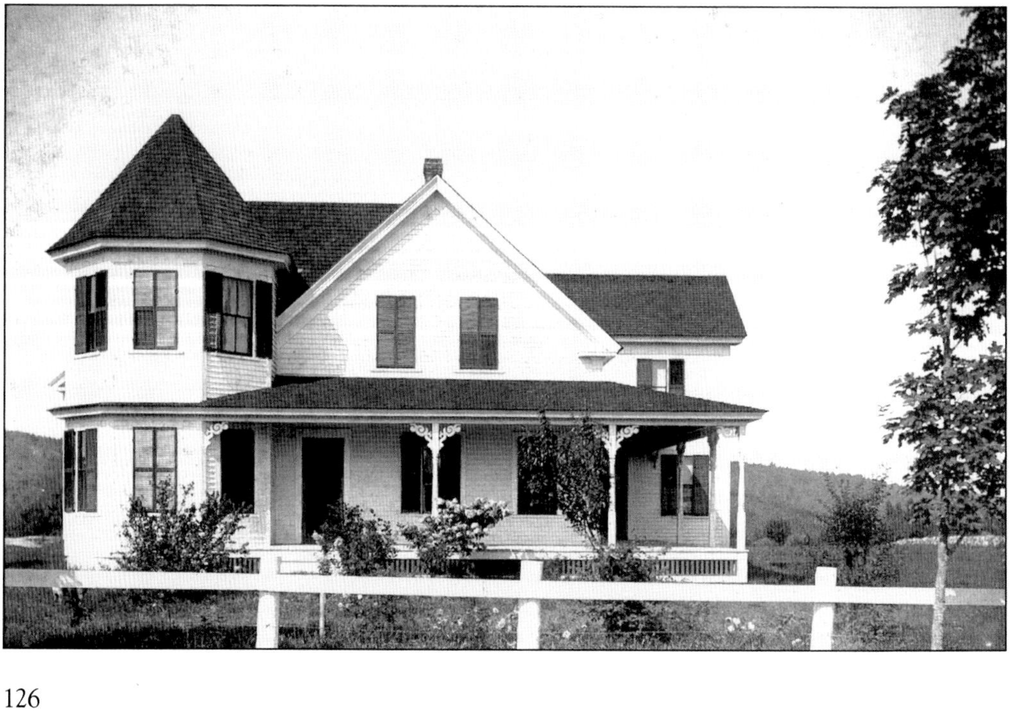

The Wakefield Historical Society was founded in 1938. In 1946, the name was changed to the Wakefield-Brookfield Historical Society, reflecting the involvement of Brookfield in the group. The society was incorporated in 1949, and of the eight incorporators, four were from Brookfield. Shown leaving the Chamberlain home for the opening of the society's new building, the Little Red Schoolhouse, are Adelaide Hughes (left), a descendant of William Chamberlain, and Louella McCausland.

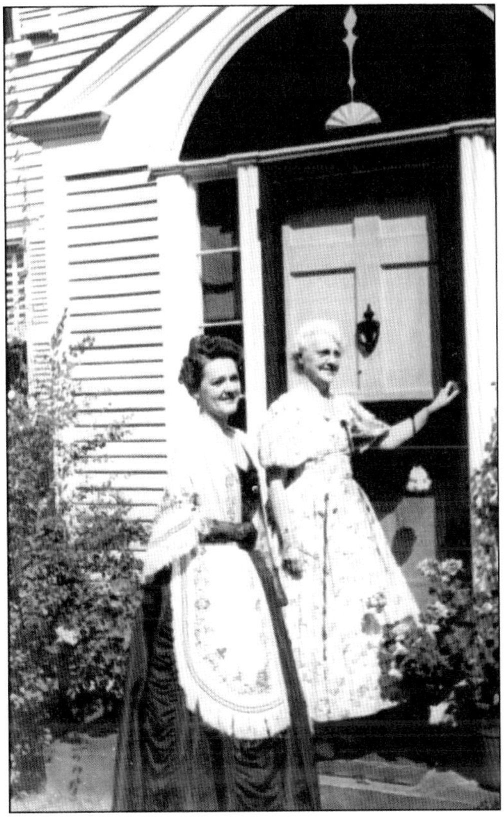

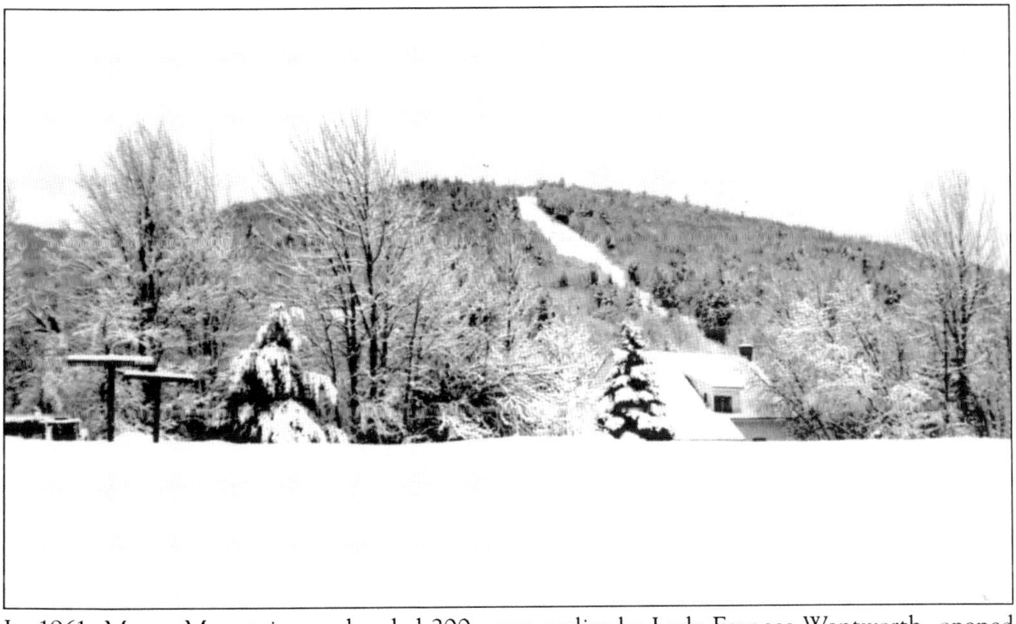

In 1961, Moose Mountain, so dreaded 200 years earlier by Lady Frances Wentworth, opened as Moose Mountain Ski Area. For many years, the mountain was popular as a family outdoor recreation area, but a lack of snow and the opening of large ski areas to the north forced its closing in the 1980s.

Discover Thousands of Local History Books Featuring Millions of Vintage Images

Arcadia Publishing, the leading local history publisher in the United States, is committed to making history accessible and meaningful through publishing books that celebrate and preserve the heritage of America's people and places.

Find more books like this at
www.arcadiapublishing.com

Search for your hometown history, your old stomping grounds, and even your favorite sports team.

Consistent with our mission to preserve history on a local level, this book was printed in South Carolina on American-made paper and manufactured entirely in the United States. Products carrying the accredited Forest Stewardship Council (FSC) label are printed on 100 percent FSC-certified paper.

MADE IN THE USA